Praxis®

Social Studies (5581) Secrets Study Guide

DEAR FUTURE EXAM SUCCESS STORY

First of all, **THANK YOU** for purchasing Mometrix study materials!

Second, congratulations! You are one of the few determined test-takers who are committed to doing whatever it takes to excel on your exam. **You have come to the right place.** We developed these study materials with one goal in mind: to deliver you the information you need in a format that's concise and easy to use.

In addition to optimizing your guide for the content of the test, we've outlined our recommended steps for breaking down the preparation process into small, attainable goals so you can make sure you stay on track.

We've also analyzed the entire test-taking process, identifying the most common pitfalls and showing how you can overcome them and be ready for any curveball the test throws you.

Standardized testing is one of the biggest obstacles on your road to success, which only increases the importance of doing well in the high-pressure, high-stakes environment of test day. Your results on this test could have a significant impact on your future, and this guide provides the information and practical advice to help you achieve your full potential on test day.

Your success is our success

We would love to hear from you! If you would like to share the story of your exam success or if you have any questions or comments in regard to our products, please contact us at **800-673-8175** or **support@mometrix.com**.

Thanks again for your business and we wish you continued success!

Sincerely,
The Mometrix Test Preparation Team

Need more help? Check out our flashcards at:
http://MometrixFlashcards.com/PraxisII

TABLE OF CONTENTS

INTRODUCTION 1
SECRET KEY #1 – PLAN BIG, STUDY SMALL 2
SECRET KEY #2 – MAKE YOUR STUDYING COUNT 3
SECRET KEY #3 – PRACTICE THE RIGHT WAY 4
SECRET KEY #4 – PACE YOURSELF 6
SECRET KEY #5 – HAVE A PLAN FOR GUESSING 7
TEST-TAKING STRATEGIES 10
UNITED STATES HISTORY 15
AMERICAN HISTORY PRE-COLUMBIAN TO 1789 15
AMERICAN HISTORY 1790 TO 1898 24
AMERICAN HISTORY 1899 TO PRESENT 41
CHAPTER QUIZ 58
WORLD HISTORY 59
WORLD HISTORY PRE-1400 59
WORLD HISTORY 1400 TO 1914 70
WORLD HISTORY 1914 TO PRESENT 77
CHAPTER QUIZ 86
GEOGRAPHY 87
CHAPTER QUIZ 101
CIVICS 102
CHAPTER QUIZ 115
ECONOMICS 116
CHAPTER QUIZ 129
PRAXIS PRACTICE TEST 130
ANSWER KEY AND EXPLANATIONS 153
HOW TO OVERCOME TEST ANXIETY 173
ONLINE RESOURCES 179

Introduction

Thank you for purchasing this resource! You have made the choice to prepare yourself for a test that could have a huge impact on your future, and this guide is designed to help you be fully ready for test day. Obviously, it's important to have a solid understanding of the test material, but you also need to be prepared for the unique environment and stressors of the test, so that you can perform to the best of your abilities.

For this purpose, the first section that appears in this guide is the **Secret Keys**. We've devoted countless hours to meticulously researching what works and what doesn't, and we've boiled down our findings to the five most impactful steps you can take to improve your performance on the test. We start at the beginning with study planning and move through the preparation process, all the way to the testing strategies that will help you get the most out of what you know when you're finally sitting in front of the test.

We recommend that you start preparing for your test as far in advance as possible. However, if you've bought this guide as a last-minute study resource and only have a few days before your test, we recommend that you skip over the first two Secret Keys since they address a long-term study plan.

If you struggle with **test anxiety**, we strongly encourage you to check out our recommendations for how you can overcome it. Test anxiety is a formidable foe, but it can be beaten, and we want to make sure you have the tools you need to defeat it.

Secret Key #1 – Plan Big, Study Small

There's a lot riding on your performance. If you want to ace this test, you're going to need to keep your skills sharp and the material fresh in your mind. You need a plan that lets you review everything you need to know while still fitting in your schedule. We'll break this strategy down into three categories.

Information Organization

Start with the information you already have: the official test outline. From this, you can make a complete list of all the concepts you need to cover before the test. Organize these concepts into groups that can be studied together, and create a list of any related vocabulary you need to learn so you can brush up on any difficult terms. You'll want to keep this vocabulary list handy once you actually start studying since you may need to add to it along the way.

Time Management

Once you have your set of study concepts, decide how to spread them out over the time you have left before the test. Break your study plan into small, clear goals so you have a manageable task for each day and know exactly what you're doing. Then just focus on one small step at a time. When you manage your time this way, you don't need to spend hours at a time studying. Studying a small block of content for a short period each day helps you retain information better and avoid stressing over how much you have left to do. You can relax knowing that you have a plan to cover everything in time. In order for this strategy to be effective though, you have to start studying early and stick to your schedule. Avoid the exhaustion and futility that comes from last-minute cramming!

Study Environment

The environment you study in has a big impact on your learning. Studying in a coffee shop, while probably more enjoyable, is not likely to be as fruitful as studying in a quiet room. It's important to keep distractions to a minimum. You're only planning to study for a short block of time, so make the most of it. Don't pause to check your phone or get up to find a snack. It's also important to **avoid multitasking**. Research has consistently shown that multitasking will make your studying dramatically less effective. Your study area should also be comfortable and well-lit so you don't have the distraction of straining your eyes or sitting on an uncomfortable chair.

The time of day you study is also important. You want to be rested and alert. Don't wait until just before bedtime. Study when you'll be most likely to comprehend and remember. Even better, if you know what time of day your test will be, set that time aside for study. That way your brain will be used to working on that subject at that specific time and you'll have a better chance of recalling information.

Finally, it can be helpful to team up with others who are studying for the same test. Your actual studying should be done in as isolated an environment as possible, but the work of organizing the information and setting up the study plan can be divided up. In between study sessions, you can discuss with your teammates the concepts that you're all studying and quiz each other on the details. Just be sure that your teammates are as serious about the test as you are. If you find that your study time is being replaced with social time, you might need to find a new team.

Secret Key #2 – Make Your Studying Count

You're devoting a lot of time and effort to preparing for this test, so you want to be absolutely certain it will pay off. This means doing more than just reading the content and hoping you can remember it on test day. It's important to make every minute of study count. There are two main areas you can focus on to make your studying count.

Retention

It doesn't matter how much time you study if you can't remember the material. You need to make sure you are retaining the concepts. To check your retention of the information you're learning, try recalling it at later times with minimal prompting. Try carrying around flashcards and glance at one or two from time to time or ask a friend who's also studying for the test to quiz you.

To enhance your retention, look for ways to put the information into practice so that you can apply it rather than simply recalling it. If you're using the information in practical ways, it will be much easier to remember. Similarly, it helps to solidify a concept in your mind if you're not only reading it to yourself but also explaining it to someone else. Ask a friend to let you teach them about a concept you're a little shaky on (or speak aloud to an imaginary audience if necessary). As you try to summarize, define, give examples, and answer your friend's questions, you'll understand the concepts better and they will stay with you longer. Finally, step back for a big picture view and ask yourself how each piece of information fits with the whole subject. When you link the different concepts together and see them working together as a whole, it's easier to remember the individual components.

Finally, practice showing your work on any multi-step problems, even if you're just studying. Writing out each step you take to solve a problem will help solidify the process in your mind, and you'll be more likely to remember it during the test.

Modality

Modality simply refers to the means or method by which you study. Choosing a study modality that fits your own individual learning style is crucial. No two people learn best in exactly the same way, so it's important to know your strengths and use them to your advantage.

For example, if you learn best by visualization, focus on visualizing a concept in your mind and draw an image or a diagram. Try color-coding your notes, illustrating them, or creating symbols that will trigger your mind to recall a learned concept. If you learn best by hearing or discussing information, find a study partner who learns the same way or read aloud to yourself. Think about how to put the information in your own words. Imagine that you are giving a lecture on the topic and record yourself so you can listen to it later.

For any learning style, flashcards can be helpful. Organize the information so you can take advantage of spare moments to review. Underline key words or phrases. Use different colors for different categories. Mnemonic devices (such as creating a short list in which every item starts with the same letter) can also help with retention. Find what works best for you and use it to store the information in your mind most effectively and easily.

Secret Key #3 – Practice the Right Way

Your success on test day depends not only on how many hours you put into preparing, but also on whether you prepared the right way. It's good to check along the way to see if your studying is paying off. One of the most effective ways to do this is by taking practice tests to evaluate your progress. Practice tests are useful because they show exactly where you need to improve. Every time you take a practice test, pay special attention to these three groups of questions:

- The questions you got wrong
- The questions you had to guess on, even if you guessed right
- The questions you found difficult or slow to work through

This will show you exactly what your weak areas are, and where you need to devote more study time. Ask yourself why each of these questions gave you trouble. Was it because you didn't understand the material? Was it because you didn't remember the vocabulary? Do you need more repetitions on this type of question to build speed and confidence? Dig into those questions and figure out how you can strengthen your weak areas as you go back to review the material.

Additionally, many practice tests have a section explaining the answer choices. It can be tempting to read the explanation and think that you now have a good understanding of the concept. However, an explanation likely only covers part of the question's broader context. Even if the explanation makes perfect sense, **go back and investigate** every concept related to the question until you're positive you have a thorough understanding.

As you go along, keep in mind that the practice test is just that: practice. Memorizing these questions and answers will not be very helpful on the actual test because it is unlikely to have any of the same exact questions. If you only know the right answers to the sample questions, you won't be prepared for the real thing. **Study the concepts** until you understand them fully, and then you'll be able to answer any question that shows up on the test.

It's important to wait on the practice tests until you're ready. If you take a test on your first day of study, you may be overwhelmed by the amount of material covered and how much you need to learn. Work up to it gradually.

On test day, you'll need to be prepared for answering questions, managing your time, and using the test-taking strategies you've learned. It's a lot to balance, like a mental marathon that will have a big impact on your future. Like training for a marathon, you'll need to start slowly and work your way up. When test day arrives, you'll be ready.

Start with the strategies you've read in the first two Secret Keys—plan your course and study in the way that works best for you. If you have time, consider using multiple study resources to get different approaches to the same concepts. It can be helpful to see difficult concepts from more than one angle. Then find a good source for practice tests. Many times, the test website will suggest potential study resources or provide sample tests.

Practice Test Strategy

If you're able to find at least three practice tests, we recommend this strategy:

Untimed and Open-Book Practice

Take the first test with no time constraints and with your notes and study guide handy. Take your time and focus on applying the strategies you've learned.

Timed and Open-Book Practice

Take the second practice test open-book as well, but set a timer and practice pacing yourself to finish in time.

Timed and Closed-Book Practice

Take any other practice tests as if it were test day. Set a timer and put away your study materials. Sit at a table or desk in a quiet room, imagine yourself at the testing center, and answer questions as quickly and accurately as possible.

Keep repeating timed and closed-book tests on a regular basis until you run out of practice tests or it's time for the actual test. Your mind will be ready for the schedule and stress of test day, and you'll be able to focus on recalling the material you've learned.

Secret Key #4 – Pace Yourself

Once you're fully prepared for the material on the test, your biggest challenge on test day will be managing your time. Just knowing that the clock is ticking can make you panic even if you have plenty of time left. Work on pacing yourself so you can build confidence against the time constraints of the exam. Pacing is a difficult skill to master, especially in a high-pressure environment, so **practice is vital**.

Set time expectations for your pace based on how much time is available. For example, if a section has 60 questions and the time limit is 30 minutes, you know you have to average 30 seconds or less per question in order to answer them all. Although 30 seconds is the hard limit, set 25 seconds per question as your goal, so you reserve extra time to spend on harder questions. When you budget extra time for the harder questions, you no longer have any reason to stress when those questions take longer to answer.

Don't let this time expectation distract you from working through the test at a calm, steady pace, but keep it in mind so you don't spend too much time on any one question. Recognize that taking extra time on one question you don't understand may keep you from answering two that you do understand later in the test. If your time limit for a question is up and you're still not sure of the answer, mark it and move on, and come back to it later if the time and the test format allow. If the testing format doesn't allow you to return to earlier questions, just make an educated guess; then put it out of your mind and move on.

On the easier questions, be careful not to rush. It may seem wise to hurry through them so you have more time for the challenging ones, but it's not worth missing one if you know the concept and just didn't take the time to read the question fully. Work efficiently but make sure you understand the question and have looked at all of the answer choices, since more than one may seem right at first.

Even if you're paying attention to the time, you may find yourself a little behind at some point. You should speed up to get back on track, but do so wisely. Don't panic; just take a few seconds less on each question until you're caught up. Don't guess without thinking, but do look through the answer choices and eliminate any you know are wrong. If you can get down to two choices, it is often worthwhile to guess from those. Once you've chosen an answer, move on and don't dwell on any that you skipped or had to hurry through. If a question was taking too long, chances are it was one of the harder ones, so you weren't as likely to get it right anyway.

On the other hand, if you find yourself getting ahead of schedule, it may be beneficial to slow down a little. The more quickly you work, the more likely you are to make a careless mistake that will affect your score. You've budgeted time for each question, so don't be afraid to spend that time. Practice an efficient but careful pace to get the most out of the time you have.

Secret Key #5 – Have a Plan for Guessing

When you're taking the test, you may find yourself stuck on a question. Some of the answer choices seem better than others, but you don't see the one answer choice that is obviously correct. What do you do?

The scenario described above is very common, yet most test takers have not effectively prepared for it. Developing and practicing a plan for guessing may be one of the single most effective uses of your time as you get ready for the exam.

In developing your plan for guessing, there are three questions to address:

- When should you start the guessing process?
- How should you narrow down the choices?
- Which answer should you choose?

When to Start the Guessing Process

Unless your plan for guessing is to select C every time (which, despite its merits, is not what we recommend), you need to leave yourself enough time to apply your answer elimination strategies. Since you have a limited amount of time for each question, that means that if you're going to give yourself the best shot at guessing correctly, you have to decide quickly whether or not you will guess.

Of course, the best-case scenario is that you don't have to guess at all, so first, see if you can answer the question based on your knowledge of the subject and basic reasoning skills. Focus on the key words in the question and try to jog your memory of related topics. Give yourself a chance to bring the knowledge to mind, but once you realize that you don't have (or you can't access) the knowledge you need to answer the question, it's time to start the guessing process.

It's almost always better to start the guessing process too early than too late. It only takes a few seconds to remember something and answer the question from knowledge. Carefully eliminating wrong answer choices takes longer. Plus, going through the process of eliminating answer choices can actually help jog your memory.

Summary: Start the guessing process as soon as you decide that you can't answer the question based on your knowledge.

How to Narrow Down the Choices

The next chapter in this book (**Test-Taking Strategies**) includes a wide range of strategies for how to approach questions and how to look for answer choices to eliminate. You will definitely want to read those carefully, practice them, and figure out which ones work best for you. Here though, we're going to address a mindset rather than a particular strategy.

Your odds of guessing an answer correctly depend on how many options you are choosing from.

Number of options left	5	4	3	2	1
Odds of guessing correctly	20%	25%	33%	50%	100%

You can see from this chart just how valuable it is to be able to eliminate incorrect answers and make an educated guess, but there are two things that many test takers do that cause them to miss out on the benefits of guessing:

- Accidentally eliminating the correct answer
- Selecting an answer based on an impression

We'll look at the first one here, and the second one in the next section.

To avoid accidentally eliminating the correct answer, we recommend a thought exercise called **the $5 challenge**. In this challenge, you only eliminate an answer choice from contention if you are willing to bet $5 on it being wrong. Why $5? Five dollars is a small but not insignificant amount of money. It's an amount you could afford to lose but wouldn't want to throw away. And while losing $5 once might not hurt too much, doing it twenty times will set you back $100. In the same way, each small decision you make—eliminating a choice here, guessing on a question there—won't by itself impact your score very much, but when you put them all together, they can make a big difference. By holding each answer choice elimination decision to a higher standard, you can reduce the risk of accidentally eliminating the correct answer.

The $5 challenge can also be applied in a positive sense: If you are willing to bet $5 that an answer choice *is* correct, go ahead and mark it as correct.

Summary: Only eliminate an answer choice if you are willing to bet $5 that it is wrong.

Which Answer to Choose

You're taking the test. You've run into a hard question and decided you'll have to guess. You've eliminated all the answer choices you're willing to bet $5 on. Now you have to pick an answer. Why do we even need to talk about this? Why can't you just pick whichever one you feel like when the time comes?

The answer to these questions is that if you don't come into the test with a plan, you'll rely on your impression to select an answer choice, and if you do that, you risk falling into a trap. The test writers know that everyone who takes their test will be guessing on some of the questions, so they intentionally write wrong answer choices to seem plausible. You still have to pick an answer though, and if the wrong answer choices are designed to look right, how can you ever be sure that you're not falling for their trap? The best solution we've found to this dilemma is to take the decision out of your hands entirely. Here is the process we recommend:

Once you've eliminated any choices that you are confident (willing to bet $5) are wrong, select the first remaining choice as your answer.

Whether you choose to select the first remaining choice, the second, or the last, the important thing is that you use some preselected standard. Using this approach guarantees that you will not be enticed into selecting an answer choice that looks right, because you are not basing your decision on how the answer choices look.

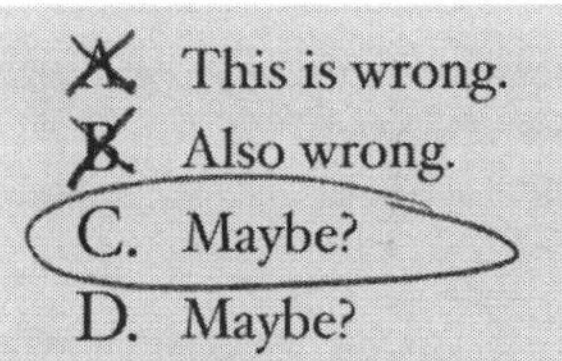

This is not meant to make you question your knowledge. Instead, it is to help you recognize the difference between your knowledge and your impressions. There's a huge difference between thinking an answer is right because of what you know, and thinking an answer is right because it looks or sounds like it should be right.

Summary: To ensure that your selection is appropriately random, make a predetermined selection from among all answer choices you have not eliminated.

Test-Taking Strategies

This section contains a list of test-taking strategies that you may find helpful as you work through the test. By taking what you know and applying logical thought, you can maximize your chances of answering any question correctly!

It is very important to realize that every question is different and every person is different: no single strategy will work on every question, and no single strategy will work for every person. That's why we've included all of them here, so you can try them out and determine which ones work best for different types of questions and which ones work best for you.

Question Strategies

☑ Read Carefully

Read the question and the answer choices carefully. Don't miss the question because you misread the terms. You have plenty of time to read each question thoroughly and make sure you understand what is being asked. Yet a happy medium must be attained, so don't waste too much time. You must read carefully and efficiently.

☑ Contextual Clues

Look for contextual clues. If the question includes a word you are not familiar with, look at the immediate context for some indication of what the word might mean. Contextual clues can often give you all the information you need to decipher the meaning of an unfamiliar word. Even if you can't determine the meaning, you may be able to narrow down the possibilities enough to make a solid guess at the answer to the question.

☑ Prefixes

If you're having trouble with a word in the question or answer choices, try dissecting it. Take advantage of every clue that the word might include. Prefixes can be a huge help. Usually, they allow you to determine a basic meaning. *Pre-* means before, *post-* means after, *pro-* is positive, *de-* is negative. From prefixes, you can get an idea of the general meaning of the word and try to put it into context.

☑ Hedge Words

Watch out for critical hedge words, such as *likely, may, can, often, almost, mostly, usually, generally, rarely,* and *sometimes.* Question writers insert these hedge phrases to cover every possibility. Often an answer choice will be wrong simply because it leaves no room for exception. Be on guard for answer choices that have definitive words such as *exactly* and *always.*

☑ Switchback Words

Stay alert for *switchbacks.* These are the words and phrases frequently used to alert you to shifts in thought. The most common switchback words are *but, although,* and *however.* Others include *nevertheless, on the other hand, even though, while, in spite of, despite,* and *regardless of.* Switchback words are important to catch because they can change the direction of the question or an answer choice.

⊘ FACE VALUE

When in doubt, use common sense. Accept the situation in the problem at face value. Don't read too much into it. These problems will not require you to make wild assumptions. If you have to go beyond creativity and warp time or space in order to have an answer choice fit the question, then you should move on and consider the other answer choices. These are normal problems rooted in reality. The applicable relationship or explanation may not be readily apparent, but it is there for you to figure out. Use your common sense to interpret anything that isn't clear.

Answer Choice Strategies

⊘ ANSWER SELECTION

The most thorough way to pick an answer choice is to identify and eliminate wrong answers until only one is left, then confirm it is the correct answer. Sometimes an answer choice may immediately seem right, but be careful. The test writers will usually put more than one reasonable answer choice on each question, so take a second to read all of them and make sure that the other choices are not equally obvious. As long as you have time left, it is better to read every answer choice than to pick the first one that looks right without checking the others.

⊘ ANSWER CHOICE FAMILIES

An answer choice family consists of two (in rare cases, three) answer choices that are very similar in construction and cannot all be true at the same time. If you see two answer choices that are direct opposites or parallels, one of them is usually the correct answer. For instance, if one answer choice says that quantity *x* increases and another either says that quantity *x* decreases (opposite) or says that quantity *y* increases (parallel), then those answer choices would fall into the same family. An answer choice that doesn't match the construction of the answer choice family is more likely to be incorrect. Most questions will not have answer choice families, but when they do appear, you should be prepared to recognize them.

⊘ ELIMINATE ANSWERS

Eliminate answer choices as soon as you realize they are wrong, but make sure you consider all possibilities. If you are eliminating answer choices and realize that the last one you are left with is also wrong, don't panic. Start over and consider each choice again. There may be something you missed the first time that you will realize on the second pass.

⊘ AVOID FACT TRAPS

Don't be distracted by an answer choice that is factually true but doesn't answer the question. You are looking for the choice that answers the question. Stay focused on what the question is asking for so you don't accidentally pick an answer that is true but incorrect. Always go back to the question and make sure the answer choice you've selected actually answers the question and is not merely a true statement.

⊘ EXTREME STATEMENTS

In general, you should avoid answers that put forth extreme actions as standard practice or proclaim controversial ideas as established fact. An answer choice that states the "process should be used in certain situations, if…" is much more likely to be correct than one that states the "process should be discontinued completely." The first is a calm rational statement and doesn't even make a definitive, uncompromising stance, using a hedge word *if* to provide wiggle room, whereas the second choice is far more extreme.

⊘ Benchmark

As you read through the answer choices and you come across one that seems to answer the question well, mentally select that answer choice. This is not your final answer, but it's the one that will help you evaluate the other answer choices. The one that you selected is your benchmark or standard for judging each of the other answer choices. Every other answer choice must be compared to your benchmark. That choice is correct until proven otherwise by another answer choice beating it. If you find a better answer, then that one becomes your new benchmark. Once you've decided that no other choice answers the question as well as your benchmark, you have your final answer.

⊘ Predict the Answer

Before you even start looking at the answer choices, it is often best to try to predict the answer. When you come up with the answer on your own, it is easier to avoid distractions and traps because you will know exactly what to look for. The right answer choice is unlikely to be word-for-word what you came up with, but it should be a close match. Even if you are confident that you have the right answer, you should still take the time to read each option before moving on.

General Strategies

⊘ Tough Questions

If you are stumped on a problem or it appears too hard or too difficult, don't waste time. Move on! Remember though, if you can quickly check for obviously incorrect answer choices, your chances of guessing correctly are greatly improved. Before you completely give up, at least try to knock out a couple of possible answers. Eliminate what you can and then guess at the remaining answer choices before moving on.

⊘ Check Your Work

Since you will probably not know every term listed and the answer to every question, it is important that you get credit for the ones that you do know. Don't miss any questions through careless mistakes. If at all possible, try to take a second to look back over your answer selection and make sure you've selected the correct answer choice and haven't made a costly careless mistake (such as marking an answer choice that you didn't mean to mark). This quick double check should more than pay for itself in caught mistakes for the time it costs.

⊘ Pace Yourself

It's easy to be overwhelmed when you're looking at a page full of questions; your mind is confused and full of random thoughts, and the clock is ticking down faster than you would like. Calm down and maintain the pace that you have set for yourself. Especially as you get down to the last few minutes of the test, don't let the small numbers on the clock make you panic. As long as you are on track by monitoring your pace, you are guaranteed to have time for each question.

⊘ Don't Rush

It is very easy to make errors when you are in a hurry. Maintaining a fast pace in answering questions is pointless if it makes you miss questions that you would have gotten right otherwise. Test writers like to include distracting information and wrong answers that seem right. Taking a little extra time to avoid careless mistakes can make all the difference in your test score. Find a pace that allows you to be confident in the answers that you select.

⊘ KEEP MOVING

Panicking will not help you pass the test, so do your best to stay calm and keep moving. Taking deep breaths and going through the answer elimination steps you practiced can help to break through a stress barrier and keep your pace.

Final Notes

The combination of a solid foundation of content knowledge and the confidence that comes from practicing your plan for applying that knowledge is the key to maximizing your performance on test day. As your foundation of content knowledge is built up and strengthened, you'll find that the strategies included in this chapter become more and more effective in helping you quickly sift through the distractions and traps of the test to isolate the correct answer.

Now that you're preparing to move forward into the test content chapters of this book, be sure to keep your goal in mind. As you read, think about how you will be able to apply this information on the test. If you've already seen sample questions for the test and you have an idea of the question format and style, try to come up with questions of your own that you can answer based on what you're reading. This will give you valuable practice applying your knowledge in the same ways you can expect to on test day.

Good luck and good studying!

United States History

Transform passive reading into active learning! After immersing yourself in this chapter, put your comprehension to the test by taking a quiz. The insights you gained will stay with you longer this way. Scan the QR code to go directly to the chapter quiz interface for this study guide. If you're using a computer, simply visit the online resources page at **mometrix.com/resources719/praxsocst** and click the Chapter Quizzes link.

American History Pre-Columbian to 1789

Prior to European colonization, the land that would become the United States was populated by millions of Native Americans belonging to hundreds of distinct tribes. Native American societies were diverse and sophisticated, with political structures, religious beliefs, domesticated animals, agricultural practices, and trade networks. Native Americans adapted their societies and cultures to the environments in which they settled, which led to distinct cultures, beliefs, practices, and languages all across the continent.

Well-Known Native Americans

The following are five well-known Native Americans and their roles in early US history:

1. **Squanto**, an Algonquian, helped early English settlers survive the hard winter by teaching them the native methods of planting corn, squash, and pumpkins.
2. **Pocahontas**, also Algonquian, became famous as a liaison with John Smith's Jamestown colony in 1607.
3. **Sacagawea**, a Shoshone, served a vital role in the Lewis and Clark expedition when the two explorers hired her as their guide in 1805.
4. **Crazy Horse** and **Sitting Bull** led Sioux and Cheyenne troops in the Battle of the Little Bighorn in 1876, soundly defeating George Armstrong Custer.
5. **Chief Joseph**, a leader of the Nez Perce who supported peaceful interaction with white settlers, attempted to relocate his tribe to Canada rather than move them to a reservation.

Major Regional Native American Groups

The major regional Native American groups and the major traits of each are as follows:

- The **Algonquians** in the eastern part of the United States lived in wigwams. The northern tribes subsisted on hunting and gathering, while those who were farther south grew crops such as corn.
- The **Iroquois**, also an east coast tribe, spoke a different language from the Algonquians and lived in rectangular longhouses.
- The **Plains tribes** lived between the Mississippi River and the Rocky Mountains. These nomadic tribes lived in teepees and followed the buffalo herds. Plains tribes included the Sioux, Cheyenne, Comanche, and Blackfoot.
- **Pueblo tribes** included the Zuni, Hopi, and Acoma. They lived in the Southwest deserts in homes made of stone or adobe. They domesticated animals and cultivated corn and beans.

- On the Pacific coast, tribes such as the **Tlingit**, **Chinook**, and **Salish** lived on fish,deer, native berries, and roots. Their rectangular homes housed large family groups, and they used totem poles.
- In the far north, the **Aleuts** and **Inuit** lived in skin tents or igloos. Talented fishermen, they built kayaks and umiaks and also hunted caribou, seals, whales, and walrus.

Review Video: Major Regional Native American Groups
Visit mometrix.com/academy and enter code: 550136

Age of Exploration

The Age of Exploration is also called the **Age of Discovery**. It is generally considered to have begun in the early 15th century and continued into the 17th century. Major developments of the **Age of Exploration** included technological advances in navigation, mapmaking, and shipbuilding. These advances led to expanded European exploration of the rest of the world. Explorers set out from several European countries, including Portugal, Spain, France, and England, seeking new routes to Asia. These efforts led to the discovery of new lands, as well as colonization in India, Asia, Africa, and North America.

Review Video: Age of Exploration
Visit mometrix.com/academy and enter code: 612972

Impact of Technological Advances in Navigation and Seafaring Exploration

For long ocean journeys, it was important for sailors to be able to find their way home even when their vessels sailed far out to sea. A variety of navigational tools enabled them to launch ambitious journeys over long distances. The **compass** and **astrolabe** were particularly important advancements. Chinese navigators used the magnetic compass in approximately 200 BC, and knowledge of the astrolabe came to Europe from Arab navigators and traders who had refined designs developed by the ancient Greeks. The Portuguese developed a ship called a **caravel** in the 1400s that incorporated navigational advancements with the ability to make long sea journeys. Equipped with this advanced vessel, the Portuguese achieved a major goal of the Age of Exploration by discovering a **sea route** from Europe to Asia in 1498.

Significance of Christopher Columbus's Voyage

In 1492, Columbus, a Genoan explorer, obtained financial backing from King Ferdinand and Queen Isabella of Spain to seek a sea route to Asia. He sought a trade route with the Asian Indies to the west. With three ships, the *Niña*, the *Pinta*, and the *Santa Maria*, he eventually landed in the **West Indies**. While Columbus failed in his effort to discover a western route to Asia, he is credited with the discovery of the **Americas**.

Review Video: Christopher Columbus
Visit mometrix.com/academy and enter code: 496598

French, Spanish, Dutch, and British Goals in Colonization of the Americas

France, Spain, the Netherlands, and England each had specific goals in the colonization of the Americas:

- Initial **French colonies** were focused on expanding the fur trade. Later, French colonization led to the growth of plantations in Louisiana, which brought numerous African slaves to the New World.

- **Spanish colonists** came to look for wealth and to convert the natives to Christianity. For some, the desire for gold led to mining in the New World, while others established large ranches.
- The **Dutch** were also involved in the fur trade and imported slaves as the need for laborers increased.
- **British colonists** arrived with various goals. Some were simply looking for additional income, while others were fleeing Britain to escape religious persecution.

Review Video: European Colonization of the Americas
Visit mometrix.com/academy and enter code: 438412

Interactions Between the Colonies and Native Americans

While there were examples of peaceful relations between Native Americans and European colonists, these two groups were often in conflict. The colonists constantly attempted to expand their territories and take Native American land. Native Americans often tried to stop the expansion of European colonies via war and diplomacy, both of which usually resulted in failure due to European advantages in technology and shifting alliances. Both the colonists and the Native Americans committed atrocities against the other in these conflicts. Many Native Americans captured in war were made slaves; however, the most fatal attack suffered by the Native Americans came in the form of disease. Foreign diseases like small pox ravaged through the Native American population. Some researchers estimate that up to 90% of the Native American population died as a result of foreign diseases brought to America by colonists.

New England Colonies

The New England colonies were New Hampshire, Connecticut, Rhode Island and Massachusetts. These colonies were founded largely to escape **religious persecution** in England. The beliefs of the **Puritans**, who migrated to America in the 1600s, significantly influenced the development of these colonies. Situated in the northeast coastal areas of America, the New England colonies featured numerous harbors as well as dense forests. The soil, however, was rocky and had a very short growing season, so was not well suited for agriculture. The economy of New England during the colonial period centered around fishing, shipbuilding and trade along with some small farms and lumber mills. Although some groups congregated in small farms, life centered mainly in towns and cities where **merchants** largely controlled the trade economy. Coastal cities such as Boston grew and thrived.

Review Video: The Massachusetts Bay Colony
Visit mometrix.com/academy and enter code: 407058

Middle or Middle Atlantic Colonies

The Middle or Middle Atlantic Colonies were New York, New Jersey, Pennsylvania, and Delaware. Unlike the New England colonies, where most colonists were from England and Scotland, the Middle Colonies founders were from various countries, including the Netherlands and Sweden. Various factors led these colonists to America. More fertile than New England, the Middle Colonies became major producers of **crops**, including rye, oats, potatoes, wheat, and barley. Some particularly wealthy inhabitants owned large farms and/or businesses. Farmers, in general, were able to produce enough to have a surplus to sell. Tenant farmers also rented land from larger landowners.

Southern Colonies

The Southern Colonies were Maryland, Virginia, North Carolina, South Carolina, and Georgia. Of the Southern Colonies, Virginia was the first permanent English colony and Georgia the last. The warm climate and rich soil of the south encouraged **agriculture**, and the growing season was long. As a result, economy in the south was based largely on labor-intensive **plantations**. Crops included tobacco, rice, and indigo, all of which became valuable cash crops. Most land in the south was controlled by wealthy plantation owners and farmers. Labor on the farms came in the form of indentured servants and African slaves. The first of these **African slaves** arrived in Virginia in 1619.

Review Video: The Southern Colonies
Visit mometrix.com/academy and enter code: 703830

Review Video: The English Colony of Virginia
Visit mometrix.com/academy and enter code: 537399

Significance of the French and Indian Wars

The **British defeat of the Spanish Armada** in 1588 led to the decline of Spanish power in Europe. This, in turn, led the British and French into battle several times between 1689 and 1748. These wars were:

- King William's War, or the Nine Years War, 1689-1697. This war was fought largely in Flanders.
- The War of Spanish Succession, or Queen Anne's War, 1702-1713
- War of Austrian Succession, or King George's War, 1740-1748

The fourth and final war, the **French and Indian War** (1754-1763), was fought largely in the North American territory and resulted in the end of France's reign as a colonial power in North America. Although the French held many advantages, including more cooperative colonists and numerous Native American allies, the strong leadership of **William Pitt** eventually led the British to victory. Costs incurred during the wars eventually led to discontent in the colonies and helped spark the **American Revolution**.

Review Video: French and Indian Wars
Visit mometrix.com/academy and enter code: 502183

Navigation Acts

The Navigation Acts, enacted in 1651, were an attempt by Britain to dominate international trade. Aimed largely at the Dutch, the acts banned foreign ships from transporting goods to the British colonies and from transporting goods to Britain from elsewhere in Europe. While the restrictions on trade angered some colonists, these acts were helpful to other American colonists who, as members of the British Empire, were legally able to provide ships for Britain's growing trade interests and use the ships for their own trading ventures. By the time the French and Indian War had ended, one-third of British merchant ships were built in the American colonies. Many colonists amassed fortunes in the shipbuilding trade.

Acts of British Parliament that Occurred After the French and Indian Wars

After the French and Indian Wars, the British Parliament passed four major acts:

1. The **Sugar Act**, 1764—this act not only required taxes to be collected on molasses brought into the colonies but gave British officials the right to search the homes of anyone suspected of violating it.
2. The **Stamp Act**, 1765—this act taxed printed materials such as newspapers and legal documents. Protests led the Stamp Act to be repealed in 1766, but the repeal also included the Declaratory Act, which stated that Parliament had the right to govern the colonies.
3. The **Quartering Act**, 1765—this act required colonists to provide accommodations and supplies for British troops. In addition, colonists were prohibited from settling west of the Appalachians until given permission by Britain.
4. The **Townshend Acts**, 1767—these acts taxed paper, paint, lead, and tea that came into the colonies. Colonists led boycotts in protest, and in Massachusetts leaders like Samuel and John Adams began to organize resistance against British rule.

Britain's Taxation of the American Colonies After the French and Indian War

The French and Indian War created circumstances for which the British desperately needed more revenue. These needs included:

- Paying off the war debt
- Defending the expanding empire
- Governing Britain's 33 far-flung colonies, including the American colonies

To meet these needs, the British passed additional laws, increasing revenues from the colonies. Because they had spent so much money to defend the American colonies, the British felt it was appropriate to collect considerably higher **taxes** from them. The colonists felt this was unfair, and many were led to protest the increasing taxes. Eventually, protest led to violence.

Triangular Trade

Triangular trade began in the colonies with ships setting off for **Africa**, carrying rum. In Africa, the rum was traded for gold or slaves. Ships then went from Africa to the **West Indies**, trading slaves for sugar, molasses, or money. To complete the triangle, the ships returned to the **colonies** with sugar or molasses to make more rum, as well as stores of gold and silver. This trade triangle violated the Molasses Act of 1733, which required the colonists to pay high duties to Britain on molasses acquired from French, Dutch, and Spanish colonies. The colonists ignored these duties, and the British government adopted a policy of salutary neglect by not enforcing them.

Review Video: The Triangular Trade
Visit mometrix.com/academy and enter code: 415470

Effects of New Laws on British-Colonial Relations

While earlier revenue-generating acts such as the Navigation Acts brought money to the colonists, the new laws after 1763 required colonists to pay money back to **Britain**. The British felt this was fair since the colonists were British subjects and since they had incurred debt protecting the Colonies. The colonists felt it was not only unfair but illegal.

The development of **local government** in America had given the colonists a different view of the structure and role of government. This made it difficult for the British to understand the colonists' protests against what the British felt was a fair and reasonable solution to the mother country's financial problems.

Factors that Led to Increasing Discontent in the American Colonies

More and more colonists were born on American soil, decreasing any sense of kinship with the far-away British rulers. Their new environment had led to new ideas of government and a strong view of the colonies as a separate entity from Britain. Colonists were allowed to **self-govern** in domestic issues, but **Britain** controlled international issues. In fact, the American colonies were largely left to form their own local government bodies, giving them more freedom than any other colonial territory. This gave the colonists a sense of **independence**, which led them to resent control from Britain. Threats during the French and Indian War led the colonists to call for unification in order to protect themselves.

Colonial and British Government Differences That Caused Tension

As new towns and other legislative districts developed in America, the colonists began to practice **representative government**. Colonial legislative bodies were made up of elected representatives chosen by male property owners in the districts. These individuals represented the interests of the districts from which they had been elected.

By contrast, in Britain, the **Parliament** represented the entire country. Parliament was not elected to represent individual districts. Instead, they represented specific classes. Because of this drastically different approach to government, the British did not understand the colonists' statement that they had no representation in the British Parliament.

Factors that Led to the Boston Massacre

With the passage of the **Stamp Act**, nine colonies met in New York to demand its repeal. Elsewhere, protest arose in New York City, Philadelphia, Boston, and other cities. These protests sometimes escalated into violence, often targeting ruling British officials. The passage of the **Townshend Acts** in 1767 led to additional tension in the colonies. The British sent troops to New York City and Boston. On March 5, 1770, protesters began to taunt the British troops, throwing snowballs. The soldiers responded by firing into the crowd. This clash between protesters and soldiers led to five deaths and eight injuries, and was christened the **Boston Massacre**. Shortly thereafter, Britain repealed the majority of the Townshend Acts.

Tea Act that Led to the Boston Tea Party

The majority of the **Townshend Acts** were repealed after the Boston Massacre in 1770, but Britain kept the tax on tea. In 1773, the **Tea Act** was passed. This allowed the East India Company to sell tea for much lower prices and also allowed them to bypass American distributors, selling directly to shopkeepers instead. Colonial tea merchants saw this as a direct assault on their business. In December of 1773, the **Sons of Liberty** boarded ships in Boston Harbor and dumped 342 chests of tea into the sea in protest of the new laws. This act of protest came to be known as the **Boston Tea Party**.

Coercive Acts Passed after the Boston Tea Party

The Coercive Acts passed by Britain in 1774 were meant to punish Massachusetts for defying British authority. These became collectively known as the **Intolerable Acts** in the colonies and mandated the following:

- Shut down ports in Boston until the city paid back the value of the tea destroyed during the Boston Tea Party
- Required that local government officials in Massachusetts be appointed by the governor rather than being elected by the people
- Allowed trials of British soldiers to be transferred to Britain rather than being held in Massachusetts
- Required locals to provide lodging for British soldiers any time there was a disturbance, even if lodging required them to stay in private homes

These acts led to the assembly of the First Continental Congress in Philadelphia on September 5, 1774. Fifty-five delegates met, representing 12 of the American colonies. They sought compromise with England over England's increasingly harsh efforts to control the colonies.

First Continental Congress

The goal of the First Continental Congress was to achieve a peaceful agreement with Britain. Made up of delegates from 12 of the 13 colonies, the Congress affirmed loyalty to Britain and the power of Parliament to dictate foreign affairs in the colonies. However, they demanded that the **Intolerable Acts** be repealed, and instituted a trade embargo with Britain until this came to pass.

In response, George III of England declared that the American colonies must submit or face military action. The British sought to end assemblies that opposed their policies. These assemblies gathered weapons and began to form militias. On April 19, 1775, the British military was ordered to disperse a meeting of the Massachusetts Assembly. A battle ensued on Lexington Common as the armed colonists resisted. The resulting battles became the **Battle of Lexington and Concord**—the first battles of the **American Revolution**.

Significance of the Second Continental Congress

The Second Continental Congress met in Philadelphia on May 10, 1775, a month after Lexington and Concord. Their discussions centered on the defense of the American colonies and how to conduct the growing war, as well as local government. The delegates also discussed declaring independence from Britain, with many members in favor of this drastic move. They established an army, and on June 15, named **George Washington** as its commander in chief. By 1776, it was obvious that there was no turning back from full-scale war with Britain. The colonial delegates of the Continental Congress signed the **Declaration of Independence** on July 4, 1776.

Review Video: The First and Second Continental Congress
Visit mometrix.com/academy and enter code: 835211

Origins and Basic Ideas of the Declaration of Independence

Penned by Thomas Jefferson and signed on July 4, 1776, the **Declaration of Independence** stated that King George III had violated the rights of the colonists and was establishing a tyrannical reign over them. Many of Jefferson's ideas of natural rights and property rights were shaped by 17th-century philosopher **John Locke**. Jefferson asserted all people's rights to "life, liberty and the pursuit of happiness." Locke's comparable idea asserted "life, liberty, and private property." Both felt that the purpose of government was to protect the rights of the people, and that individual rights were more important than individuals' obligations to the state.

Review Video: Declaration of Independence
Visit mometrix.com/academy and enter code: 256838

Battles of the Revolutionary War

The following are five major battles of the Revolutionary War and their significance:

- The **Battle of Lexington and Concord** (April 1775) is considered the first engagement of the Revolutionary War.
- The **Battle of Bunker Hill** (June 1775) was one of the bloodiest of the entire war. Although American troops withdrew, about half of the British army was lost. The colonists proved they could stand against professional British soldiers. In August, Britain declared that the American colonies were officially in a state of rebellion.
- The first colonial victory occurred in Trenton, New Jersey, when Washington and his troops **crossed the Delaware River** on Christmas Day, 1776, for a December 26 surprise attack on British and Hessian troops.
- The **Battle of Saratoga** effectively ended a plan to separate the New England colonies from their Southern counterparts. The surrender of British general John Burgoyne led to France joining the war as allies of the Americans and is generally considered a turning point of the war.
- On October 19, 1781, General Cornwallis surrendered after a defeat in the **Battle of Yorktown**, ending the Revolutionary War.

Review Video: The American Revolutionary War
Visit mometrix.com/academy and enter code: 935282

Significance of the Treaty of Paris

The Treaty of Paris was signed on September 3, 1783, bringing an official end to the Revolutionary War. In this document, Britain officially recognized the United States of America as an **independent nation**. The treaty established the Mississippi River as the country's western border. The treaty also restored Florida to Spain, while France reclaimed African and Caribbean colonies seized by the British in 1763. On November 25, 1783, the last British troops departed from the newly born United States of America.

Significance of the Articles of Confederation

A precursor to the Constitution, the **Articles of Confederation** represented the first attempt of the newly independent colonies to establish the basics of government. The Continental Congress approved the Articles on November 15, 1777. They went into effect on March 1, 1781, following ratification by the thirteen states. The articles prevented a central government from gaining too much power, instead giving power to a **congressional body** made up of **delegates** from all thirteen states. However, the individual states retained final authority.

Without a strong central **executive**, though, this weak alliance among the new states proved ineffective in settling disputes or enforcing laws. The idea of a weak central government needed to be revised. Recognition of these weaknesses eventually led to the drafting of a new document, the **Constitution**.

> **Review Video: Articles of Confederation**
> Visit mometrix.com/academy and enter code: 927401

Initial Proposition and Draft of the Constitution

Delegates from twelve of the thirteen states (Rhode Island was not represented) met in Philadelphia in May of 1787, initially intending to revise the Articles of Confederation. However, it quickly became apparent that a simple revision would not provide the workable governmental structure the newly formed country needed. After vowing to keep all the proceedings secret until the final document was completed, the delegates set out to draft what would eventually become the **Constitution of the United States of America**. By keeping the negotiations secret, the delegates were able to present a completed document to the country for ratification, rather than having every small detail hammered out by the general public.

General Structure of Government Proposed by the Delegates

The delegates agreed that the new nation required a **strong central government** but that its overall power should be **limited**. The various branches of the government should have **balanced power**, so that no one group could control the others. Final power belonged to the **citizens** who voted officials into office based on who would provide the best representation.

Objections Against the Constitution

Once the Constitution was drafted, it was presented for approval by the states. Nine states needed to approve the document for it to become official. However, debate and discussion continued. Major **concerns** included:

- There was no bill of rights to protect individual freedoms.
- States felt too much power was being handed over to the central government.
- Voters wanted more control over their elected representatives.

Discussion about necessary changes to the Constitution was divided into two camps: Federalists and Anti-Federalists. **Federalists** wanted a strong central government. **Anti-Federalists** wanted to prevent a tyrannical government from developing if a central government held too much power

Major Players in the Federalist and Anti-Federalist Camps

Major Federalist leaders included Alexander Hamilton, John Jay, and James Madison. They wrote a series of letters, called the **Federalist Papers**, aimed at convincing the states to ratify the Constitution. These were published in New York papers. Anti-Federalists included Thomas Jefferson and Patrick Henry. They argued against the Constitution as it was originally drafted in a series of **Anti-Federalist Papers**.

The final compromise produced a strong central government controlled by checks and balances. A **Bill of Rights** was also added, becoming the first ten amendments to the Constitution. These amendments protected rights such as freedom of speech, freedom of religion, and other basic rights. Aside from various amendments added throughout the years, the United States Constitution has remained unchanged.

Individuals Who Formed the First Administration of the New Government

The individuals who formed the first administration of the new government were:

- **George Washington**—elected as the first President of the United States in 1789
- **John Adams**—finished second in the election and became the first Vice President
- **Thomas Jefferson**—appointed by Washington as Secretary of State
- **Alexander Hamilton**—appointed Secretary of the Treasury

The Virginia Plan, the New Jersey Plan, and the Great Compromise

Disagreement immediately occurred between delegates from large states and those from smaller states. James Madison and Edmund Randolph (the governor of Virginia) felt that representation in Congress should be based on state population. This was the **Virginia Plan**. The **New Jersey Plan**, presented by William Paterson from New Jersey, proposed that each state should have equal representation. Finally, Roger Sherman from Connecticut formulated the **Connecticut Compromise**, also called the Great Compromise. The result was the familiar structure we have today. Each state has the equal representation of two Senators in the Senate, with the number of representatives in the House of Representatives based on population. This is called a **bicameral congress**. Both houses may draft bills, but financial matters must originate in the House of Representatives.

The Three-fifths Compromise and Number of Representatives for Each State

During debate on the US Constitution, a disagreement arose between the Northern and Southern states involving how **slaves** should be counted when determining a state's quota of representatives. In the South, large numbers of slaves were commonly used to run plantations. Delegates wanted slaves to be counted to determine the number of representatives but not counted to determine the amount of taxes the states would pay. The Northern states wanted exactly the opposite arrangement. The final decision was to count three-fifths of the slave population both for tax purposes and to determine representation. This was called the **Three-fifths Compromise**.

Provisions of the Commerce Compromise

The Commerce Compromise also resulted from a North/South disagreement. In the North, the economy was centered on **industry and trade**. The Southern economy was largely **agricultural**. The Northern states wanted to give the new government the ability to regulate exports as well as trade between the states. The South opposed this plan. Another compromise was in order. In the end, Congress received regulatory power over all trade, including the ability to collect **tariffs** on exported goods. In the South, this raised another red flag regarding the slave trade, as they were concerned about the effect on their economy if tariffs were levied on slaves. The final agreement allowed importing slaves to continue for twenty years without government intervention. Import taxes on slaves were limited, and after the year 1808, Congress could decide whether to allow continued imports of slaves.

American History 1790 to 1898

Alien and Sedition Acts

When **John Adams** became president, a war was raging between Britain and France. While Adams and the Federalists backed the British, Thomas Jefferson and the Democratic-Republican Party supported the French. The United States nearly went to war with France during this time period, while France worked to spread its international standing and influence under the leadership of **Napoleon Bonaparte**. The **Alien and Sedition Acts** grew out of this conflict and made it illegal to speak in a hostile fashion against the existing government. They also allowed the president to deport anyone in the US who was not a citizen and who was suspected of treason or treasonous activity. When Jefferson became the third president in 1800, he repealed these four laws and pardoned anyone who had been convicted under them.

Development of Political Parties in Early US Government

Many in the US were against political parties after seeing the way parties, or factions, functioned in Britain. The factions in Britain were more interested in personal profit than the overall good of the country, and they did not want this to happen in the US.

However, the differences of opinion between Thomas Jefferson and Alexander Hamilton led to the formation of **political parties**. Hamilton favored a stronger central government, while Jefferson felt that more power should remain with the states. Jefferson was in favor of strict Constitutional interpretation, while Hamilton believed in a more flexible approach. As others joined the two camps, Hamilton backers began to call themselves **Federalists**, while those supporting Jefferson became identified as **Democratic-Republicans**.

Development of the Whig, the Democratic, and the Republican Parties

Thomas Jefferson was elected president in 1800 and again in 1804. The **Federalist Party** began to decline, and its major figure, Alexander Hamilton, died in a duel with Aaron Burr in 1804. By 1816, the Federalist Party had virtually disappeared.

New parties sprang up to take its place. After 1824, the **Democratic-Republican Party** suffered a split. The **Whigs** rose, backing John Quincy Adams and industrial growth. The new Democratic Party formed in opposition to the Whigs, and their candidate, Andrew Jackson, was elected as president in 1828.

By the 1850s, issues regarding slavery led to the formation of the **Republican Party**, which was anti-slavery, while the Democratic Party, with a larger interest in the South, favored slavery. This Republican/Democrat division formed the basis of today's **two-party system**.

Significance of Marbury v. Madison

The main duty of the Supreme Court today is **judicial review**. This power was largely established by **Marbury v. Madison**. When John Adams was voted out of office in 1800, he worked during his final days in office to appoint Federalist judges to Supreme Court positions, knowing Jefferson, his replacement, held opposing views. As late as March 3, the day before Jefferson was to take office, Adams made last-minute appointments referred to as "Midnight Judges." One of the late appointments was William Marbury. The next day, March 4, Jefferson ordered his Secretary of State, James Madison, not to deliver Marbury's commission. This decision was backed by Chief Justice Marshall, who determined that the **Judiciary Act of 1789**, which granted the power to deliver commissions, was illegal in that it gave the Judicial Branch powers not granted in the Constitution. This case set precedent for the Supreme Court to nullify laws it found to be **unconstitutional**.

Review Video: Marbury v Madison
Visit mometrix.com/academy and enter code: 573964

Political Motivations Behind France Selling the Louisiana Purchase

With tension still high between France and Britain, Napoleon was in need of money to support his continuing war efforts. To secure necessary funds, he decided to sell the **Louisiana Territory** to the US. President **Thomas Jefferson** wanted to buy New Orleans, feeling US trade was made vulnerable to both Spain and France at that port. Instead, Napoleon sold him the entire territory for the bargain price of $15 million. The Louisiana Territory was larger than all the rest of the United States put together, and it eventually became 15 additional states.

Federalists in Congress were opposed to the purchase. They feared that the Louisiana Purchase would extend slavery, and that further western growth would weaken the power of the northern states.

Lewis and Clark Expedition

The purchase of the **Louisiana Territory** from France in 1803 more than doubled the size of the United States. President Thomas Jefferson wanted to have the area mapped and explored, since much of the territory was wilderness. He chose Meriwether Lewis and William Clark to head an expedition into the Louisiana Territory. After two years, Lewis and Clark returned, having traveled all the way to the Pacific Ocean. They brought maps, detailed journals, and a multitude of information about the wide expanse of land they had traversed. The **Lewis and Clark Expedition** opened up the west in the Louisiana Territory and beyond for further exploration and settlement.

Review Video: Purpose of the Lewis and Clark Expedition
Visit mometrix.com/academy and enter code: 570657

Causes and Result of the War of 1812

The War of 1812 grew out of the continuing tension between France and Great Britain. Napoleon continued striving to conquer Britain, while the US continued trade with both countries but favored France and the French colonies. Because of what Britain saw as an alliance between America and France, they determined to bring an end to trade between the two nations.

With the British preventing US trade with the French and the French preventing trade with the British, James Madison's presidency introduced acts to **regulate international trade**. If either Britain or France removed their restrictions, America would not trade with the other country. Napoleon acted first, and Madison prohibited trade with England. England saw this as the US formally siding with the French, and war ensued in 1812.

The **War of 1812** has been called the **Second American Revolution**. It established the superiority of the US naval forces and reestablished US independence from Britain and Europe.

The British had two major objections to America's continued trade with France. First, they saw the US as helping France's war effort by providing supplies and goods. Second, the United States had grown into a competitor, taking trade and money away from British ships and tradesmen. In its attempts to end American trade with France, the British put into effect the **Orders in Council**, which made any and all French-owned ports off-limits to American ships. They also began to seize American ships and conscript their crews.

Review Video: Overview of the War of 1812
Visit mometrix.com/academy and enter code: 507716

Review Video: Opinions About the War of 1812
Visit mometrix.com/academy and enter code: 274558

Major Military Events of the War of 1812

Two major naval battles, at **Lake Erie** and **Lake Champlain**, kept the British from invading the US via Canada. American attempts to conquer Canadian lands were not successful.

In another memorable British attack, the British invaded Washington, DC and burned the White House on August 24, 1814. Legend has it that **Dolley Madison**, the First Lady, salvaged the portrait of George Washington from the fire. On Christmas Eve, 1814, the **Treaty of Ghent** officially ended the war. However, Andrew Jackson, unaware that the war was over, managed another victory at New Orleans on January 8, 1815. This victory improved American morale and led to a new wave of national pride and support known as the "**Era of Good Feelings**."

Influence of the American System on American Economics

Spurred by the trade conflicts of the War of 1812 and supported by Henry Clay among others, the **American System** set up tariffs to help protect American interests from competition with overseas products. Reducing competition led to growth in employment and an overall increase in American industry. The higher tariffs also provided funds for the government to pay for various improvements. Congress passed high tariffs in 1816 and also chartered a federal bank. The **Second Bank of the United States** was given the job of regulating America's money supply.

McCulloch v. Maryland

Judicial review was further exercised by the Supreme Court in **McCulloch v. Maryland**. When Congress chartered a national bank, the **Second Bank of the United States**, Maryland voted to tax any bank business dealing with banks chartered outside the state, including the federally chartered bank. Andrew McCulloch, an employee of the Second Bank of the US in Baltimore, refused to pay this tax. The resulting lawsuit from the State of Maryland went to the Supreme Court for judgment.

John Marshall, Chief Justice of the Supreme Court, stated that Congress was within its rights to charter a national bank. In addition, the State of Maryland did not have the power to levy a tax on the federal bank or on the federal government in general. In cases where state and federal government collided, precedent was set for the **federal government** to prevail.

Effects of the Missouri Compromise on the Tensions Between the North and South

By 1819, the United States had developed a tenuous balance between slave and free states, with exactly 22 senators in Congress from each faction. However, Missouri was ready to join the union. As a slave state, it would tip the balance in Congress. To prevent this imbalance, the **Missouri Compromise** brought the northern part of Massachusetts into the union as Maine, establishing it as a free state to balance the admission of Missouri as a slave state. In addition, the remaining portion of the Louisiana Purchase was to remain free north of **latitude 36°30'**. Since cotton did not grow well this far north, this limitation was acceptable to congressmen representing the slave states.

However, the proposed Missouri constitution presented a problem, as it outlawed immigration of free blacks into the state. Another compromise was in order, this time proposed by **Henry Clay**. According to this new compromise, Missouri would never pass a law that prevented anyone from entering the state. Through this and other work, Clay earned his title of the "**Great Compromiser**."

Review Video: The Missouri Compromise
Visit mometrix.com/academy and enter code: 848091

Monroe Doctrine

On December 2, 1823, President Monroe delivered a message to Congress in which he introduced the **Monroe Doctrine**. In this address, he stated that any attempts by European powers to establish new colonies on the North American continent would be considered interference in American politics. The US would stay out of European matters, and expected Europe to offer America the same courtesy. This approach to foreign policy stated in no uncertain terms that America would not tolerate any new European colonies in the New World, and that events occurring in Europe would no longer influence the policies and doctrines of the US.

Review Video: What was the Monroe Doctrine?
Visit mometrix.com/academy and enter code: 953021

Effect of the Treaty of Paris on Native Americans

After the Revolutionary War, the **Treaty of Paris**, which outlined the terms of surrender of the British to the Americans, granted large parcels of land to the US that were occupied by Native Americans. The new government attempted to claim the land, treating the natives as a conquered people. This approach proved unenforceable.

Next, the government tried purchasing the land from the Native Americans via a series of **treaties** as the country expanded westward. In practice, however, these treaties were not honored, and Native Americans were simply dislocated and forced to move farther and farther west, often with military action, as American expansion continued.

Indian Removal Act of 1830 and the Treaty of New Echota

The Indian Removal Act of 1830 gave the new American government power to form treaties with Native Americans. In theory, America would claim land east of the Mississippi in exchange for land west of the Mississippi, to which the natives would relocate voluntarily. In practice, many tribal leaders were forced into signing the treaties, and relocation at times occurred by force.

The **Treaty of New Echota** in 1835 was supposedly a treaty between the US government and Cherokee tribes in Georgia. However, the treaty was not signed by tribal leaders but rather by a small portion of the represented people. The leaders protested and refused to leave, but President Martin Van Buren enforced the treaty by sending soldiers. During their forced relocation, more than 4,000 Cherokees died on what became known as the **Trail of Tears**.

Review Video: Indian Removal Act
Visit mometrix.com/academy and enter code: 666738

Jacksonian Democracy vs. Preceding Political Climate

Jacksonian Democracy is largely seen as a shift from politics favoring the wealthy to politics favoring the common man. The right to vote was given to all free white males, not just property owners, as had been the case previously. Jackson's approach favored the patronage system, laissez-faire economics, and relocation of the Native American tribes from the Southeast portion of the country. Jackson opposed the formation of a federal bank and allowed the Second Bank of the United States to collapse by vetoing a bill to renew the charter. Jackson also faced the challenge of the **Nullification Crisis** when South Carolina claimed that it could ignore or nullify any federal law it considered unconstitutional. Jackson sent troops to the state to enforce the protested tariff laws, and a compromise engineered by Henry Clay in 1833 settled the matter for the time being.

Second Great Awakening

Led by Protestant evangelical leaders, the **Second Great Awakening** occurred between 1800 and 1830. Several missionary groups grew out of the movement, including the **American Home Missionary Society**, which formed in 1826. The ideas behind the Second Great Awakening focused on personal responsibility, both as an individual and in response to injustice and suffering. The **American Bible Society** and the **American Tract Society** provided literature, while various traveling preachers spread the word. New denominations arose, including the Latter-day Saints and Seventh-day Adventists.

Another movement associated with the Second Great Awakening was the **temperance movement**, focused on ending the production and use of alcohol. One major organization behind the temperance movement was the **Society for the Promotion of Temperance**, formed in 1826 in Boston.

Attitudes Toward Education in the Early 19th Century

Horace Mann, among others, felt that schools could help children become better citizens, keep them away from crime, prevent poverty, and help American society become more unified. His *Common School Journal* brought his ideas of the importance of education into the public consciousness and proposed his suggestions for an improved American education system. Increased literacy led to increased awareness of current events, Western expansion, and other major developments of the time period. Public interest and participation in the arts and literature also increased. By the end of the 19th century, all children had access to a **free public elementary education**.

Development of Economic Trends as the US Continued to Grow

In the Northeast, the economy mostly depended on **manufacturing, industry, and industrial development**. This led to a dichotomy between rich business owners and industrial leaders and the much poorer workers who supported their businesses. The South continued to depend on **agriculture**, especially on large-scale farms or plantations worked mostly by slaves and indentured servants. In the West, where new settlements had begun to develop, the land was largely wild. Growing communities were essentially **agricultural**, raising crops and livestock. The differences between regions led each to support different interests both politically and economically.

Industrial Activity Before and After 1800

During the 18th century, goods were often manufactured in houses or small shops. With increased technology allowing for the use of machines, **factories** began to develop. In factories, a large volume of salable goods could be produced in a much shorter amount of time. Many Americans, including increasing numbers of **immigrants**, found jobs in these factories, which were in constant need of labor. Another major invention was the **cotton gin**, which significantly decreased the processing time of cotton and was a major factor in the rapid expansion of cotton production in the South.

Development of Labor Movements in the 1800s

In 1751, a group of bakers held a protest in which they stopped baking bread. This was technically the first American **labor strike**. In the 1830s and 1840s, labor movements began in earnest. Boston's masons, carpenters, and stoneworkers protested the length of the workday, fighting to reduce it to ten hours. In 1844, a group of women in the textile industry also fought to reduce their workday to ten hours, forming the **Lowell Female Labor Reform Association**. Many other protests occurred and organizations developed through this time period with the same goal in mind.

Major Ideas Driving American Foreign Policy

The three major ideas driving American foreign policy during its early years were:

- **Isolationism**—the early US government did not intend to establish colonies, though they did plan to grow larger within the bounds of North America.
- **No entangling alliances**—both George Washington and Thomas Jefferson were opposed to forming any permanent alliances with other countries or becoming involved in other countries' internal issues.
- **Nationalism**—a positive patriotic feeling about the United States blossomed quickly among its citizens, particularly after the War of 1812, when the US once again defeated Britain. The Industrial Revolution also sparked increased nationalism by allowing even the most far-flung areas of the US to communicate with each other via telegraph and the expanding railroad.

Effects of Manifest Destiny on American Politics

In the 1800s, many believed America was destined by God to expand west, bringing as much of the North American continent as possible under the umbrella of the US government. With the Northwest Ordinance and the Louisiana Purchase, over half of the continent became American. However, the rapid and relentless expansion brought conflict with the Native Americans, Great Britain, Mexico, and Spain. One result of "**Manifest Destiny**" was the **Mexican-American War** from 1846 to 1848. By the end of the war, Texas, California, and a large portion of what is now the American Southwest joined the growing nation. Conflict also arose over the **Oregon Territory**, shared by the US and Britain. In 1846, President James Polk resolved this problem by compromising with Britain, establishing a US boundary south of the 49th parallel.

Review Video: Manifest Destiny
Visit mometrix.com/academy and enter code: 957409

Mexican-American War

Spain had held colonial interests in America since the 1540s—earlier even than Great Britain. In 1810, **Mexico** revolted against Spain, becoming a free nation in 1821. **Texas** followed suit, declaring its independence after an 1836 revolution. In 1844, the Democrats pressed President Tyler to annex Texas. Unlike his predecessor, Andrew Jackson, Tyler agreed to admit Texas into the Union, and in 1845, Texas became a state.

During Mexico's war for independence, the nation incurred $4.5 million in war debts to the US. Newly elected James K. Polk offered to forgive the debts in return for New Mexico and Upper California, but Mexico refused. In 1846, war was declared in response to a Mexican attack on American troops that President Polk had moved into a disputed zone between the Rio Grande and Nueces River. As US victory grew more certain, dispute arose over how to handle slavery in any newly acquired territory. The **Wilmot Proviso**, though it was never passed, was a large source of contention, as it aimed to prohibit slavery in any territory acquired from Mexico—sowing further seeds of tension between the North and the South. The Mexican-American War ended in 1848 with Mexico agreeing to sell California and its remaining territory north of the Rio Grande.

Review Video: The Mexican-American War
Visit mometrix.com/academy and enter code: 271216

Review Video: Sectional Crisis: The Wilmot Proviso
Visit mometrix.com/academy and enter code: 974842

Popular Sovereignty and the Compromise of 1850

In addition to the pro-slavery and anti-slavery factions, a third group rose, who felt that each individual state should decide whether to allow or permit slavery within its borders. The idea that a state could make its own choices was referred to as **popular sovereignty**.

When California applied to join the union in 1849, the balance of congressional power was again threatened. The **Compromise of 1850** introduced a group of laws meant to bring an end to the conflict:

- California's admittance as a free state
- The outlaw of the slave trade in Washington, DC
- An increase in efforts to capture escaped slaves
- The right of New Mexico and Utah territories to decide individually whether to allow slavery

In spite of these measures, debate raged each time a new state prepared to enter the union.

Gadsden Purchase and the 1853 Post-War Treaty with Mexico

After the Mexican-American war, a **second treaty** in 1853 determined hundreds of miles of America's southwest borders. In 1854, the **Gadsden Purchase** was finalized, providing even more territory to aid in the building of the transcontinental railroad. This purchase added what would eventually become the southernmost regions of Arizona and New Mexico to the growing nation. The modern outline of the United States was by this time nearly complete.

Kansas-Nebraska Act Trigger of Additional Conflict

With the creation of the Kansas and Nebraska territories in 1854, another debate began. Congress allowed popular sovereignty in these territories, but slavery opponents argued that the Missouri Compromise had already made slavery illegal in this region. In Kansas, two separate governments arose, one pro-slavery and one anti-slavery. Conflict between the two factions rose to violence, leading Kansas to gain the nickname of "**Bleeding Kansas**."

Review Video: Sectional Crisis: The Kansas-Nebraska Act
Visit mometrix.com/academy and enter code: 982119

Early Leaders in the Women's Rights Movement

The women's rights movement began in the 1840s, with leaders including Elizabeth Cady Stanton, Sojourner Truth, Ernestine Rose, and Lucretia Mott. In 1869, Elizabeth Cady Stanton and Susan B. Anthony formed the **National Woman Suffrage Association**, fighting for women's right to vote.

In 1848, in Seneca Falls, the first women's rights convention was held, with about 300 attendees. The two-day **Seneca Falls Convention** discussed the rights of women to vote (suffrage) as well as equal treatment in careers, legal proceedings, etc. The convention produced a "Declaration of Sentiments," which outlined a plan for women to attain the rights they deserved. **Frederick Douglass** supported the women's rights movement, as well as the abolition movement. In fact, women's rights and abolition movements often went hand-in-hand during this time period.

Review Video: The Women's Rights Movement in America
Visit mometrix.com/academy and enter code: 987734

EVENTS AND DEVELOPMENTS THAT BROUGHT THE NORTH AND SOUTH INTO CONFLICT

The conflict between the North and South coalesced around the issue of **slavery**, but other elements contributed to the growing disagreement. Though most farmers in the South worked small farms with little or no slave labor, the huge plantations run by the South's rich depended on slaves or indentured servants to remain profitable. They had also become more dependent on **cotton**, with slave populations growing in concert with the rapid increase in cotton production. In the North, a more diverse agricultural economy and the growth of **industry** made slaves rarer. The **abolitionist movement** grew steadily, with Harriet Beecher Stowe's *Uncle Tom's Cabin* giving many an idea to rally around. A collection of anti-slavery organizations formed, with many actively working to free slaves in the South, often bringing them to the northern states or Canada.

DRED SCOTT DECISION

Abolitionist factions coalesced around the case of **Dred Scott**, using his case to test the country's laws regarding slavery. Scott, a slave, had been taken by his owner from Missouri, which was a slave state. He then traveled to Illinois, a free state, then on to the Minnesota Territory, also free based on the Missouri Compromise. After several years, he returned to Missouri, and his owner subsequently died. Abolitionists took Scott's case to court, stating that Scott was no longer a slave but free, since he had lived in free territory. The case went to the Supreme Court.

The Supreme Court stated that, because Scott, as a slave, was not a US citizen, his time in free states did not change his status. He also did not have the right to sue. In addition, the Court determined that the **Missouri Compromise** was unconstitutional, stating that Congress had overstepped its bounds by outlawing slavery in the territories.

Review Video: The Dred Scott Act
Visit mometrix.com/academy and enter code: 364838

ANTI-SLAVERY ORGANIZATIONS

Five anti-slavery organizations and their significance are:

- **American Colonization Society**—Protestant churches formed this group, aimed at returning black slaves to Africa. Former slaves subsequently formed Liberia, but the colony did not do well, as the region was not well-suited for agriculture.
- **American Anti-Slavery Society**—William Lloyd Garrison, a Quaker, was the major force behind this group and its newspaper, *The Liberator.*
- **Philadelphia Female Anti-Slavery Society**—this women-only group was formed by Margaretta Forten because women were not allowed to join the Anti-Slavery Society formed by her father.
- **Anti-Slavery Convention of American Women**—this group continued meeting even after pro-slavery factions burned down their original meeting place.
- **Female Vigilant Society**—this organization raised funds to help the Underground Railroad, as well as slave refugees.

INCIDENTS AT HARPER'S FERRY AND JOHN BROWN'S ROLE

John Brown, an abolitionist, had participated in several anti-slavery activities, including killing five pro-slavery men in retaliation, after the sacking of Lawrence, Kansas, an anti-slavery town. He and other abolitionists also banded together to pool their funds and build a runaway slave colony.

In 1859, Brown seized a federal arsenal in **Harper's Ferry**, located in what is now West Virginia. Brown intended to seize guns and ammunition and lead a slave rebellion. **Robert E. Lee** captured

Brown and 21 followers, who were subsequently tried and hanged. While Northerners took the executions as an indication that the government supported slavery, Southerners were of the opinion that most of the North supported Brown and were, in general, anti-slavery.

Presidential Candidates for the 1860 Election

The 1860 presidential candidates represented four different parties, each with a different opinion on slavery:

- **John Breckinridge**, representing the Southern Democrats, was pro-slavery but urged compromise to preserve the Union.
- **Abraham Lincoln**, of the Republican Party, was anti-slavery.
- **Stephen Douglas**, of the Northern Democrats, felt that the issue should be determined locally, on a state-by-state basis.
- **John Bell**, of the Constitutional Union Party, focused primarily on keeping the Union intact.

In the end, Abraham Lincoln won both the popular and electoral election. Southern states, who had sworn to secede from the Union if Lincoln was elected, did so, led by South Carolina and followed by the rest of the Deep South (Mississippi, Alabama, Georgia, Louisiana, Florida, and Texas). These states established the **Confederate States of America**, with its capital in Montgomery, Alabama. The president of the CSA was **Jefferson Davis**. Outgoing US President Buchanan claimed that he had no constitutional authority to stop the secession, but upon entering office, Lincoln attempted to maintain control of all Southern forts. This led to the firing on **Ft. Sumter** (SC) by the Confederates. As Lincoln called for aid, the Upper South (Virginia, Arkansas, North Carolina, and Tennessee) seceded as well, and the CSA made Richmond, Virginia its new capital.

Compromises to Save the Union

The US government made a number of compromises in an attempt to preserve the Union after Lincoln's election. The **Crittenden Compromise** extended the line of the Missouri Compromise and promised federal protection of slavery south of that line. The **House of Representatives Compromise** offered an extension of the Missouri Compromise and a Constitutional amendment to protect slavery. The **Virginia Peace Convention** produced an offer to extend the line of the Missouri Compromise and establish that slavery can never be outlawed except by the permission of the owner. Finally, Congress offered $300 for each slave. The South said that this was not enough money, and the North was appalled by the offer, regardless. It became clear that such compromises would not be enough to save the Union.

North vs. South in the Civil War

The Northern states had significant advantages, including:

- **Larger population**—the North consisted of 24 states, while the South had 11.
- **Better transportation and finances**—with railroads primarily in the North, supply chains were much more dependable, as was overseas trade.
- **Raw materials**—the North held the majority of America's gold, as well as iron, copper, and other minerals vital to wartime.

The South's advantages included the following:

- **Better-trained military officers**—many of the Southern officers were West Point trained and had commanded in the Mexican and Indian wars.
- **Familiarity with weapons**—the climate and lifestyle of the South meant most of the people were experienced with both guns and horses. The industrial North had less extensive experience.
- **Defensive position**—the South felt that victory was guaranteed, since they were protecting their own lands, while the North would be invading.
- **Well-defined goals**—the South fought an ideological war to be allowed to govern themselves and preserve their way of life. The North originally fought to preserve the Union and later to free the slaves.

Review Video: American Civil War: North vs. South Overview
Visit mometrix.com/academy and enter code: 370788

Benefit of the Emancipation Proclamation on the Union's Military Strategy

The Emancipation Proclamation, issued by President Lincoln on January 1, 1863, freed all slaves in **Confederate states** that were still in rebellion against the Union. While the original proclamation did not free any slaves in the states actually under Union control, it did set a precedent for the emancipation of slaves as the war progressed.

The **Emancipation Proclamation** worked in the Union's favor, as many freed slaves and other black troops joined the **Union Army**. Almost 200,000 blacks fought in the Union army, and over 10,000 served in the navy. By the end of the war, over 4 million slaves had been freed, and in 1865 slavery was abolished in the **13th amendment** to the Constitution.

Review Video: The Civil War: The Emancipation Proclamation
Visit mometrix.com/academy and enter code: 181778

Major Events of the Civil War

Six major events of the Civil War and their outcomes or significance are:

- The **First Battle of Bull Run** (July 21, 1861)—this was the first major land battle of the war. Observers, expecting to enjoy an entertaining skirmish, set up picnics nearby. Instead, they found themselves witness to a bloodbath. Union forces were defeated, and the battle set the course of the Civil War as long, bloody, and costly.
- The **Capture of Fort Henry** by Ulysses S. Grant—this battle in February of 1862 marked the Union's first major victory.
- The **Battle of Gettysburg** (July 1-3, 1863)—often seen as the turning point of the war, Gettysburg also saw the largest number of casualties of the war, with over 50,000 dead, wounded, or missing. Robert E. Lee was defeated, and the Confederate army, significantly crippled, withdrew.
- The **Overland Campaign** (May and June of 1864)—Grant, now in command of all the Union armies, led this high casualty campaign that eventually positioned the Union for victory.
- **Sherman's March to the Sea**—William Tecumseh Sherman, in May of 1864, conquered Atlanta. He then continued to Savannah, destroying vast amounts of property as he went.
- Following Lee's defeat at the Appomattox Courthouse, General Grant accepted **Lee's surrender** in the home of Wilmer McLean in Appomattox, Virginia on April 9, 1865.

Impact of the Civil War across America

The Civil War impacted various people in America in remarkable ways. The people most affected were likely African Americans, who were at the center of the divide between the North and the South. Many African Americans directly fought in the war on both sides. Those in the Southern states were ultimately freed as a result of the Emancipation Proclamation of 1863. Soldiers in the war saw brutal warfare and faced physical and psychological repercussions of combat. It has long been said about the Civil War that soldiers often knew or were related to the very people they were fighting. This was especially so in states that hosted battles or lied on the borders between Southern and Northern states, such as Virginia and Tennessee. Others affected included women and children who were, in some cases, located fairly near the fights and played roles as suppliers, medics, and activists, leading to some precursors to the women's rights movement. In the reconstruction, economic, political, legal, and emotional fallout had to be dealt with, leading to many decades of repair following the war.

Circumstances of Lincoln's Assassination

The Civil War ended with the surrender of the South on April 9, 1865. Five days later, Lincoln and his wife, Mary, went to the play *Our American Cousin* at the Ford Theater. John Wilkes Booth, who did not know that the war was over, did his part in a plot to help the Confederacy by shooting Lincoln. He was carried from the theater to a nearby house, where he died the next morning. Booth was tracked down and killed by Union soldiers twelve days later.

Review Video: Overview of the American Civil War
Visit mometrix.com/academy and enter code: 239557

Goals of Reconstruction and the Freedmen's Bureau

In the aftermath of the Civil War, the South was left in chaos. From 1865 to 1877, government on all levels worked to help restore order to the South, ensure civil rights to the freed slaves, and bring the Confederate states back into the Union. This became known as the **Reconstruction period**. In 1866, Congress passed the **Reconstruction Acts**, placing former Confederate states under military rule and stating the grounds for readmission into the Union.

The **Freedmen's Bureau** was formed to help freedmen both with basic necessities like food and clothing and also with employment and finding of family members who had been separated during the war. Many in the South felt the Freedmen's Bureau worked to set freed slaves against their former owners. The Bureau was intended to help former slaves become self-sufficient, and to keep them from falling prey to those who would take advantage of them. It eventually closed due to lack of funding and to violence from the **Ku Klux Klan**.

Policies of the Radical and Moderate Republicans

The **Radical Republicans** wished to treat the South quite harshly after the war. **Thaddeus Stevens**, the House Leader, suggested that the Confederate states be treated as if they were territories again, with ten years of military rule and territorial government before they would be readmitted. He also wanted to give all black men the right to vote. Former Confederate soldiers would be required to swear they had never supported the Confederacy (knows as the "Ironclad Oath") in order to be granted full rights as American citizens.

In contrast, the **moderate Republicans** wanted only black men who were literate or who had served as Union troops to be able to vote. All Confederate soldiers except troop leaders would also be able to vote. Before his death, **Lincoln** had favored a more moderate approach to

Reconstruction, hoping this approach might bring some states back into the Union before the end of the war.

PHASES OF RECONSTRUCTION

The three phases of Reconstruction are:

- **Presidential Reconstruction**—largely driven by President Andrew Johnson's policies, the presidential phase of Reconstruction was lenient on the South and allowed continued discrimination against and control over blacks.
- **Congressional Reconstruction**—Congress, controlled largely by Radical Republicans, took a different stance, providing a wider range of civil rights for blacks and greater control over Southern government. Congressional Reconstruction is marked by military control of the former Confederate States.
- **Redemption**—gradually, the Confederate states were readmitted into the Union. During this time, white Democrats took over the government of most of the South. In 1877, President Rutherford Hayes withdrew the last federal troops from the South.

CARPETBAGGERS AND SCALAWAGS

The chaos in the South attracted a number of people seeking to fill the power vacuums and take advantage of the economic disruption. **Scalawags** were southern whites who aligned with freedmen to take over local governments. Many in the South who could have filled political offices refused to take the necessary oath required to grant them the right to vote, leaving many opportunities for Scalawags and others. **Carpetbaggers** were Northerners who traveled to the South for various reasons. Some provided assistance, while others sought to make money or to acquire political power during this chaotic period.

BLACK CODES AND THE CIVIL RIGHTS BILL

The Black Codes were proposed to control freed slaves. They would not be allowed to bear arms, assemble, serve on juries, or testify against whites. Schools would be segregated, and unemployed blacks could be arrested and forced to work. The **Civil Rights Act** countered these codes, providing much wider rights for the freed slaves.

Andrew Johnson, who became president after Lincoln's death, supported the Black Codes and vetoed the Civil Rights Act in 1865 and again in 1866. The second time, Congress overrode his veto, and it became law.

Two years later, Congress voted to **impeach** Johnson, the culmination of tensions between Congress and the president. He was tried and came within a single vote of being convicted, but ultimately was acquitted and finished his term in office.

PURPOSE OF THE THIRTEENTH, FOURTEENTH, AND FIFTEENTH AMENDMENTS

The Thirteenth, Fourteenth and Fifteenth Amendments were all passed shortly after the end of the Civil War:

- The **Thirteenth Amendment** was ratified by the states on December 6, 1865. This amendment prohibited slavery in the United States.
- The **Fourteenth Amendment** overturned the Dred Scott decision and was ratified July 9, 1868. American citizenship was redefined: a citizen was any person born or naturalized in the US, with all citizens guaranteed equal legal protection by all states. It also guaranteed citizens of any race the right to file a lawsuit or serve on a jury.

- The **Fifteenth Amendment** was ratified on February 3, 1870. It states that no citizen of the United States can be denied the right to vote based on race, color, or previous status as a slave.

Black Southerners and Segregation

Most Southern Democrats supported **segregation**, or the separation of the races. Although the **Civil Rights Act of 1875** had outlawed segregated restaurants and hotels, among other things, the Supreme Court ruled in 1883 that this act violated the 14th amendment because only states, and not individuals, could be forbidden from segregation. The **Jim Crow laws** were those rules that segregated black people and white people. Although de facto (by custom) segregation had existed in the North for years, the South began to implement segregation de jure (by law). In **Plessy v. Ferguson** (1896), the Supreme Court ruled that accommodations should be "separate but equal." In **Cummings v. Board of Education** (1898), the Supreme Court allowed public schools to be segregated.

Developments in Transportation

As America expanded its borders, it also developed new technology to travel the rapidly growing country. Roads and railroads traversed the nation, with the **Transcontinental Railroad** eventually allowing travel from one coast to the other. Canals and steamboats simplified water travel and made shipping easier and less expensive. The **Erie Canal** (1825) connected the Great Lakes to the Hudson River. Other canals connected other major waterways, further facilitating transportation and the shipment of goods.

Transcontinental Railroad

In 1869, the **Union Pacific Railroad** completed the first section of a planned **transcontinental railroad**. This section went from Omaha, Nebraska to Sacramento, California. Ninety percent of the workers were Chinese, working in very dangerous conditions for very low pay. With the rise of the railroad, products were much more easily transported across the country. While this was positive overall for industry throughout the country, it was often damaging to family farmers, who found themselves paying high shipping costs for smaller supply orders while larger companies received major discounts.

Measures to Limit Immigration in the 19th Century

In 1870, the **Naturalization Act** put limits on US citizenship, allowing full citizenship only to whites and those of African descent. The **Chinese Exclusion Act of 1882** put limits on Chinese immigration. The **Immigration Act of 1882** taxed immigrants, charging 50 cents per person. These funds helped pay administrative costs for regulating immigration. **Ellis Island** opened in 1892 as a processing center for those arriving in New York. The year 1921 saw the **Emergency Quota Act** passed, also known as the **Johnson Quota Act**, which severely limited the number of immigrants allowed into the country.

Agriculture in the 19th Century

Technological Advances in Agricultural Changes

During the mid-1800s, irrigation techniques improved significantly. Advances occurred in cultivation and breeding, as well as fertilizer use and crop rotation. In the Great Plains, also known as the Great American Desert, the dense soil was finally cultivated with steel plows. In 1892, gasoline-powered tractors arrived, and they were widely used by 1900. Other advancements in agriculture's toolset included barbed wire fences, combines, silos, deep-water wells, and the cream separator.

Major Actions That Helped Improve Agriculture

Four major government actions that helped improve US agriculture in the 19th century are:

- The **Department of Agriculture** came into being in 1862, working for the interests of farmers and ranchers across the country.
- The **Morrill Land-Grant Acts** were a series of acts passed between 1862 and 1890, allowing land-grant colleges.
- In conjunction with land-grant colleges, the **Hatch Act of 1887** brought agriculture experiment stations into the picture, helping discover new farming techniques.
- In 1914, the **Smith-Lever Act** provided cooperative programs to help educate people about food, home economics, community development, and agriculture. Related agriculture extension programs helped farmers increase crop production to feed the rapidly growing nation.

Inventors from the 1800s

Major inventors from the 1800s and their inventions include:

- Alexander Graham Bell—the telephone
- Orville and Wilbur Wright—the airplane
- Richard Gatling—the machine gun
- Walter Hunt, Elias Howe, and Isaac Singer—the sewing machine
- Nikola Tesla—alternating current motor
- George Eastman—the Kodak camera
- Thomas Edison—the first commercially practical light bulbs, motion pictures, and the phonograph
- Samuel Morse—the telegraph
- Charles Goodyear—vulcanized rubber
- Cyrus McCormick—the reaper
- George Westinghouse—the transformer, the air brake

This was an active period for invention, with about 700,000 patents registered between 1860 and 1900.

Gilded Age

The time period from the end of the Civil War to the beginning of the First World War is often referred to as the **Gilded Age**, or the **Second Industrial Revolution**. The US was changing from an agricultural-based economy to an **industrial economy**, with rapid growth accompanying the shift. In addition, the country itself was expanding, spreading into the seemingly unlimited west.

This time period saw the beginning of banks, department stores, chain stores, and trusts—all familiar features of the modern-day landscape. Cities also grew rapidly, and large numbers of immigrants arrived in the country, swelling the urban ranks.

> **Review Video: The Gilded Age: An Overview**
> Visit mometrix.com/academy and enter code: 684770

Factors Leading to the Development of the Populist Party

A major **recession** struck the United States during the 1890s, with crop prices falling dramatically. **Drought** compounded the problems, leaving many American farmers in crippling debt. The **Farmers' Alliance** formed in 1875, drawing the rural poor into a single political entity.

Recession also affected the more industrial parts of the country. The **Knights of Labor**, formed in 1869 by **Uriah Stephens**, was able to unite workers into a union to protect their rights. Dissatisfied by views espoused by industrialists, the Farmers Alliance and the Knights of Labor, joined to form the **Populist Party**, also known as the People's Party, in 1892. Some of the elements of the party's platform included:

- National currency
- Graduated income tax
- Government ownership of railroads as well as telegraph and telephone systems
- Secret ballots for voting
- Immigration restriction
- Single-term limits for president and vice-president

The Populist Party was in favor of decreasing elitism and making the voice of the common man more easily heard in the political process.

Growth of the Labor Movement Through the Late 19th Century

One of the first large, well-organized strikes occurred in 1892. Called the **Homestead Strike**, it occurred when the Amalgamated Association of Iron and Steel Workers struck against the Carnegie Steel Company. Gunfire ensued, and Carnegie was able to eliminate the plant's union. In 1894, workers in the American Railway Union, led by Eugene Debs, initiated the **Pullman Strike** after the Pullman Palace Car Co. cut their wages by 28 percent. President Grover Cleveland called in troops to break up the strike on the grounds that it interfered with mail delivery. Mary Harris "Mother" Jones organized the **Children's Crusade** to protest child labor. A protest march proceeded to the home of President Theodore Roosevelt in 1903. Jones also worked with the United Mine Workers of America and helped found the **Industrial Workers of the World**.

Panic of 1893

Far from a US-centric event, the **Panic of 1893** was an economic crisis that affected most of the globe. As a response, President Grover Cleveland repealed the **Sherman Silver Purchase Act**, afraid it had caused the downturn rather than boosting the economy as intended. The Panic led to bankruptcies, with banks and railroads going under and factory unemployment rising as high as 25 percent. In the end, the **Republican Party** regained power due to the economic crisis.

Progressive Era

From the 1890s to the end of the First World War, **Progressives** set forth an ideology that drove many levels of society and politics. The Progressives were in favor of workers' rights and safety and wanted measures taken against waste and corruption. They felt science could help improve society and that the government could—and should—provide answers to a variety of social problems. Progressives came from a wide variety of backgrounds but were united in their desire to improve society.

Muckrakers and the Progressive Movement

"Muckrakers" was a term used to identify aggressive investigative journalists who exposed scandals, corruption, and many other wrongs in late 19th-century society. Among these intrepid writers were:

- **Ida Tarbell**—she exposed John D. Rockefeller's Standard Oil Trust.
- **Jacob Riis**—a photographer, he brought the living conditions of the poor in New York to the public's attention.

- **Lincoln Steffens**—he worked to expose political corruption in municipal government.
- **Upton Sinclair**—his book *The Jungle* led to reforms in the meat-packing industry.

Through the work of these journalists, many new policies came into being, including workmen's compensation, child labor laws, and trust-busting.

Dealings with Native Americans Through the End of the 19th Century

America's westward expansion led to conflict and violent confrontations with Native Americans such as the **Battle of Little Bighorn**. In 1876, the American government ordered all Native Americans to relocate to reservations. Lack of compliance led to the **Dawes Act** in 1887, which ordered assimilation rather than separation: Native Americans were offered American citizenship and a piece of their tribal land if they would accept the lot chosen by the government and live on it separately from the tribe. This act remained in effect until 1934. Reformers also forced Native American children to attend **boarding schools**, where they were not allowed to speak their native language and were immersed into a Euro-American culture and religion. Children were often abused in these schools and were indoctrinated to abandon their identity as Native Americans.

In 1890, the massacre at **Wounded Knee**, accompanied by Geronimo's surrender, led the Native Americans to work to preserve their culture rather than fight for their lands.

Review Video: Government Dealings with Native Americans Through 1900
Visit mometrix.com/academy and enter code: 635645

Native Americans in Wartime Through the Beginning of the 20th Century

The **Spanish-American War** (1898) saw a number of Native Americans serving with Teddy Roosevelt in the Rough Riders. Apache scouts accompanied General John J. Pershing to Mexico, hoping to find **Pancho Villa**. More than 17,000 Native Americans were drafted into service for **World War I**, though at the time, they were not considered legal citizens. In 1924, Native Americans were finally granted official citizenship by the **Indian Citizenship Act**.

After decades of relocation, forced assimilation, and genocide, the number of Native Americans in the US has greatly declined. Though many Native Americans have chosen—or have been forced—to assimilate, about 300 reservations exist today, with most of their inhabitants living in abject poverty.

Review Video: Wartime Role of Native Americans
Visit mometrix.com/academy and enter code: 419128

Events Leading up to the Spanish-American War

Spain had controlled **Cuba** since the 15th century. Over the centuries, the Spanish had quashed a variety of revolts. In 1886, slavery ended in Cuba, and another revolt was rising.

In the meantime, the US had expressed interest in Cuba, offering Spain $130 million for the island in 1853, during Franklin Pierce's presidency. In 1898, the Cuban revolt was underway. In spite of various factions supporting the Cubans, the US President, William McKinley, refused to recognize the rebellion, preferring negotiation over involvement in war. Then, the *Maine*, a US battleship in Havana Harbor, was blown up, killing 266 crew members. The US declared war two months later, and the war ended with a **Spanish surrender** in less than four months.

American History 1899 to Present

Influence of Big Stick Diplomacy on American Foreign Policy in Latin America

Theodore Roosevelt's famous quote, "Speak softly and carry a big stick," is supposedly of African origins, at least according to Roosevelt. He used this proverb to justify expanded involvement in foreign affairs during his tenure as President. The US military was deployed to protect American interests in **Latin America**. Roosevelt also worked to maintain an equal or greater influence in Latin America than those held by European interests. As a result, the US Navy grew larger, and the US generally became more involved in foreign affairs. Roosevelt felt that if any country was left vulnerable to control by Europe due to economic issues or political instability, the US had not only a right to intervene but was **obligated** to do so. This led to US involvement in Cuba, Nicaragua, Haiti, and the Dominican Republic over several decades leading into the First and Second World Wars.

Importance of the Panama Canal

Initial work began on the **Panama Canal** in 1881, though the idea had been discussed since the 1500s. The canal greatly reduces the length and time needed to sail from one ocean to the other by connecting the Atlantic to the Pacific through the Isthmus of Panama, which joins South America to North America. Before the canal was built, travelers had to sail around the entire perimeter of South America to reach the West Coast of the US. The French began the work after successfully completing the **Suez Canal**, which connected the Mediterranean Sea to the Red Sea. However, due to disease and high expense, the work moved slowly, and after eight years, the company went bankrupt, suspending work. The US purchased the holdings, and the first ship sailed through the canal in 1914. The Panama Canal was constructed as a lock-and-lake canal, with ships lifted on locks to travel from one lake to another over the rugged, mountainous terrain. In order to maintain control of the Canal Zone, the US assisted Panama in its battle for independence from **Colombia**.

Taft's Dollar Diplomacy vs. Roosevelt's Diplomatic Theories

During William Howard Taft's presidency, Taft instituted "**Dollar Diplomacy**." This approach was America's effort to influence Latin America and East Asia through economic rather than military means. Taft saw past efforts in these areas to be political and warlike, while his efforts focused on peaceful economic goals. His justification of the policy was to protect the **Panama Canal**, which was vital to US trade interests.

In spite of Taft's assurance that Dollar Diplomacy was a peaceful approach, many interventions proved violent. During Latin American revolts, such as those in **Nicaragua**, the US sent troops to settle the revolutions. Afterward, bankers moved in to help support the new leaders through loans. Dollar Diplomacy continued until 1913, when Woodrow Wilson was elected president.

Growth of Civil Rights for African Americans

Marcus Garvey founded the **Universal Negro Improvement Association and African Communities League (UNIA-ACL)**, which became a large and active organization focused on building black nationalism. In 1909, the **National Association for the Advancement of Colored People (NAACP)** came into being, working to defeat Jim Crow laws. The NAACP also helped prevent racial segregation from becoming federal law, fought against lynchings, helped black soldiers in WWI become officers, and helped defend the Scottsboro Boys, who were unjustly accused of rape.

Wilson's Approach to International Diplomacy

Turning away from Taft's "Dollar Diplomacy," Wilson instituted a foreign policy he referred to as "**moral diplomacy**." This approach still influences American foreign policy today.

Wilson felt that **representative government and democracy** in all countries would lead to worldwide stability. Democratic governments, he felt, would be less likely to threaten American interests. He also saw the US and Great Britain as the great role models in this area, as well as champions of world peace and self-government. Free trade and international commerce would allow the US to speak out regarding world events.

Main elements of Wilson's policies included:

- Maintaining a strong military
- Promoting democracy throughout the world
- Expanding international trade to boost the American economy

THE SIXTEENTH, SEVENTEENTH, EIGHTEENTH, AND NINETEENTH AMENDMENTS

The early 20th century saw several amendments made to the US Constitution:

- The **Sixteenth Amendment** (1913) established a federal income tax.
- The **Seventeenth Amendment** (1913) allowed popular election of senators.
- The **Eighteenth Amendment** (1919) prohibited the sale, production, and transportation of alcohol. This amendment was later repealed by the Twenty-first Amendment.
- The **Nineteenth Amendment** (1920) gave women the right to vote.

These amendments largely grew out of the Progressive Era, as many citizens worked to improve American society.

GOALS OF THE ANTI-DEFAMATION LEAGUE

In 1913, the Anti-Defamation League was formed to prevent anti-Semitic behavior and practices. Its actions also worked to prevent all forms of racism and to prevent individuals from being discriminated against for any reason involving their race. They spoke against the Ku Klux Klan, as well as other racist or anti-Semitic organizations. This organization still works to fight discrimination against all minorities.

ROLE OF THE FEDERAL TRADE COMMISSION IN ELIMINATING TRUSTS

Muckrakers such as Ida Tarbell and Lincoln Steffens brought to light the damaging trend of trusts—huge corporations working to monopolize areas of commerce so they could control prices and distribution. The **Sherman Antitrust Act** and the **Clayton Antitrust Act** set out guidelines for competition among corporations and set out to eliminate these trusts. The **Federal Trade Commission** was formed in 1914 in order to enforce antitrust measures and ensure that companies were operated fairly and did not create controlling monopolies.

MAJOR EVENTS OF WORLD WAR I

World War I occurred from 1914 to 1918 and was fought largely in Europe. The rise in **nationalism** at the beginning of the 20th century helped contribute to the possibility of war. There was also some conflict between the **imperialist** (France, Britain, and the US) and the **non-imperialist** (Germany, Italy) nations. Many large nations were seeking economic expansion outside of their own borders, and the competition for foreign markets was intense. There was also a complex system of entangling alliances; many countries were involved in several different alliances at the same time. The spark for World War I, though, was the assassination of **Archduke Franz Ferdinand**, heir to the throne of Austria-Hungary, in April of 1914 by a Serbian nationalist. When Emperor Franz Joseph declared war on Serbia, it set off a chain reaction that involved virtually every nation in Europe. At the beginning of the conflict, Woodrow Wilson declared the US neutral. Eventually, however, the US joined the war. Major events influencing US involvement included:

- **Sinking of the *Lusitania***—the British passenger liner RMS *Lusitania* was sunk by a German U-boat in 1915. Among the 1,000 civilian victims were over 100 American citizens. Outraged by this act, many Americans began to push for US involvement in the war, using the *Lusitania* as a rallying cry.
- **German U-boat aggression**—Wilson continued to keep the US out of the war, using as his 1916 reelection slogan, "He kept us out of war." While he continued to work toward an end of the war, German U-boats began to indiscriminately attack American and Canadian merchant ships carrying supplies to Germany's enemies in Europe.
- **Zimmerman Telegram** —the final event that brought the US into World War I was the interception of the Zimmerman Telegram (also known as the Zimmerman Note) on January 17th, 1917. In this telegram, Germany proposed forming an alliance with Mexico if the US entered the war.

Efforts in the US During World War I Supporting the War Effort

American **railroads** came under government control in December 1917. The widespread system was consolidated into a single system, with each region assigned a director. This greatly increased the efficiency of the railroad system, allowing the railroads to supply both domestic and military needs. Control returned to private ownership in 1920. In 1918, **telegraph, telephone, and cable services** also came under Federal control, to be returned to private management the next year. The **American Red Cross** supported the war effort by knitting clothes for Army and Navy troops. They also helped supply hospital and refugee clothing and surgical dressings. Over 8 million people participated in this effort. To generate wartime funds, the US government sold **Liberty Bonds**. In four issues, they sold nearly $25 billion—more than one-fifth of Americans purchased them. After the war, a fifth bond drive was held but sold "**Victory Liberty Bonds**."

Review Video: WWI Overview
Visit mometrix.com/academy and enter code: 659767

Influence of Wilson's Fourteen Points on Final Peace Treaties

President Woodrow Wilson proposed **Fourteen Points** as the basis for a peace settlement to end the war. Presented to the US Congress in January 1918, the Fourteen Points included:

- Five points outlining **general ideals**
- Eight points to resolve **immediate problems** of political and territorial nature
- One point proposing an **organization of nations** (the League of Nations) with the intent of maintaining world peace

In November of that same year, Germany agreed to an **armistice**, assuming the final treaty would be based on the Fourteen Points. However, during the peace conference in Paris 1919, there was much disagreement, leading to a final agreement that punished Germany and the other Central Powers much more than originally intended. Henry Cabot Lodge, who had become the Foreign Relations Committee chairman in 1918, wanted an unconditional surrender from Germany and was concerned about the article in the **Treaty of Versailles** that gave the League of Nations power to declare war without a vote from the US Congress. A **League of Nations** was included in the Treaty of Versailles at Wilson's insistence. The Senate rejected the Treaty of Versailles, and in the end, Wilson refused to concede to Lodge's demands. As a result, the US did not join the League of Nations.

Origins of the Red Scare

World War I created many jobs, but after the war ended, these jobs disappeared, leaving many unemployed. In the wake of these employment changes, the **International Workers of the World** and the **Socialist Party**, headed by Eugene Debs, became more and more visible. Workers initiated strikes in an attempt to regain the favorable working conditions that had been put into place before the war. Unfortunately, many of these strikes became violent, and the actions were blamed on "Reds," or Communists, for trying to spread their views into America. With the recent Bolshevik Revolution in Russia, many Americans feared a similar revolution might occur in the US. The **Red Scare** ensued, with many individuals jailed for supposedly holding communist, anarchist, or socialist beliefs.

Major Changes and Events that Took Place in America During the 1920s

The post-war 1920s saw many Americans moving from the farm to the city, with growing prosperity in the US. The **Roaring Twenties**, or the **Jazz Age**, was driven largely by growth in the automobile and entertainment industries. Individuals like Charles Lindbergh, the first aviator to make a solo flight across the Atlantic Ocean, added to the American admiration of individual accomplishment. Telephone lines, distribution of electricity, highways, the radio, and other inventions brought great changes to everyday life.

Review Video: 1920's
Visit mometrix.com/academy and enter code: 124996

Prohibition

The Eighteenth Amendment was ratified by most states in 1919, making the manufacture, sale, transportation, importation, and exportation of alcohol illegal; however, this change was not enforced with much success. Instead of curbing the production and consumption of alcohol, Prohibition led to the creation of a large, illegal alcohol market dominated by organized crime. Criminal organizations, like the Mafia crime syndicate, grew massively in power and influence during the 1920s and 1930s by cornering the market on the production, distribution, and sale of alcohol. Americans continued to drink alcohol in speakeasies—hidden, illegal drinking establishments. The huge illegal market for alcohol contributed to increased crime and unregulated, sometimes dangerous, alcohol.

Major Cultural Movements of the 1920s Influenced by African Americans

The **Harlem Renaissance** saw a number of African-American artists settling in Harlem in New York. This community produced a number of well-known artists and writers, including Langston Hughes, Nella Larsen, Zora Neale Hurston, Claude McKay, Countee Cullen, and Jean Toomer. The growth of jazz, also largely driven by African Americans, defined the **Jazz Age**. Its unconventional, improvisational style matched the growing sense of optimism and exploration of the decade. Originating as an offshoot of the blues, jazz began in New Orleans. Some significant jazz musicians were Duke Ellington, Louis Armstrong, and Jelly Roll Morton. **Big Band** and **Swing Jazz** also developed in the 1920s. Well-known musicians of this movement included Bing Crosby, Frank Sinatra, Count Basie, Benny Goodman, Billie Holiday, Ella Fitzgerald, and The Dorsey Brothers.

American Civil Liberties Union

The American Civil Liberties Union (**ACLU**), founded in 1920, grew from the American Union Against Militarism. The ACLU helped conscientious objectors avoid going to war during WWI, and also helped those being prosecuted under the **Espionage Act** (1917) and the **Sedition Act** (1918), many of whom were immigrants. Their major goals were to protect immigrants and other citizens who were threatened with prosecution for their political beliefs, and to support labor unions, which were also under threat by the government during the Red Scare.

Womens' Suffrage

The Nineteenth Amendment gave **women the right to vote**. This amendment was proposed on June 4, 1919, and was ratified on August 18, 1920. An amendment to give women the right to vote was first introduced in Congress in 1878, but it failed to pass. For the next four decades, the amendment was reintroduced in every session of Congress but was defeated each time. The involvement of women in the war effort during World War I spawned increased support for women's suffrage. Finally, in 1918, the House of Representatives approved the amendment to grant women suffrage, but the Senate defeated it. In 1919, the Senate also passed the amendment and sent it to the states for approval, where it was ratified in 1920.

Provisions and Importance of the National Origins Act of 1924

The National Origins Act (Johnson-Reed Act) placed limitations on **immigration**. The number of immigrants allowed into the US was based on the population of each nationality of immigrants who were living in the country in 1890. Only two percent of each nationality's 1890 population numbers were allowed to immigrate. This led to great disparities between immigrants from various nations, and Asian immigration was not allowed at all. Some of the impetus behind the Johnson-Reed Act came as a result of paranoia following the **Russian Revolution**. Fear of communist influences in the US led to a general fear of immigrants.

Ku Klux Klan

In 1866, Confederate Army veterans came together to fight against Reconstruction in the South, forming a group called the **Ku Klux Klan (KKK)**. With white supremacist beliefs, including anti-Semitism, nativism, anti-Catholicism, and overt racism, this organization relied heavily on violence to get its message across. In 1915, they grew again in power, using a film called *The Birth of a Nation*, by D.W. Griffith, to spread their ideas. In the 1920s, the reach of the KKK spread far into the north and midwest, and members controlled a number of state governments. Its membership and power began to decline during the Great Depression but experienced a resurgence later.

The Great Depression

The **Great Depression** was the largest economic downturn in the history of the United States. It began in 1929 with the stock market crash and ended around 1939. The Great Depression grew out of several factors that had developed over the previous years, including:

- Growing economic disparity between the rich and middle classes, with the rich amassing wealth much more quickly than the lower classes
- Disparity in economic distribution in industries
- Growing use of credit, leading to an inflated demand for some goods
- Government support of new industries rather than agriculture
- Risky stock market investments, leading to the stock market crash

Additional factors contributing to the Depression also included the **Labor Day Hurricane** in the Florida Keys (1935) and the **Great Hurricane of 1938** in New England, along with the **Dust Bowl** in the Great Plains, which destroyed crops and resulted in the displacement of as many as 2.5 million people.

Review Video: Causes of the Great Depression
Visit mometrix.com/academy and enter code: 635912

The Dust Bowl

The Dust Bowl (1930-1941) was a period of American history characterized by a high incidence of dust storms in the Great Plains region. The instability of the world agriculture market during World War I led to overproduction in the 1920s. Even lands previously considered unsuitable for agricultural use were leveled and developed. This excessive activity devastated the Great Plains, eliminating the natural vegetation that could have prevented the massive soil movement that occurred during the drought and strong winds of the 1930s, and resulted in widespread crop failure. In turn, the Dust Bowl led to millions of people being displaced from their homes and hundreds of thousands migrating to California in search of work and better living conditions. On their journeys, however, these migrants faced poor conditions, starvation, and dehydration. Even when they arrived in California, many of them struggled to find work. The work that was available was often hard labor, like picking cotton. Migrants also faced hostility and even phyisical violence from locals. They were often forced to live in roadside camps, which were sometimes the target of arson.

Franklin D. Roosevelt's Election and New Deal

Franklin D. Roosevelt was elected president in 1932 with his promise of a "**New Deal**" for Americans. His goals were to provide government work programs to provide jobs, wages, and relief to numerous workers throughout the beleaguered US. Congress gave Roosevelt almost free rein to produce relief legislation. The goals of this legislation were:

- **Relief**—creating jobs for the high numbers of unemployed
- **Recovery**—stimulating the economy through the National Recovery Administration
- **Reform**—passing legislation to prevent future, similar economic crashes

The Roosevelt Administration also passed legislation regarding ecological issues, including the Soil Conservation Service, aimed at preventing another Dust Bowl.

Roosevelt's Alphabet Organizations

So-called "alphabet organizations" set up during Roosevelt's administration included:

- **Civilian Conservation Corps** (CCC)—provided jobs in the forestry service
- **Agricultural Adjustment Administration** (AAA)—increased agricultural income by adjusting both production and prices
- **Tennessee Valley Authority** (TVA)—organized projects to build dams in the Tennessee River for flood control and production of electricity, resulting in increased productivity for industries in the area, and easier navigation of the Tennessee River
- **Public Works Administration** (PWA) and Civil Works Administration (CWA)—provided a multitude of jobs, initiating over 34,000 projects
- **Works Progress Administration** (WPA)—helped unemployed persons to secure employment on government work projects or elsewhere

Actions Taken During the Roosevelt Administration to Prevent Future Crashes

The Roosevelt administration passed several laws and established several institutions to initiate the "reform" portion of the New Deal, including:

- **Glass-Steagall Act**—separated investment from commercial banking
- **Securities Exchange Commission (SEC)**—helped regulate Wall Street investment practices, making them less dangerous to the overall economy

- **Wagner Act**—provided worker and union rights to improve relations between employees and employers
- **Social Security Act of 1935**—provided pensions as well as unemployment insurance

Other actions focused on insuring bank deposits and adjusting the value of American currency. Most of these regulatory agencies and government policies and programs still exist today.

Major Regulations Regarding Labor During the Great Depression

Three major regulations regarding labor that were passed after the Great Depression are:

- **Davis-Bacon Act** (1931)—provided fair compensation for contractors and subcontractors.
- The **Wagner Act** (1935)—also known as the National Labor Relations Act, it established that unions were legal, protected members of unions, and required collective bargaining. This act was later amended by the Taft-Hartley Act of 1947 and the Landrum-Griffin Act of 1959, which further clarified certain elements.
- **Walsh-Healey Act** (1936)—established a minimum wage, child labor laws, safety standards, and overtime pay.

World War II

America's Introduction to WWII

After the First World War, the US became obsessed with isolating itself from foreign conflicts. The **Nye Committee** studied the war and determined that it had been fought for financial reasons and could have been avoided. Isolationist parties achieved some popularity during this period, including the **America First Committee**, led by Charles Lindbergh, and **SOS** (Stop Organized Slaughter). The **Neutrality Laws** of 1935-7 declared that the US could not sell weapons to another country in a time of war and that US citizens could not travel on the ships of a nation at war. In 1937, FDR delivered the **Quarantine Speech**, in which he asserted that the Nazi "disease" must be contained. Finally, after conflict in Europe had escalated considerably, FDR declared that the US needed to help Britain and be an "arsenal of democracy in the world." The **Neutrality Act of 1940** made it legal for the US to sell weapons on a cash and carry basis. In August of 1941, FDR and Churchill drew up the **Atlantic Charter**, which vowed to destroy Nazism, protect the right of self-determination, and create a World Peace Organization.

Buildup to the Attack on Pearl Harbor

A number of events had created a stormy relationship between the US and Japan long before the invasion of Pearl Harbor, but the conflict reached a boiling point after President Roosevelt froze all Japanese assets in the US and cut Japan off from US oil and steel. America also had a cordial relationship at this time with Japan's longtime rival, China. The Japanese launched surprise attacks both on the American naval base at **Pearl Harbor** and on the **Philippines**, where they hoped to secure some oil.

US Involvement in WWII Concerning Europe and Africa

After the Japanese attack on Pearl Harbor in 1941, the US declared **war** on Japan, after which Germany declared war on the US. Before going after Japan, however, the US first attacked Germany; this was done because the US underestimated Japan industrially and militarily, and because the US feared Britain was on the verge of defeat. **Operation Overlord**, the Allied invasion of the European continent at Normandy, was led in part by General **Dwight D. Eisenhower**. The American generals Omar Bradley and George Patton took part in the **Allied Operation Torch**, aimed at taking back North Africa. At the **Battle of the Bulge**, in Belgium, the Germans tried to break the Allied lines, but were unsuccessful, in part because of the heroism of American soldiers.

US Involvement in WWII Concerning Asia and the Pacific

The US strategy for controlling the Pacific was known as "island hopping." In the **Coral Sea Battle of 1942**, Americans stopped the Japanese from taking Australia and New Guinea. In the same year, the **Doolittle raids** of Japanese naval bases boosted American morale. In the **Battle of Midway** (1942), the US sunk four Japanese aircraft carriers. In the **Battle of Leyte Gulf**, General Douglas MacArthur took back the Philippines and also took control of Iwo Jima and Okinawa. During this period, a team of American scientists led by Robert Oppenheimer was developing the **atomic bomb** in Los Alamos, New Mexico. Japan was warned several times by President Truman that the bomb would be used if they did not surrender. Surely enough, Americans dropped atomic bombs on **Hiroshima** on August 6, 1945, and on **Nagasaki** three days later. Japanese leaders surrendered aboard the USS Missouri on August 15, 1945.

The Holocaust is the name given to the systematic killing of Jews, Gypsies, homosexuals, and others by the Nazis. **Anti-Semitism** had existed in Europe for a long time, but the Nazis gave it renewed emphasis and, after making numerous false claims about Jews, began persecuting them upon Hitler's rise to power in 1933. Jews were disenfranchised, forced into ghettos, had their property taken, and were finally sent to work and be killed in **concentration camps**. Approximately 6 million Jews were killed during the **Holocaust**. As the situation for the Germans became more dire in the Second World War, Hitler sought to implement what he called the "final solution," in which hundreds of thousands were killed just before the fall of Nazi Germany.

Interventionist and Isolationist Approaches in World War II

When war broke out in Europe in 1939, President Roosevelt stated that the US would remain **neutral**. However, his overall approach was considered "**interventionist**," as he was willing to provide aid to the Allies without actually entering the conflict. Thus, the US supplied a wide variety of war materials to the Allied nations in the early years of the war.

Isolationists believed the US should not provide any aid to the Allies, including supplies. They felt Roosevelt, by assisting the Allies, was leading the US into a war for which it was not prepared. Led by Charles Lindbergh, the Isolationists believed that any involvement in the European conflict endangered the US by weakening its national defense.

Sequence of Events that Led the US to Declare War and Enter World War II

In 1937, Japan invaded China, prompting the US to eventually halt exports to Japan. Roosevelt also did not allow Japanese interests to withdraw money held in US banks. In 1941, **General Tojo** rose to power as the Japanese prime minister. Recognizing America's ability to bring a halt to Japan's expansion, he authorized the bombing of **Pearl Harbor** on December 7. The US responded by declaring war on Japan. Partially because of the **Tripartite Pact** among the Axis Powers, Germany and Italy then declared war on the US, later followed by Bulgaria, Hungary, and other Axis nations.

Review Video: World War II Overview
Visit mometrix.com/academy and enter code: 759402

Occurrences of World War II that Led to the Surrender of Germany

In 1941, **Hitler** violated the non-aggression pact he had signed with Stalin two years earlier by invading the USSR. **Stalin** then joined the **Allies**. Stalin, Roosevelt, and Winston Churchill planned to defeat Germany first, then Japan, bringing the war to an end.

In 1942-1943, the Allies drove **Axis** forces out of Africa. In addition, the Germans were soundly defeated at Stalingrad.

The **Italian Campaign** involved Allied operations in Italy between July 1943 and May 1945, including Italy's liberation. On June 6, 1944, known as **D-Day**, the Allies invaded France at Normandy. Soviet troops moved on the eastern front at the same time, driving German forces back. By April 25, 1945, Berlin was surrounded by Soviet troops. On May 7, Germany surrendered.

Major Events of World War II that Led to the Surrender of Japan

War continued with **Japan** after Germany's surrender. Japanese forces had taken a large portion of Southeast Asia and the Western Pacific, all the way to the Aleutian Islands in Alaska. **General Doolittle** bombed several Japanese cities while American troops scored a victory at Midway. Additional fighting in the Battle of the Coral Sea further weakened Japan's position. As a final blow, the US dropped two **atomic bombs** on Japan, one on Hiroshima and the other on Nagasaki. This was the first time atomic bombs had been used in warfare, and the devastation was horrific and demoralizing. Japan surrendered on September 2, 1945, which became **V-J Day** in the US.

The 442nd Regimental Combat Team, Tuskegee Airmen, and Navajo Code Talkers

The 442nd Regimental Combat Team consisted of Japanese-Americans fighting in Europe for the US. The most highly decorated unit per member in US history, they suffered a 93% casualty rate during the war. The **Tuskegee Airmen** were African American aviators, the first black Americans allowed to fly for the military. In spite of being ineligible to become official navy pilots, they flew over 15,000 missions and were highly decorated. The **Navajo Code Talkers** were native Navajo who used their traditional language to transmit information among Allied forces. Because Navajo is a highly-complex and unwritten language and not simply a code, the Axis powers were never able to translate it. The use of Navajo Code Talkers to transmit information was instrumental in the taking of Iwo Jima and other major victories of the war.

Circumstances and Opportunities for Women During World War II

Women served widely in the military during WWII, working in numerous positions, including the **Flight Nurses Corps**. Women also moved into the workforce while men were overseas, leading to over 19 million women in the US workforce by 1944. **Rosie the Riveter** stood as a symbol of these women and a means of recruiting others to take needed positions. Women, as well as their families left behind during wartime, also grew **Victory Gardens** to help provide food.

Japanese-American Internment During World War II

Following the attack on Pearl Harbor, the American government began to suspect that people of Japanese ancestry in America may be operating as spies for Japan, though there was little evidence for this. Just a couple of months after the attack, President Franklin D. Roosevelt signed Executive Order 9066, which allowed the government to declare Military Exclusion Zones for the purpose of national security. This made it legal for the military to remove people or other perceived threats from these exclusion zones. As a result, over 100,000 people of Japanese ancestry were removed from their homes in these areas and placed into internment camps. These camps were hastily built and offered poor living conditions. Children interned in these camps did not have access to a full education, and many Japanese-Americans lost their businesses and homes as a result of their internment.

In **Korematsu v. US** (1944), the Supreme Court ruled that the internment camps were legal, but in **ex parte Endo** (1944), the Court adjusted its decision to state that the US could only intern those whose disloyalty could be proven. Japanese internment ended in 1945, but the effects of internment on Japanese-Americans endured.

Importance of the Atomic Bomb During World War II

The atomic bomb, developed during WWII, was the most powerful bomb ever invented. A single bomb, carried by a single plane, held enough power to destroy an entire city. This devastating effect was demonstrated with the bombing of **Hiroshima** and **Nagasaki** in 1945 in what later became a controversial move, but ended the war. The bombings resulted in as many as 150,000 immediate deaths and many more as time passed after the bombings, mostly due to **radiation poisoning**.

Whatever the arguments against the use of "The Bomb," the post-WWII era saw many countries develop similar weapons to match the newly expanded military power of the US. The impact of those developments and use of nuclear weapons continues to haunt international relations today.

Importance of the Yalta Conference and the Potsdam Conference

In February 1945, Joseph Stalin, Franklin D. Roosevelt, and Winston Churchill met in Yalta to discuss the post-war treatment of the **Axis nations**, particularly Germany. Though Germany had not yet surrendered, its defeat was imminent. After Germany's official surrender, Joseph Stalin, Harry Truman (Roosevelt's successor), and Clement Attlee (replacing Churchill partway through the conference) met to formalize those plans. This meeting was called the **Potsdam Conference**. Basic provisions of these agreements included:

- Dividing Germany and Berlin into four zones of occupation
- Demilitarization of Germany
- Poland remaining under Soviet control
- Outlawing the Nazi Party
- Trials for Nazi leaders
- Relocation of numerous German citizens
- The USSR joining the United Nations, established in 1945
- Establishment of the United Nations Security Council, consisting of the US, the UK, the USSR, China, and France

Agreements Made with Post-War Japan

General Douglas MacArthur led the American **military occupation of Japan** after the country surrendered. The goals of the US occupation included removing Japan's military and making the country a democracy. A 1947 constitution removed power from the emperor and gave it to the people, as well as granting voting rights to women. Japan was no longer allowed to declare war, and a group of 28 government officials were tried for war crimes. In 1951, the US finally signed a peace treaty with Japan. This treaty allowed Japan to rearm itself for purposes of self-defense but stripped the country of the empire it had built overseas.

US Treatment of Immigrants During and After World War II

In 1940, the US passed the **Alien Registration Act**, which required all aliens older than fourteen to be fingerprinted and registered. They were also required to report changes of address within five days.

Tension between whites and Japanese immigrants in **California**, which had been building since the beginning of the century, came to a head with the bombing of **Pearl Harbor** in 1941. Believing that even those Japanese living in the US were likely to be loyal to their native country, the president ordered numerous Japanese to be arrested on suspicion of subversive action and isolated in exclusion zones known as **War Relocation Camps**. Approximately 120,000 Japanese-Americans, two-thirds of them US citizens, were sent to these camps during the war.

General State of the US After World War II

Following WWII, the US became the strongest political power in the world, becoming a major player in world affairs and foreign policies. The US determined to stop the spread of **communism**, having named itself the "**arsenal of democracy**" during the war. In addition, America emerged with a greater sense of itself as a single, integrated nation, with many regional and economic differences diminished. The government worked for greater equality, and the growth of communications increased contact among different areas of the country. Both the aftermath of the Great Depression and the necessities of WWII had given the government greater **control** over various institutions as well as the economy. This also meant that the American government took on greater responsibility for the well-being of its citizens, both in the domestic arena, such as providing basic needs, and in protecting them from foreign threats. This increased role of providing basic necessities for all Americans has been criticized by some as "**the welfare state**."

Fear of Communism Following World War II

After World War II, America became greatly concerned with the spread of communism, which was being propagated mainly by the Soviet Union and the communist party in China. A series of policies in America, Western Europe, and the Soviet Union brought the anti-communist and communist groups ever closer to open conflict. As these tensions grew in the international community, Americans became increasingly paranoid about the spread of **Communism**. There were numerous investigations aimed at weeding Communist spies out of the government, and two people, Julius and Ethel Rosenberg, were executed for spying. The leader of much of this was Senator **Joseph McCarthy**, who was famous for promoting and prolonging the "**Red Scare**" as the often-termed witch-hunt for communists in the government was known (Soviet communications released after the fall of the Soviet Union confirmed the vast majority of his accusations). The tide of anti-communism extended into a general disapproval of organized labor. The **Taft-Hartley Act** restricted the ability of labor unions markedly. In order to survive, the nation's two largest labor unions combined, forming the **AFL-CIO**.

US Policy Toward Immigrants After World War II

Prior to WWII, the US had been limiting **immigration** for several decades. After WWII, policy shifted slightly to accommodate political refugees from Europe and elsewhere. So many people were displaced by the war that in 1946, the UN formed the **International Refugee Organization** to deal with the problem. In 1948, the US Congress passed the **Displaced Persons Act**, which allowed over 400,000 European refugees to enter the US, most of them concentration camp survivors and refugees from Eastern Europe.

In 1952, the **United States Escapee Program (USEP)** increased the quotas, allowing refugees from communist Europe to enter the US, as did the **Refugee Relief Act**, passed in 1953. At the same time, however, the **Internal Security Act of 1950** allowed deportation of declared communists, and Asians were subjected to a quota based on race, rather than country of origin. Later changes included:

- **Migration and Refugee Assistance Act** (1962)—provided aid for refugees in need
- **Immigration and Nationality Act** (1965)—ended quotas based on nation of origin
- **Immigration Reform and Control Act** (1986)—prohibited the hiring of illegal immigrants but also granted amnesty to about three million illegals already in the country

Accomplishments of Harry S. Truman

Harry S. Truman took over the presidency from Franklin D. Roosevelt near the end of WWII. He made the final decision to drop atomic bombs on Japan and played a major role in the final decisions regarding the treatment of post-war Germany. On the domestic front, Truman initiated a 21-point plan known as the **Fair Deal**. This plan expanded Social Security, provided public housing, and made the Fair Employment Practice Committee permanent. Truman helped support Greece and Turkey (which were under threat from the USSR), supported South Korea against communist North Korea, and helped with recovery in Western Europe. He also participated in the formation of **NATO**, the North Atlantic Treaty Organization.

Events and Importance of the Korean War

The Korean War began in 1950 and ended in 1953. For the first time in history, a world organization—the **United Nations**—played a military role in a war. North Korea sent communist troops into South Korea, seeking to bring the entire country under communist control. The UN sent out a call to member nations, asking them to support South Korea. Truman sent troops, as did many other UN member nations. The war ended three years later with a **truce** rather than a peace treaty, and Korea remains divided at the **38th parallel north**, with communist rule remaining in the North and a democratic government ruling the South.

Effects of US Cold War Foreign Policy Acts on the International Relationships

The following are US Cold War foreign policy acts and how they affected international relationships, especially between the US and the Soviet Union:

- **Marshall Plan**—this sent aid to war-torn Europe after WWII, largely focusing on preventing the spread of communism.
- **Containment Policy**—proposed by George F. Kennan, the containment policy focused on containing the spread of Soviet communism.
- **Truman Doctrine**—Harry S. Truman stated that the US would provide both economic and military support to any country threatened by Soviet takeover.
- **National Security Act**—passed in 1947, this act reorganized the government's military departments into the Department of Defense and created the Central Intelligence Agency and the National Security Council.

The combination of these acts led to the **Cold War**, with Soviet communists attempting to spread their influence and the US and other countries trying to contain or stop this spread.

Accomplishments of Dwight D. Eisenhower

Eisenhower carried out a middle-of-the-road foreign policy and brought the US several steps forward in equal rights. He worked to minimize tensions during the Cold War and negotiated a peace treaty with Russia after the death of Stalin. He enforced desegregation by sending troops to Little Rock Central High School in Arkansas, as well as ordering the desegregation of the military. Organizations formed during his administration included the Department of Health, Education, and Welfare, and the National Aeronautics and Space Administration (NASA).

Effect of the Arms Race on Post WWII International Relations

After World War II, major nations, particularly the US and USSR, rushed to develop highly advanced weapons systems such as the **atomic bomb** and later the **hydrogen bomb**. These countries seemed determined to outpace each other with the development of numerous, deadly weapons. These weapons were expensive and extremely dangerous, and it is possible that the war between US and Soviet interests remained "cold" due to the fear that one side or the other would use these powerful weapons.

TECHNOLOGICAL ADVANCES THAT OCCURRED THROUGHOUT THE 1900S

Numerous technological advances throughout the 1900s led to more effective treatment of diseases, more efficient communication and transportation, and new means of generating power. Advances in **medicine** increased the human lifespan in developed countries, and near-instantaneous **communication** opened up a myriad of possibilities. Some of these advances include:

- Discovery of penicillin (1928)
- Supersonic air travel (1947)
- Nuclear power plants (1951)
- Orbital satellite leading to manned space flight (Sputnik, 1957)
- First man on the moon (1969)

NATO, WARSAW PACT, AND THE BERLIN WALL

NATO, the **North Atlantic Treaty Organization**, came into being in 1949. It essentially amounted to an agreement among the US and Western European countries that an attack on any one of these countries was to be considered an attack against the entire group. Under the influence of the Soviet Union, the Eastern European countries of the USSR, Bulgaria, East Germany, Poland, Romania, Albania, Hungary, and Czechoslovakia responded with the **Warsaw Pact**, which created a similar agreement among those nations. In 1961, a wall was built to separate communist East Berlin from democratic West Berlin. This was a literal representation of the "**Iron Curtain**" that separated the democratic and communist countries throughout the world.

PRESIDENCY OF JOHN F. KENNEDY

Although his term was cut short by his assassination, **JFK** instituted economic programs that led to a period of continuous expansion in the US unmatched since before WWII. He formed the Alliance for Progress and the Peace Corps, organizations intended to help developing nations. He also oversaw the passage of new civil rights legislation and drafted plans to attack poverty and its causes, along with support of the arts. Kennedy's presidency ended when he was assassinated by **Lee Harvey Oswald** in 1963.

EVENTS OF THE CUBAN MISSILE CRISIS

The Cuban Missile Crisis occurred in 1962, during John F. Kennedy's presidency. Russian Premier **Nikita Khrushchev** decided to place nuclear missiles in **Cuba** to protect the island from invasion by the US. An American U-2 plane flying over the island photographed the missile bases as they were being built. Tensions rose, with the US concerned about nuclear missiles so close to its shores, and the USSR concerned about American missiles that had been placed in **Turkey**. Eventually, the missile sites were removed, and a US naval blockade turned back Soviet ships carrying missiles to Cuba. During negotiations, the US agreed to remove their missiles from Turkey and agreed to sell surplus wheat to the USSR. A telephone hotline between Moscow and Washington was set up to allow instant communication between the two heads of state to prevent similar incidents in the future.

ACCOMPLISHMENTS OF THE LYNDON B. JOHNSON PRESIDENCY

Kennedy's vice president, **Lyndon Johnson**, assumed the presidency after Kennedy's **assassination**. He supported civil rights bills, tax cuts, and other wide-reaching legislation that Kennedy had also supported. Johnson saw America as a "**Great Society**," and enacted legislation to fight disease and poverty, renew urban areas, and support education and environmental conservation. Medicare and Medicaid were instituted under his administration. He continued

Kennedy's support of space exploration, and he is also known, although less positively, for his handling of the **Vietnam War**.

Factors That Led to the Growth of the Civil Rights Movement

In the 1950s, post-war America was experiencing a rapid growth in prosperity; however, African Americans found themselves left behind. Racial segregation and discrimination were still legalized at this time and disproportionately affected black Americans and other minority groups. The civil rights movement arose to abolish legalized discrimination and provide equality for all Americans. While there were many different ideologies that made up the civil rights movement, the movement is largely characterized by peaceful protest and civil disobedience.

- **Rosa Parks**—often called the "mother of the Civil Rights Movement," her refusal to give up her seat on the bus to a white man served as a seed from which the movement grew.
- **Martin Luther King, Jr.**—the best-known leader of the movement, King drew on Gandhi's beliefs and encouraged non-violent opposition. He led a march on Washington in 1963, received the Nobel Peace Prize in 1964, and was assassinated in 1968.
- **Malcolm X**—espousing less peaceful means of change, Malcolm X became a Black Muslim and supported black nationalism.

Policies and Legislation Enacted Expanding Minority Rights

Several major acts have been passed, particularly since WWII, to protect the rights of minorities in America. These include:

- Civil Rights Act (1964)
- Voting Rights Act (1965)
- Age Discrimination Act (1967)
- Americans with Disabilities Act (1990)

Other important movements for civil rights included a prisoner's rights movement, movements for immigrant rights, and the women's rights movement. The National Organization for Women (NOW) was established in 1966 and worked to pass the Equal Rights Amendment. The amendment was passed, but not enough states ratified it for it to become part of the US Constitution.

Impact of Stokely Carmichael, Adam Clayton Powell, and Jesse Jackson

- **Stokely Carmichael**—Carmichael originated the term "Black Power" and served as head of the Student Nonviolent Coordinating Committee. He believed in black pride and black culture and felt separate political and social institutions should be developed for blacks.
- **Adam Clayton Powell**—chairman of the Coordinating Committee for Employment, he led rent strikes and other actions, as well as a bus boycott, to increase the hiring of blacks.
- **Jesse Jackson**—Jackson was selected to head the Chicago Operation Breadbasket in 1966, and went on to organize boycotts and other actions. He also had an unsuccessful run for president.

Events of the Civil Rights Movement

Major events of the Civil Rights Movement include:

- **Montgomery Bus Boycott**—in 1955, Rosa Parks refused to give her seat on the bus to a white man. As a result, she was tried and convicted of disorderly conduct and of violating local ordinances. A 381-day bus boycott ensued, protesting segregation on public buses.

- **Desegregation of Little Rock**—in 1957, after the Supreme Court decision on Brown v. Board of Education, which declared "separate but equal" unconstitutional, the Arkansas school board voted to desegregate their schools. Even though Arkansas was considered progressive, its governor brought in the Arkansas National Guard to prevent nine black students from entering Central High School in Little Rock. President Eisenhower responded by federalizing the National Guard and ordering them to stand down.
- **Birmingham Campaign**—protestors organized a variety of actions such as sit-ins and an organized march to launch a voting campaign. When the City of Birmingham declared the protests illegal, the protestors, including Martin Luther King, Jr., persisted and were arrested and jailed.
- **March on Washington**—on August 28, 1963, more than 200,000 people marched on Washington, D.C. to advocate for civil and economic rights for African Americans. Dr. Martin Luther King Jr., positioned near the Lincoln Memorial, gave his famous "I Have a Dream" speech. This march was heavily influential in passing the Civil Rights Act of 1964.

Pieces of Legislation Passed as a Result of the Civil Rights Movement

Other pieces of legislation passed as a result of the Civil Rights movement include:

- **Brown v. Board of Education** (1954)—the Supreme Court declared that "separate but equal" accommodations and services were unconstitutional.
- **Civil Rights Act of 1964**—this declared discrimination illegal in employment, education, or public accommodation.
- **Voting Rights Act of 1965**—this act ended various activities practiced, mostly in the South, to bar blacks from exercising their voting rights. These included poll taxes and literacy tests.
- **Fair Housing Act of 1968**—this act prohibited discrimination in the sale, purchase, and rental of housing.

Other pieces of legislation that expanded minority rights include the Age Discrimination Act (1967) and the Americans with Disabilities Act (1990). Other important movements for civil rights included prisoners' rights movements, movements for immigrant rights, and the women's rights movement. The National Organization for Women (NOW) was established in 1966 and worked to pass the Equal Rights Amendment. The amendment was passed, but not enough states ratified it for it to become part of the US Constitution.

Events of the Richard Nixon Presidency

Richard Nixon is best known for the **Watergate scandal** during his presidency, but other important events marked his tenure as president, including:

- End of the Vietnam War
- Improved diplomatic relations between the US and China, and the US and the USSR
- National Environmental Policy Act passed, providing for environmental protection
- Compulsory draft ended
- Supreme Court legalized abortion in Roe v. Wade (subsequently overturned in 2022)
- Watergate

The Watergate scandal of 1972 ended Nixon's presidency. Rather than face impeachment and removal from office, he **resigned** in 1974.

US Perspective on the Progression of the Vietnam War

After World War II, the US pledged, as part of its foreign policy, to come to the assistance of any country threatened by **communism**. When Vietnam was divided into a communist North and democratic South, much like Korea before it, the eventual attempts by the North to unify the country under Communist rule led to intervention by the US. On the home front, the **Vietnam War** became more and more unpopular politically, with Americans growing increasingly discontent with the inability of the US to achieve the goals it had set for the Asian country. When President **Richard Nixon** took office in 1969, his escalation of the war led to protests at Kent State in Ohio, during which several students were killed by National Guard troops. Protests continued, eventually resulting in the end of the compulsory draft in 1973. In that same year, the US departed Vietnam. In 1975, the South surrendered, and Vietnam became a unified country under communist rule.

Events of the Gerald Ford Presidency

Gerald Ford was appointed to the vice presidency after Nixon's vice president **Spiro Agnew** resigned in 1973 under charges of tax evasion. With Nixon's resignation, Ford became president.

Ford's presidency saw negotiations with Russia to limit nuclear arms, as well as struggles to deal with inflation, economic downturn, and energy shortages. Ford's policies sought to reduce governmental control of various businesses and reduce the role of government overall. He also worked to prevent escalation of conflicts in the Middle East.

End of the Cold War and the Dissolution of the Soviet Union

In the late 1980s, **Mikhail Gorbachev** led the Soviet Union. He introduced a series of reform programs. **Ronald Reagan** famously urged Gorbachev to tear down the **Berlin Wall** as a gesture of growing freedom in the Eastern Bloc, and in 1989 it was demolished, ending the separation of East and West Germany. The Soviet Union relinquished its power over the various republics in Eastern Europe, and they became independent nations with their own individual governments. In 1991, the **USSR** was dissolved and the Cold War also came to an end.

Review Video: The End of the Cold War
Visit mometrix.com/academy and enter code: 278032

Events of the Jimmy Carter Presidency

Jimmy Carter was elected as president in 1976. Faced with a budget deficit, high unemployment, and continued inflation, Carter also dealt with numerous matters of international diplomacy, including:

- **Torrijos-Carter Treaties**—the US gave control of the Panama Canal to Panama.
- **Camp David Accords**—negotiations between Anwar el-Sadat, the president of Egypt, and Menachem Begin, the Israeli Prime Minister, led to a peace treaty between Egypt and Israel.
- **Strategic Arms Limitation Talks (SALT)**—these led to agreements and treaties between the US and the Soviet Union.
- **Iran Hostage Crisis**—after the Shah of Iran was deposed, an Islamic cleric, Ayatollah Khomeini, came to power. The shah came to the US for medical treatment, and Iran demanded his return so he could stand trial. In retaliation, a group of Iranian students stormed the US Embassy in Iran. Fifty-two American hostages were held for 444 days.

Jimmy Carter was awarded the **Nobel Peace Prize** in 2002.

Events of the Ronald Reagan Presidency

Ronald Reagan, at 69, became the oldest American president. The two terms of his administration included notable events such as:

- Reaganomics, also known as supply-side, trickle-down, or free-market economics, involving major tax cuts
- Economic Recovery Tax Act of 1981
- First female justice appointed to the Supreme Court—Sandra Day O'Connor
- Massive increase in the national debt—from $1 trillion to $3 trillion
- Reduction of nuclear weapons via negotiations with Mikhail Gorbachev
- Iran-Contra scandal—cover-up of US involvement in revolutions in El Salvador and Nicaragua
- Deregulation of savings and loan industry
- Loss of the space shuttle *Challenger*

Events of the George H. W. Bush Presidency

Reagan's presidency was followed by a term under his former vice president, **George H. W. Bush**. Bush's run for president included the famous "**thousand points of light**" speech, which was instrumental in increasing his standing in the election polls. During Bush's presidency, numerous international events took place, including:

- Fall of the Berlin wall and Germany's unification
- Panamanian dictator Manuel Noriega captured and tried on drug and racketeering charges
- Dissolution of the Soviet Union
- Gulf War, or Operation Desert Storm, triggered by Iraq's invasion of Kuwait
- Tiananmen Square Massacre in Beijing, China
- Ruby Ridge
- The arrival of the World Wide Web

Events of the William Clinton Presidency

William Jefferson "Bill" Clinton was the second president in US history to be impeached, but he was not convicted, and maintained high approval ratings in spite of the impeachment. Major events during his presidency included:

- Family and Medical Leave Act
- "Don't Ask, Don't Tell," a compromise position regarding homosexuals serving in the military
- North American Free Trade Agreement, or NAFTA
- Defense of Marriage Act
- Oslo Accords
- Siege at Waco, Texas, involving the Branch Davidians led by David Koresh
- Bombing of the Murrah Federal Building in Oklahoma City, Oklahoma
- Troops sent to Haiti, Bosnia, and Somalia to assist with domestic problems in those areas

EVENTS OF THE GEORGE W. BUSH PRESIDENCY

George W. Bush, son of George H. W. Bush, became president after Clinton. Major events during his presidency included:

- September 11, 2001, al-Qaeda terrorists hijack commercial airliners and fly into the World Trade Center towers and the Pentagon, killing nearly 3,000 Americans
- US troops sent to Afghanistan to hunt down al-Qaeda leaders, including the head of the organization, Osama Bin Laden; beginning of the War on Terror
- US troops sent to Iraq, along with a multinational coalition, to depose Saddam Hussein and prevent his deployment of suspected weapons of mass destruction
- Subprime mortgage crisis and near collapse of the financial industry, leading to the Great Recession; first of multiple government bailouts of the financial industry

EVENTS OF THE BARACK OBAMA PRESIDENCY

In 2008, Barack Obama, a senator from Illinois, became the first African American US president. His administration focused on improving the lot of a country suffering from a major recession. His major initiatives included:

- Economic bailout packages
- Improvements in women's rights
- Moves to broaden LGBT rights
- Health care reform legislation
- Reinforcement of the war in Afghanistan

EVENTS OF THE DONALD TRUMP PRESIDENCY

In 2016, Donald Trump, previously a real estate developer and television personality, was elected 45th president after a tumultuous election in which he won the electoral college but lost the popular vote. Marked by tension between the administration and domestic media, Trump's initiatives included:

- Appointing three Supreme Court Justices: Neil Gorsuch, Brett Kavanaugh, and Amy Coney Barrett
- Passing a major tax reform bill
- Enacting travel and emigration restrictions on eight nations: Iran, Libya, Syria, Yemen, Somalia, Chad, North Korea, and Venezuela
- Recognizing Jerusalem, rather than Tel Aviv, as the capital of Israel
- Responding to the novel coronavirus (SARS-CoV-2) outbreak

Almost completely along party lines, Donald Trump was impeached by the House on charges of abuse of power and obstruction of Congress; he was acquitted by the Senate.

Chapter Quiz

Ready to see how well you retained what you just read? Scan the QR code to go directly to the chapter quiz interface for this study guide. If you're using a computer, simply visit the online resources page at **mometrix.com/resources719/praxsocst** and click the Chapter Quizzes link.

World History

Transform passive reading into active learning! After immersing yourself in this chapter, put your comprehension to the test by taking a quiz. The insights you gained will stay with you longer this way. Scan the QR code to go directly to the chapter quiz interface for this study guide. If you're using a computer, simply visit the online resources page at **mometrix.com/resources719/praxsocst** and click the Chapter Quizzes link.

World History Pre-1400

Different Periods of Prehistory

History begins when people started recording their existence with writing systems, but the vast majority of human existence occurred during prehistoric times. Because writing systems were not yet invented, much of our information about prehistory comes from archaeology and anthropology, which use physical remains and environmental evidence to uncover insights into humanity before we developed systems of recording our experiences.

- **Lower Paleolithic or Early Stone Age**— early humans were hunter-gatherers who lived in small groups or tribes and used crude tools like needles, hatchets, awls, and cutting tools made of stone, wood, and other natural materials.
- **Middle Paleolithic or Middle Stone Age**, beginning approximately 300,000 BC—stone tools became more sophisticated, local traditions were developed, and communities became more complex.
- **Upper Paleolithic or Late Stone Age**—Humans began to develop a wider variety of tools. These tools were better made and more specialized. They also began to wear clothes, organize in groups with definite social structures, and practice art. Most lived in caves during this time period.
- **Bronze Age**, beginning approximately 3000 BC—metals are discovered, and the first civilizations emerge as humans become more technologically advanced.
- **Iron Age**, beginning 1200 to 1000 BC—metal tools replace stone tools as humans develop knowledge of smelting.

Anthropology

Anthropology is the study of human culture. Anthropologists study groups of humans, how they relate to each other, and the similarities and differences between these different groups and cultures. Anthropological research takes two approaches: **cross-cultural research** and **comparative research**. Most anthropologists work by living among different cultures and participating in those cultures in order to learn about them.

There are four major **divisions** within anthropology:

- Biological anthropology
- Cultural anthropology
- Linguistic anthropology
- Archaeology

Science of Archaeology

Archaeology is the study of past human cultures by evaluating what they leave behind. This can include bones, buildings, art, tools, pottery, graves, and even trash. Archaeologists maintain detailed notes and records of their findings and use special tools to evaluate what they find. Photographs, notes, maps, artifacts, and surveys of the area can all contribute to the evaluation of an archaeological site. By studying all these elements of numerous archeological sites, scientists have been able to theorize that humans or near-humans have existed for about 600,000 years. Before that, more primitive humans are believed to have appeared about one million years ago. These humans eventually developed into **Cro-Magnon man**, and then **Homo sapiens**, or modern man.

Neolithic Period

The Neolithic period, also known as the **New Stone Age**, refers to that stage of human cultural evolution in which man developed stone tools, settled in villages, and began making crafts. In order to begin living in towns, man had to learn how to domesticate animals and sustain agriculture; formerly, in the Paleolithic and Mesolithic periods, man had subsisted through hunting, fishing, and gathering. The **Neolithic period** is said to have ended when urban civilizations began, or when metal tools or writing began. Because the designation of Neolithic depends on these factors, anthropologists date its occurrence differently for different regions and populations. At present, anthropologists believe that the earliest Neolithic culture was in southwest Asia between 8000 and 6000 BC.

Requirements for Early Civilizations and States

While historians and archaeologists don't all agree on exactly what makes a civilization, many consider the following features defining characteristics of civilizations:

- Urban centers
- Complex social structures
- Centralized government
- Organized religion
- Monumental architecture
- Writing systems
- Economic systems and trade
- Division of labor

The **earliest civilizations** developed in river valleys where reliable, fertile land was easily found, including:

- The Nile River Valley in Egypt
- Mesopotamia
- The Indus Valley
- Hwang Ho in China

The very earliest civilizations developed in the **Tigris-Euphrates valley** in Mesopotamia, which is now part of Iraq, and in Egypt's **Nile valley**. These civilizations arose between 5000 and 3000 BC. The area where these civilizations grew is known as the Fertile Crescent. Geography and the availability of water made large-scale human habitation possible. The walled city of Uruk, which was built in Sumer (southern Mesopotamia), is often considered the first city ever constructed.

Importance of Rivers and Water to the Growth of Early Civilizations

The earliest civilizations are also referred to as **fluvial civilizations** because they were founded near rivers. Rivers and the water they provide were vital to these early groupings, offering:

- Water for drinking, cultivating crops, and caring for domesticated animals
- A gathering place for wild animals that could be hunted
- Rich soil deposits as a result of regular flooding

Irrigation techniques helped direct water where it was most needed, to sustain herds of domestic animals and to nourish crops of increasing size and quality.

Fertile Crescent

James Breasted, an archaeologist from the University of Chicago, popularized the term "**Fertile Crescent**" to describe the area in Southwest Asia and the Mediterranean basin where the earliest civilizations arose. The region includes modern-day Iraq, Syria, Lebanon, Israel, Palestine, and Jordan. It is bordered on the south by the Syrian and Arabian Deserts, the west by the Mediterranean Sea, and to the north and east by the Taurus and Zagros Mountains, respectively. This area not only provided the raw materials for the development of increasingly advanced civilizations but also saw waves of migration and invasion, leading to the earliest wars and genocides as groups conquered and absorbed each other's cultures and inhabitants.

Ancient Civilizations of Mesopotamia and the Near East

These cultures controlled different areas of Mesopotamia and the Near East during various time periods but were similar in that they were **autocratic**: a single ruler served as the head of the government and often was the main religious ruler as well. These rulers were often tyrannical, militaristic leaders who controlled all aspects of life, including law, trade, and religious activity. Portions of the legacies of these civilizations remain in cultures today. These include mythologies, religious systems, mathematical innovations, and even elements of various languages.

The Near East was home to many distinct cultures and civilizations in the ancient world. These cultures controlled different areas of Mesopotamia and the Near East during various time periods but were similar in that they were **autocratic**: a single ruler served as the head of the government and often was the main religious ruler as well. These rulers were often tyrannical, militaristic leaders who controlled all aspects of life, including law, trade, and religious activity. Portions of the legacies of these civilizations remain in cultures today. These include mythologies, religious systems, mathematical innovations, and even elements of various languages.

The Sumerians

Sumer, located in the southern part of Mesopotamia, consisted of a dozen **city-states**. Each city-state had its own patron gods, and the leader of each city-state also served as the high priest. Cultural legacies of Sumer include:

- The invention of writing
- The invention of the wheel
- The first library—established in Assyria by Ashurbanipal
- The Hanging Gardens of Babylon—one of the Seven Wonders of the Ancient World

- First written laws—Ur-Nammu's Codes and the Codes of Hammurabi
- The *Epic of Gilgamesh*—the first recorded epic story

Review Video: Early Mesopotamia: The Sumerians
Visit mometrix.com/academy and enter code: 939880

The Babylonians

The Babylonians conquered the Sumerians and established a city on the Euphrates River in approximately 1750 BC One of the most famous Babylonian rulers was Hammurabi, an Amorite leader who established the famous Code of Hammurabi, an extremely detailed set of laws. This marked the first time that a set of rules governing every aspect of social life was applied to an entire people.

The Amorites

A group of Semitic-speaking people often referred to as the Amorites existed in Mesopotamia for a long time, but the early history of this group is not well known. Some scholars believe the term actually referred to multiple different groups of people from the west. The earliest records of them paint the Amorites as a nomadic, potentially uncivilized, people who made incursions into established territories, oftentimes stealing from communities; however, they eventually assimilated into Mesopotamia and added elements of their own culture. The Amorites are best known for their period of rule over the kingdom of Babylonia.

The Hittites

The Hittites conquered the Babylonian civilization but adopted their religion, laws, and literature. Overall, the Hittites tended to tolerate other religions, unlike many other contemporary cultures, and absorbed foreign gods into their own belief systems rather than forcing their religion onto peoples they conquered. The Hittite Empire reached its peak in 1600-1200 BC. After a war with Egypt, which weakened them severely, they were eventually conquered by the Assyrians.

The Assyrians

The Assyrians developed powerful military technologies, such as horse-drawn chariots and iron weapons, that allowed them to eventually build one of the world's oldest empires. They had a long and complex history, at times being subjects under the rule of other civilizations, like the Babylonians. At their peak (c. 911-612 BC), they were one of the most powerful civilizations in the world, and they were able to maintain their empire for hundreds of years.

The Chaldeans

The Chaldeans were a Semitic people who ruled over the Neo-Babylonian Empire. Originally a separate tribal group, they largely assimilated into Babylonian culture. The Neo-Babylonian Empire ultimately fell to the Persian Empire in 539 BC.

The Persian Empire

The Persian Empire (Achaemenid Empire) were conquerors, but those they conquered were often allowed to keep their own laws, customs, and religious traditions rather than being forced to accept those of their conquerors. They are recognized for their centralized bureaucratic administration and complex infrastructure. They mainly practiced Zoroastrianism, a religion that was heavily influential before it declined after the spread of Islam in the region.

HEBREWS

The Hebrew or ancient Israelite culture emerged in the Levant in the second century BC. They developed the monotheistic religion that eventually developed into modern Judaism and Christianity. The Hebrew history is well-preserved and contains detailed descriptions of conquests against them from Egypt, Assyria, Babylon, Persia, and Rome, many of which can be confirmed from artifacts of other cultures. Despite being conquered by a variety of empires, their cultural identity has survived and still exists today.

EGYPT

Egypt was one of the most powerful and culturally significant civilizations in the ancient world. Its history is often broken up into a few distinct eras: the Old Kingdom, the First Intermediate Period, the Middle Kingdom, the Second Intermediate Period, the New Kingdom, the Third Intermediate Period, and the Late Period. These eras cover a span of around 3,000 years, beginning approximately in the year 3150 BC, when Menes (an Egyptian ruler whose identity is debated) united Upper and Lower Egypt, and ending around 332 BC, when Alexander the Great conquered the region.

Egypt was centered around the Nile River, which had a predictable annual flooding schedule that the Egyptians used to grow large surpluses of crops. The Egyptians traded these surplus crops with nearby civilizations, particularly Mesopotamia. This trade formed one of the chief bases of their wealth and influence.

During its long history, Ancient Egypt contributed many technological and cultural innovations in the fields of religion, art, engineering, astronomy, medicine, and more. They are renowned for their impressive monuments, temples, and tombs, including the Great Pyramids and the Sphinx of Giza. On many of these monuments is a complex script developed by the Egyptians called hieroglyphics. This is a written language that uses pictures and other symbols to represent words, ideas, and sounds. It was often used to record important events, such as battles, and the lives of important people, such as the Pharaoh (the modern title attributed to the king of Egypt).

KUSHITES

Kush, or Cush, was located in Nubia, south of ancient Egypt, and the earliest existing records of this civilization were found in Egyptian texts. At one time, Kush was the largest empire on the Nile River, ruling not only Nubia but Upper and Lower Egypt as well.

In Neolithic times, Kushites lived in villages, with buildings made of mud bricks. They were settled rather than nomadic and practiced hunting and fishing, cultivated grain, and also herded cattle. Kerma, the capital, was a major center of trade.

Kush determined leadership through matrilineal descent of their kings, as did Egypt. Their heads of state, the Kandake or Kentake, were female. Their polytheistic religion included the primary Egyptian gods as well as regional gods, including a lion-headed god, which is commonly found in African cultures. Kush was conquered by the Aksumite Empire in the 4th century AD.

PHOENICIANS

Skilled seafarers and navigators, the Phoenicians were a maritime civilization mostly along the coast of the Levant region. They were highly skilled in trade and developed a purple dye that was in great demand in the ancient world. They were also skilled glass and metal workers. They devised a phonetic alphabet, using symbols to represent individual sounds rather than whole words or syllables.

MINOANS

The Minoans lived on the island of Crete, just off the coast of Greece. This civilization reigned from approximately 4000 to 1400 BC and is considered to be the first advanced civilization in Europe. The Minoans developed writing systems known to linguists as **Linear A** and **Linear B**. Linear A has not yet been translated; Linear B evolved into classical Greek script. "Minoans" is not the name they used for themselves but is instead a variation on the name of King Minos, a king in Greek mythology believed by some to have been a denizen of Crete. The Minoan civilization subsisted on trade, and their way of life was often disrupted by earthquakes and volcanoes. Much is still unknown about the Minoans, and archaeologists continue to study their architecture and archaeological remains. The Minoan culture eventually fell to Greek invaders and was supplanted by the **Mycenaean civilization**.

MYCENAEANS

In contrast to the Minoans, whom they displaced, the **Mycenaeans** relied more on conquest than on trade. Mycenaean states included Sparta, Athens, and Corinth. The history of this civilization, including the **Trojan War**, was recorded by the Greek poet **Homer**. His work was largely considered mythical until archaeologists discovered evidence of the city of **Troy** in Hisarlik, Turkey. Archaeologists continue to add to the body of information about this ancient culture, translating documents written in Linear B, a script derived from the Minoan Linear A. It is theorized that the Mycenaean civilization was eventually destroyed in either a Dorian invasion or an attack by Greek invaders from the north.

DORIAN INVASION

A Dorian invasion does not refer to an invasion by a particular group of people, but rather is a hypothetical theory to explain the end of the **Mycenaean civilization** and the growth of **classical Greece**. Ancient tradition refers to these events as "the return of the Heracleidae," or the sons (descendants) of Hercules. Archaeologists and historians still do not know exactly who conquered the Mycenaeans, but it is believed to have occurred around 1200 BC, contemporaneous with the destruction of the **Hittite civilization** in what is now modern Turkey. The Hittites speak of an attack by people of the Aegean Sea, or the "Sea People." Only Athens was left intact.

ANCIENT INDIA

The civilizations of ancient India gave rise to both **Hinduism** and **Buddhism**, major world religions that have influenced countries far from their place of origin. Practices such as yoga, increasingly popular in the West, can trace their roots to these earliest Indian civilizations, and the poses are still formally referred to by Sanskrit names. Literature from ancient India includes the *Mahabharata* containing the *Bhagavad Gita*, the *Ramayana*, *Arthashastra*, and the *Vedas*, a collection of sacred texts. Indo-European languages, including English, find their beginnings in these ancient cultures. Ancient Indo-Aryan languages such as Sanskrit are still used in some formal Hindu practices.

INDUS VALLEY CIVILIZATION

The Indus Valley Civilization (IVC) was an urban civilization that arose in the Indus Valley, located in between the modern countries of Iran, India, and Pakistan. These ancient humans developed the concept of zero in mathematics, practiced an early form of the Hindu religion, and developed the caste system which is still prevalent in India today. Archeologists are still uncovering information about this highly developed ancient civilization.

Earliest Civilizations in China

Many historians believe **Chinese civilization** is the oldest uninterrupted civilization in the world. The **Neolithic age** in China goes back to 10,000 BC, with agriculture in China beginning as early as 5000 BC. Their system of writing dates to 1500 BC. The Yellow River served as the center for the earliest Chinese settlements. In Ningxia, in northwest China, there are carvings on cliffs that date back to the Paleolithic Period, indicating the extreme antiquity of Chinese culture. Literature from ancient China includes Confucius' *Analects*, the *Tao Te Ching*, and a variety of poetry.

Ancient Cultures in the Americas

Less is known of ancient American civilizations since less was left behind. Some of the more well-known cultures include:

- The **Norte Chico civilization** in Peru, an agricultural society of up to 30 individual communities, existed over 5,000 years ago. This culture is also known as the Caral-Supe civilization, and is the oldest known civilization in the Americas.
- The **Anasazi**, or Ancestral Pueblo People, lived in what is now the southwestern United States. Emerging about 1200 BC, the Anasazi built complex adobe dwellings and were the forerunners of later Pueblo Indian cultures.
- The **Maya** emerged in southern Mexico and northern Central America as early as 2600 BC. They developed a written language and a complex calendar.

Greece

After the fall of Mycenaean civilization came a dark age out of which would spring one of the most influential cultures in the western world: Greece. While much was lost after the fall of the Mycenaeans, including writing, the Ancient Greeks, in the Archaic Period (800-500 BC) and the Classical Period (500-323 BC), went on to make fundamental achievements in politics, philosophy, history, drama, literature, art, mathematics, and science. They colonized areas all across the Mediterranean and spread their culture around the world. Their culture was heavily influential in shaping the Roman Empire and later civilizations, including those that exist today.

Spartans vs. Athenians

Both powerful Greek city-states, Sparta and Athens fought each other in the **Peloponnesian War** (431-404 BC). Despite their proximity, the Spartans and the Athenians nurtured contrasting cultures:

- The **Spartans**, located in Peloponnesus, were ruled by an oligarchic military state. They practiced farming, disallowed trade for Spartan citizens, and valued military arts and strict discipline. They emerged as the strongest military force in the area and maintained this status for many years. In one memorable encounter, a small group of Spartans held off a huge army of Persians at Thermopylae.
- The **Athenians** were centered in Attica, where the land was rocky and unsuitable for farming. Like the Spartans, they descended from invaders who spoke Greek. Their government was very different from Sparta's; it was in Athens that democracy was created by Cleisthenes of Athens in 508 BC. Athenians excelled in art, theater, architecture, and philosophy.

Contributions of Ancient Greece That Still Exist Today

Ancient Greece made numerous major contributions to cultural development, including:

- **Theater**—Aristophanes and other Greek playwrights laid the groundwork for modern theatrical performance.
- **Alphabet**—the Greek alphabet, derived from the Phoenician alphabet, developed into the Roman alphabet, and then into our modern-day alphabet.
- **Geometry**—Pythagoras and Euclid pioneered much of the system of geometry still taught today. Archimedes made various mathematical discoveries, including calculating a very accurate value of pi.
- **Historical writing**—much of ancient history doubles as mythology or religious texts. Herodotus and Thucydides made use of research and interpretation to record historical events.
- **Philosophy**—Socrates, Plato, and Aristotle served as the fathers of Western philosophy. Their work is still required reading for philosophy students.

Review Video: Ancient Greece Timeline
Visit mometrix.com/academy and enter code: 800829

Alexander the Great

Born to Philip II of Macedon and tutored by Aristotle, **Alexander the Great** is considered one of the greatest conquerors in history. He conquered Egypt and the Achaemenid/Persian Empire, a powerful empire founded by Cyrus the Great that spanned three continents, and he traveled as far as India and the Iberian Peninsula. Alexander the Great died at an early age and, though his cause of death is not known for certain, one hypothesis is that he succumbed to malaria at the early age of 32. His conquering efforts spread Greek culture into the east. This cultural diffusion left a greater mark on history than did his empire, which fell apart due to internal conflict not long after his death. Trade between the East and West increased, as did an exchange of ideas and beliefs that influenced both regions greatly. The **Hellenistic traditions** his conquest spread were prevalent in Byzantine culture until as late as the 15th century.

Persian Wars

The Persian Empire, ruled by **Cyrus the Great**, encompassed an area from the Black Sea to Afghanistan and beyond into Central Asia. After the death of Cyrus, **Darius I** became king in 522 BC. The empire reached its zenith during his reign, and Darius attempted to conquer Greece as well. From 499 to 449 BC, the Greeks and Persians fought in the **Persian Wars**. The **Peace of Callias** brought an end to the fighting, after the Greeks were able to repel the invasion.

Battles of the Persian Wars included:

- The **Battle of Marathon**—heavily outnumbered Greek forces managed to achieve victory.
- The **Battle of Thermopylae**—a small band of Spartans held off a throng of Persian troops for several days before Persia defeated the Greeks and captured an evacuated Athens.
- The **Battle of Salamis**—this was a naval battle that again saw outnumbered Greeks achieving victory.
- The **Battle of Plataea**—this was another Greek victory, but one in which they outnumbered the Persians. This ended the invasion of Greece.

Maurya Empire

The Maurya Empire was a large, powerful empire established in India. It was one of the largest ever to rule in the Indian subcontinent and existed from 322 to 185 BC, ruled by **Chandragupta Maurya** after the withdrawal from India of Alexander the Great. The Maurya Empire was highly developed, including a standardized economic system, waterways, and private corporations. Trade to the Greeks and others became common, with goods including silk, exotic foods, and spices. Religious development included the rise of Buddhism and Jainism. The laws of the Maurya Empire protected not only civil and social rights of the citizens, but they also protected animals, establishing protected zones for economically important creatures such as elephants, lions, and tigers. This period of time in Indian history was largely peaceful, perhaps due to the strong Buddhist beliefs of many of its leaders. The empire finally fell after a succession of weak leaders and was taken over by **Demetrius**, a Greco-Bactrian king who took advantage of this lapse in leadership to conquer southern Afghanistan and Pakistan around 180 BC, forming the **Indo-Greek Kingdom**.

Hinduism

Hinduism is the traditional religion of India. It is expressed in an individual's philosophy and behavior, rather than in the performance of any specific rituals. **Hinduism** does not claim a founder but has evolved slowly over thousands of years; the first Hindu writings date back to the third millennium BC. There are a few concepts that are common to all permutations of Hinduism, such as the **Vedas**, which are considered to be the sacred texts of the religion. The chief aim in life for a Hindu is to be liberated from the cycle of suffering and rebirth. Hindus believe in **reincarnation** and that a person's conduct in this life will affect his or her position in the next (**karma**). Although Hinduism is frequently associated with the caste system, the two are actually unrelated.

Buddhism

Buddhism was created by **Gautama Siddhartha** (otherwise known as Buddha) in about 528 B.C. It was in part a response to Hinduism, which Buddha felt had become bloated with worldliness and politics. Traditional Buddhism is based upon the **Four Noble Truths**: existence is suffering, suffering is caused by desire, an end of suffering will come with Nirvana, and Nirvana will come with the practice of the **Eightfold Path**. The steps of the Eightfold Path are as follows: right views, right resolve, right speech, right action, right livelihood, right effort, right mindfulness, and right concentration. Buddhism did not receive any official sanction for a long time but did eventually spread and take hold in India, China, Japan, and elsewhere.

Development and Growth of the Chinese Empires

In China, history was divided into a series of **dynasties**. The most famous of these, the **Han dynasty**, existed from 206 BC to AD 220. Accomplishments of the Chinese empires included:

- Building the Great Wall of China
- Numerous inventions, including paper, paper money, printing, and gunpowder
- High level of artistic development
- Silk production

The Chinese dynasties were comparable to Rome as far as their artistic and intellectual accomplishments, as well as the size and scope of their influence.

Confucianism and Taoism

Confucianism was founded by Confucius (551–479 BC), who lived around the same time as Buddha. This faith was designed to relieve conflict in all arenas, from that which existed among families to that between Heaven and Earth. Confucius defined "appropriate" social roles for people of different ages, sexes, and social ranks; by assuming these roles, Confucians attempt to create a more peaceful world.

Taoism originated in China at approximately the same time as Confucianism. Taoism strives to create harmony between humans and the natural world. Unlike Confucianism, which has a significant political aspect and is largely monistic, Taoism values natural goodness and expressiveness over social order and is largely dualistic.

Roman Empire and Republic

Rome began humbly, in a single town that grew out of Etruscan settlements and traditions, founded, according to legend, by twin brothers Romulus and Remus, who were raised by wolves. Romulus killed Remus, and from his legacy grew Rome. A thousand years later, the **Roman Empire** covered a significant portion of the known world, from what is now Scotland, across Europe, and into the Middle East. **Hellenization**, or the spread of Greek culture throughout the world, served as an inspiration and a model for the spread of Roman culture. Rome brought in belief systems of conquered peoples as well as their technological and scientific accomplishments, melding the disparate parts into a Roman core. Rome began as a **republic** ruled by consuls, but after the assassination of **Julius Caesar**, it became an **empire** led by emperors. Rome's overall government was autocratic, but local officials came from the provinces where they lived. This limited administrative system was probably a major factor in the long life of the empire.

Review Video: Roman Republic Part One
Visit mometrix.com/academy and enter code: 360192

Review Video: Roman Republic Part Two
Visit mometrix.com/academy and enter code: 881514

Development of the Byzantine Empire from the Roman Empire

In the early 4th century, the Roman Empire split, with the eastern portion becoming the Eastern Empire, or the **Byzantine Empire**. In AD 330, **Constantine** founded the city of **Constantinople**, which became the center of the Byzantine Empire. Its major influences came from Mesopotamia and Persia, in contrast to the Western Empire, which maintained traditions more closely linked to Greece and Carthage. Byzantium's position gave it an advantage over invaders from the West and the East, as well as control over trade from both regions. It protected the Western empire from invasion from the Persians and the Ottomans, and practiced a more centralized rule than in the West. The Byzantines were famous for lavish art and architecture, as well as the Code of Justinian, which collected Roman law into a clear system. The Byzantine Empire finally fell to the **Ottomans** in 1453.

Early Christianity

Early Christianity was a mass of competing doctrines, including various groups such as the Gnostics and Arians who all sought to have their view legitimized as the truth. Eventually, the **orthodox church**, through an ecumenical council of bishops, created in the 4th century AD the canon of New Testament texts which exists today. The apostles had created a hierarchy of bishops, priests, and deacons who stressed obedience to duly constituted church authority. By the middle of the 2nd century, Christianity began to attract intellectuals in the **Roman Empire**. Although Christians were still liable to be persecuted in the farther reaches of the empire, many turned to the Church as the empire crumbled. For many, the christian church was all that was left of civilization and would rebuild Europe over the next millennium.

Significance of the Nicene Creed

The **Byzantine Empire** was Christian-based but incorporated Greek language, philosophy, and literature and drew its law and government policies from Rome. However, there was as yet no unified doctrine of Christianity, as it was a relatively new religion that had spread rapidly and without a great deal of organization. In 325, the **First Council of Nicaea** addressed this issue. From this conference came the **Nicene Creed**, addressing the Trinity and other basic Christian beliefs. The **Council of Chalcedon** in 451 further defined the view of the Trinity.

Factors That Led to the Fall of the Western Roman Empire

Germanic tribes, including the Visigoths, Ostrogoths, Vandals, Saxons, and Franks, controlled most of Europe. The Roman Empire faced major opposition on that front. The increasing size of the empire also made it harder to manage, leading to dissatisfaction throughout the empire as Roman government became less efficient. Germanic tribes refused to adhere to the Nicene Creed, instead following **Arianism**, which led the Roman Catholic Church to declare them heretics. The **Franks** proved a powerful military force in their defeat of the Muslims in 732. In 768, **Charlemagne** became king of the Franks. These tribes waged several wars against Rome, including the invasion of Britannia by the Angles and Saxons. Far-flung Rome lost control over this area of its empire, and eventually, Rome itself was **invaded**.

Iconoclasm and Conflicts of Roman Catholic and Eastern Orthodox Churches

Emperor Leo III ordered the destruction of all icons throughout the Byzantine Empire. Images of Jesus were replaced with crosses, and images of Jesus, Mary, or other religious figures were considered blasphemy on the grounds of idolatry. **Pope Gregory II** called a synod to discuss the issue. The synod declared that the images were not heretical and that strong disciplinary measures would result for anyone who destroyed them. Leo's response was an attempt to kill Pope Gregory, but this plan ended in failure.

Effect of the Viking Invasions on the Culture of England and Europe

Vikings invaded Northern France in the 10th century, eventually becoming the **Normans**. Originating in Scandinavia, the **Vikings** were accomplished seafarers with advanced knowledge of trade routes. With overpopulation plaguing their native lands, they began to travel. From the 8th to the 11th centuries, they spread throughout Europe, conquering and colonizing. Vikings invaded and colonized England in several waves, including the **Anglo-Saxon invasions** that displaced Roman control. Their influence remained significant in England, affecting everything from the language of the country to place names and even the government and social structure. By 900, Vikings had settled in **Iceland**. They proceeded then to **Greenland** and eventually to **North America**, arriving in the New World even before the Spanish and British who claimed the lands several centuries later. They also traded with the Byzantine Empire until the 11th century, when their significant level of activity came to an end.

West vs. East 10th-Century Events

In **Europe**, the years AD 500-1000 are largely known as the **Dark Ages**. In the 10th century, numerous Viking invasions disrupted societies that had been more settled under Roman rule. Vikings settled in Northern France, eventually becoming the Normans. By the 11th century, Europe would rise again into the **High Middle Ages** with the beginning of the **Crusades**.

In **China**, wars also raged. This led the Chinese to make use of gunpowder for the first time in warfare.

In the **Americas**, the **Mayan Empire** was winding down while the **Toltec** became more prominent. **Pueblo** Indian culture was also at its zenith.

In the **East**, the **Muslims** and the **Byzantine Empire** were experiencing a significant period of growth and development.

World History 1400 to 1914

Feudalism in Europe in the Middle Ages

A major element of the social and economic life of Europe, **feudalism** developed as a way to ensure European rulers would have the wherewithal to quickly raise an army when necessary. **Vassals** swore loyalty and promised to provide military service for lords, who in return offered a **fief**, or a parcel of land, for them to use to generate their livelihood. Vassals could work the land themselves, have it worked by **peasants** or **serfs**—workers who had few rights and were little more than slaves—or grant the fief to someone else. The king legally owned all the land, but in return, promised to protect the vassals from invasion and war. Vassals returned a certain percentage of their income to the lords, who in turn, passed a portion of their income on to the king. A similar practice was **manorialism**, in which the feudal system was applied to a self-contained manor. These manors were often owned by the lords who ran them but were usually included in the same system of loyalty and promises of protection that drove feudalism.

Review Video: The Middle Ages: Feudalism
Visit mometrix.com/academy and enter code: 165907

Effect of Black Death on Medieval Politics and Economic Conditions

The Black Death, believed to be **bubonic plague**, most likely came to Europe on fleas carried by rats on sailing vessels. The plague killed more than a third of the entire population of Europe and effectively ended **feudalism** as a political system. Many who had formerly served as peasants or serfs found different work, as a demand for skilled labor grew. Nation-states grew in power, and in the face of the pandemic, many began to turn away from faith in God and toward the ideals of ancient Greece and Rome for government and other beliefs.

Review Video: Black Death (An Overview)
Visit mometrix.com/academy and enter code: 431857

Influence of the Roman Catholic Church Over Medieval Society

The Roman Catholic Church extended significant influence both politically and economically throughout medieval society. The church supplied **education**, as there were no established schools or universities. To a large extent, the church had filled a power void left by various invasions throughout the former Roman Empire, leading it to exercise a role that was far more **political** than religious. Kings were heavily influenced by the pope and other church officials, and churches controlled large amounts of land throughout Europe.

Progression of the Crusades and Major Figures Involved

The Crusades began in the 11th century and continued into the 15th. The major goal of these various military ventures was to slow the progression of Muslim forces into Europe and to expel them from the **Holy Land**, where they had taken control of Jerusalem and Palestine. Alexius I, the Byzantine emperor, called for help from **Pope Urban** II when Palestine was taken. In 1095, the pope, hoping to reunite Eastern and Western Christianity, encouraged all Christians to help the cause. Amidst great bloodshed, this crusade recaptured **Jerusalem**, but over the next centuries, Jerusalem and other areas of the Holy Land changed hands numerous times. The **Second Crusade** (1147-1149) consisted of an unsuccessful attempt to retake Damascus. The **Third Crusade**, under Pope Gregory VIII, attempted to recapture Jerusalem but failed. The **Fourth Crusade**, under Pope Innocent III, attempted to come into the Holy Land via Egypt. The Crusades led to greater power for the pope and the Catholic Church in general and also opened numerous trading and cultural routes between Europe and the East.

Political Developments in India Through the 11th Century

After the Mauryan dynasty, the **Guptas** ruled India, maintaining a long period of peace and prosperity in the area. During this time, the Indian people invented the decimal system and the concept of zero. They produced cotton and calico, as well as other products in high demand in Europe and Asia, and developed a complex system of medicine. The Gupta Dynasty ended in the 6th century. First, the **Huns** invaded, and then the **Hephthalites** (an Asian nomadic tribe) destroyed the weakened empire. In the 14th century, **Tamerlane**, a Muslim who envisioned restoring Genghis Khan's empire, expanded India's borders and founded the **Mogul Empire**. His grandson Akbar promoted freedom of religion and built a widespread number of mosques, forts, and other buildings throughout the country.

Development of Chinese and Japanese Governments Through the 11th Century

After the Mongols, led by Genghis Khan and his grandson Kublai Khan, unified the Mongol Empire, **China** was led by the **Ming Dynasty** (1368-1644) and the **Manchu (also known as Qing) Dynasty** (1644-1912). Both dynasties were isolationist, ending China's interaction with other countries until the 18th century. The Ming Dynasty was known for its porcelain, while the Manchus focused on farming and road construction as the population grew.

Japan developed independently of China but borrowed the Buddhist religion, the Chinese writing system, and other elements of Chinese society. Ruled by the divine emperor, Japan basically functioned on a feudal system led by **daimyo**, or warlords, and soldiers known as **samurai**. Japan remained isolationist, not interacting significantly with the rest of the world until the 1800s.

Ming Dynasty

The Ming dynasty lasted in China from AD 1368 to 1644. This dynasty was established by a Buddhist monk, **Zhu Yuanzhang**, who quickly became obsessed with consolidating power in the central government and was known for the brutality with which he achieved his ends. It was during the **Ming dynasty** that China developed and introduced its famous civil service examinations, rigorous tests on the **Confucian classics**. The future of an ambitious Chinese youth depended on his performance on this exam. The capital was transferred from Nanjing to Beijing during this period, and the **Forbidden City** was constructed inside the new capital. The Ming period, despite its constant expansionary wars, also continued China's artistic resurgence; the porcelain of this period is especially admired.

Developments in Africa Through the 11th Century

Much of Africa was difficult to traverse early on, due to the large amount of desert and other inhospitable terrain. **Egypt** remained important, though most of the northern coast became Muslim as their armies spread through the area. **Ghana** rose as a trade center in the 9th century, lasting into the 12th century, primarily trading in gold, which it exchanged for Saharan salt. **Mali** rose somewhat later, with the trade center Timbuktu becoming an important exporter of goods such as iron, leather, and tin. Mali also dealt in agricultural trade, becoming one of the most significant trading centers in West Africa. The Muslim religion dominated, and technological advancement was sparse.

African culture was largely defined through migration, as Arab merchants and others settled on the continent, particularly along the east coast. Scholars from the Muslim nations gravitated to Timbuktu, which in addition to its importance in trade, had also become a magnet for those seeking Islamic knowledge and education.

History of Islam and Its Role in Bringing Unity to the Middle East

Born in AD 570, **Muhammad** began preaching around 613, leading his followers in a new religion called **Islam**, which means "submission to God's will." Before this time, the Arabian Peninsula was inhabited largely by Bedouins, nomads who battled amongst each other and lived in tribal organizations. But by the time Muhammad died in 632, most of Arabia had become Muslim to some extent.

Muhammad conquered **Mecca**, where a temple called the **Kaaba** had long served as a center of the nomadic religions. He declared this temple the most sacred of Islam, and Mecca as the holy city. His writings became the **Koran**, or **Qur'an**, divine revelations he said had been delivered to him by the angel Gabriel.

Muhammad's teachings gave the formerly tribal Arabian people a sense of unity that had not existed in the area before. After his death, the converted Muslims of Arabia conquered a vast territory, creating an empire and bringing advances in literature, technology, science, and art as Europe was declining under the scourge of the Black Death. Literature from this period includes the *Arabian Nights* and the *Rubaiyat* of Omar Khayyam.

Later in its development, Islam split into two factions; the **Shiite** and the **Sunni** Muslims. Conflict continues today between these groups.

Ottoman Empire

By 1400, the Ottomans had grown in power in Anatolia and had begun attempts to take Constantinople. In 1453, they finally conquered the Byzantine capital and renamed it **Istanbul**. The **Ottoman Empire's** major strength, much like Rome before it, lay in its ability to unite widely disparate people through religious tolerance. This tolerance, which stemmed from the idea that Muslims, Christians, and Jews were fundamentally related and could coexist, enabled the Ottomans to develop a widely varied culture. They also believed in just laws and just government, with government centered in a monarch, known as the **sultan**.

Renaissance

The French word "renaissance" means "rebirth." This is the term used to describe a period of history and cultural movement that occurred after the Middle Ages. During this time, interest rose again in the beliefs and politics of ancient Greece and Rome. Art, literature, music, science, and philosophy all burgeoned during the Renaissance and experience rapid progress.

Many of the ideas of the Renaissance began in **Florence, Italy** in the 14th century, spurred by the **Medici** family. Education for the upper classes expanded to include law, math, reading, writing, and classical Greek and Roman works. As the Renaissance progressed, the world was presented through art and literature in a realistic way that had never been explored before. This **realism** drove culture to new heights.

Review Video: The Renaissance
Visit mometrix.com/academy and enter code: 123100

Humanism

The term "humanism" was attributed long after the Renaissance but represents a foundational collection of ideas that propelled much of the developments that occurred during the Renaissance in art, politics, education, and many other fields. Humanists believed that the study of classics from Ancient Greece and Rome was essential to understanding humanity, virtues, ethics, and peoples' roles in society. The study of humanity was given precedence over the study of religion, though religion and humanism were not mutually exclusive, and many religious people also held many humanist beliefs. Humanism did not represent a formal school of thought or encompassing philosophy. It was, rather, a general intellectual movement that placed education—specifically of classical texts—at the forefront. Some of the main subjects of Renaissance humanism were:

- Private and civic virtue
- Latin
- Grammar and rhetoric
- Literature and poetry
- Moral philosophy

Renaissance Artists, Authors, and Scientists

Artists of the Renaissance included Leonardo da Vinci, also an inventor; Michelangelo, also an architect; and others who focused on realism in their work. In **literature**, major contributions came from humanist authors like Petrarch, Erasmus, Sir Thomas More, and Boccaccio, who believed man should focus on reality rather than on the ethereal. Shakespeare, Cervantes, and Dante followed in their footsteps, and their works found a wide audience thanks to Gutenberg's development of the printing press.

Scientific developments of the Renaissance included the work of Copernicus, Galileo, and Kepler, who challenged the geocentric philosophies of the day by proving that the earth was not the center of the solar system.

Two Phases of the Reformation Period

The Reformation period arose near the later part of the Renaissance and consisted of both the Protestant and the Catholic Reformation. The **Protestant Reformation** rose in Germany when **Martin Luther** protested abuses of the Catholic Church. **John Calvin** led the movement in Switzerland, while in England, King Henry VIII made use of the Reformation's ideas to further his own political goals. The **Catholic Reformation**, or **Counter-Reformation**, occurred in response to the Protestant movement, leading to various changes in the Catholic Church. Some provided wider tolerance of different religious viewpoints, but others actually increased the persecution of those deemed to be heretics.

From a **religious** standpoint, the Reformation occurred due to abuses by the Catholic Church such as indulgences and dispensations, religious offices being offered up for sale, and an increasingly dissolute clergy. **Politically**, the Reformation was driven by increased power of various ruling monarchs, who wished to take all power to themselves rather than allowing power to remain with the church. They also had begun to chafe at papal taxes and the church's increasing wealth. The ideas of the Protestant Revolution removed power from the Catholic Church and the Pope himself, playing nicely into the hands of those monarchs, such as Henry VIII, who wanted out from under the church's control.

Review Video: Martin Luther and the Reformation
Visit mometrix.com/academy and enter code: 691828

Review Video: The Counter-Reformation
Visit mometrix.com/academy and enter code: 950498

Review Video: The Protestants
Visit mometrix.com/academy and enter code: 583582

Developments of the Scientific Revolution

In addition to holding power in the political realm, church doctrine also governed scientific belief. During the **Scientific Revolution**, however, which began during the renaissance, astronomers and other scientists began to amass evidence that challenged the church's scientific doctrines. These scientists employed the scientific method and emergent theories and technologies to make new discoveries about the universe. It was during the Scientific Revolution that many huge scientific discoveries were made, and the very nature of knowledge gathering changed. Major figures of the Scientific Revolution included:

- **Nicolaus Copernicus**—wrote *On the Revolutions of the Celestial Spheres*, arguing that the earth revolved around the sun
- **Tycho Brahe**—cataloged astronomical observations
- **Johannes Kepler**—developed laws of planetary motion
- **Galileo Galilei**—defended the heliocentric theories of Copernicus and Kepler, discovered four moons of Jupiter, and died under house arrest by the church, charged with heresy
- **Isaac Newton**—discovered gravity; studied optics, calculus, and physics; and believed the workings of nature could be studied and proven through observation

Review Video: The Scientific Revolution
Visit mometrix.com/academy and enter code: 974600

Major Ideas of the Enlightenment

The Enlightenment (also called the Age of Reason) began in the late 17th century and lasted until around the late 18th century. It came partially as a result of the reformation, which diminished some of the power of the Christian Church. This allowed more freedom of expression and thought. During this time in Europe and North America, philosophers and scientists began to rely more and more on **observation** and logic to support their ideas rather than building on past beliefs, particularly those held by the church. A focus on **ethics and reason** drove their work. Through reason, they believed, some of the universe's most difficult questions—be them in ethics, politics, or science — could be answered. Major philosophers of the Enlightenment included:

- **Rene Descartes**—while often considered a pre-Enlightenment thinker, Descartes's philosophical work was instrumental to the development of philosophy in the Enlightenment. He believed that in order to know something, everything must first be put into doubt until it could be proved. He believed the senses could not be fully trusted to represent reality, but that reason may be relied upon to understand the foundational aspects of existence. He famously wrote, "I think, therefore I am," which is his assertion that the very fact that he is thinking is evidence that he really exists.
- **David Hume**—he pioneered empiricism and skepticism, believing that truth could only be found through direct experience and that what others said to be true was always suspect.
- **Immanuel Kant**—he believed in self-examination and observation and that the root of morality lay within human beings.
- **Jean-Jacques Rousseau**—he developed the idea of the social contract, that government existed by the agreement of the people, and that the government was obligated to protect the people and their basic rights. His ideas heavily influenced the founding fathers.

Review Video: Age of Enlightenment
Visit mometrix.com/academy and enter code: 143022

American Revolution vs. French Revolution

Both the American and French Revolution came about as a protest against the excesses and overly controlling nature of their respective monarchs. In **America**, the British colonies had been left mostly to self-govern until the British monarchs began to increase control, spurring the colonies to revolt. In **France**, the nobility's excesses had led to increasingly difficult economic conditions, with inflation, heavy taxation, and food shortages creating great burdens on the lower classes. Both revolutions led to the development of republics to replace the monarchies that were displaced. However, the French Revolution eventually led to the rise of the dictator **Napoleon Bonaparte**, while the American Revolution produced a working **republic** from the beginning.

Events and Figures of the French Revolution

In 1789, **King Louis XVI**, faced with a huge national debt, convened parliament. The **Third Estate**, or Commons, a division of the French parliament, then claimed power, and the king's resistance led to the storming of the **Bastille**, the royal prison. The people established a constitutional monarchy. When King Louis XVI and Marie Antoinette attempted to leave the country, they were executed on the guillotine. From 1793 to 1794, **Robespierre** and extreme radicals, the **Jacobins**, instituted a **Reign of Terror**, executing tens of thousands of nobles as well as anyone considered an enemy of the Revolution. Robespierre was then executed as well, and the **Directory** came into power, leading to a temporary return to bourgeois values. This governing body proved incompetent and corrupt, allowing **Napoleon Bonaparte** to come to power in 1799, first as a dictator, then as emperor. While the French Revolution threw off the power of a corrupt monarchy, its immediate results were likely not what the original perpetrators of the revolt had intended.

Review Video: The French Revolution: Napoleon Bonaparte
Visit mometrix.com/academy and enter code: 876330

Industrial Revolution

Effects of the Industrial Revolution on Society

The Industrial Revolution began in Great Britain in the 18th century, bringing coal- and steam-powered machinery into widespread use. Industry began a period of rapid growth with these developments. Goods that had previously been produced in small workshops or even in homes were produced more efficiently and in much larger quantities in **factories**. Where society had been largely agrarian-based, the focus swiftly shifted to an **industrial** outlook. As electricity and internal combustion engines replaced coal and steam as energy sources, even more drastic and rapid changes occurred. Western European countries, in particular, turned to colonialism, taking control of portions of Africa and Asia to ensure access to the raw materials needed to produce factory goods. Specialized labor became very much in demand, and businesses grew rapidly, creating monopolies, increasing world trade, and developing large urban centers. Even agriculture changed fundamentally as the Industrial Revolution led to a second **Agricultural Revolution** with the addition of new technology to advance agricultural production.

Review Video: Industrialization
Visit mometrix.com/academy and enter code: 893924

First and Second Phases of the Industrial Revolution

The **first phase** of the Industrial Revolution took place from roughly 1750 to 1830. The textile industry experienced major changes as more and more elements of the process became mechanized. Mining benefited from the steam engine. Transportation became easier and more widely available as waterways were improved and the railroad came into prominence. In the **second phase**, from 1830 to 1910, industries further improved in efficiency, and new industries were introduced as photography, various chemical processes, and electricity became more widely available to produce new goods or new, improved versions of old goods. Petroleum and hydroelectricity became major sources of power. During this time, the Industrial Revolution spread out of Western Europe and into the US and Japan.

Political, Social and Economic Side Effects of the Industrial Revolution

The Industrial Revolution led to widespread education, a wider franchise, and the development of mass communication in the political arena. **Economically**, conflicts arose between companies and their employees, as struggles for fair treatment and fair wages increased. Unions gained power and became more active. Government regulation over industries increased, but at the same time, growing businesses fought for the right to free enterprise. In the **social** sphere, populations increased and began to concentrate around centers of industry. Cities became larger and more densely populated. Scientific advancements led to more efficient agriculture, greater supply of goods, and increased knowledge of medicine and sanitation, leading to better overall health.

Review Video: The Industrial Revolution
Visit mometrix.com/academy and enter code: 372796

Causes and Progression of the Russian Revolution of 1905

In Russia, rule lay in the hands of the **czars**, and the overall structure was **feudalistic**. Beneath the czars was a group of rich nobles, landowners whose lands were worked by peasants and serfs. The **Russo-Japanese War** (1904-1905) made conditions much worse for the lower classes. When peasants demonstrated outside the czar's Winter Palace, the palace guard fired upon the crowd. The demonstration had been organized by a trade union leader, and after the violent response, many unions and political parties blossomed and began to lead numerous strikes. When the economy ground to a halt, Czar Nicholas II signed a document known as the **October Manifesto**, which established a constitutional monarchy and gave legislative power to parliament. However, he violated the manifesto shortly thereafter, disbanding parliament and ignoring the civil liberties granted by the manifesto. This eventually led to the **Bolshevik Revolution**.

World History 1914 to Present

Nationalism and Its Effect on Society Through the 18th and 19th Centuries

Nationalism, put simply, is a strong belief in, identification with, and allegiance to a particular nation and people. **Nationalistic belief** unified various areas that had previously seen themselves as fragmented, which led to **patriotism** and, in some cases, **imperialism**. As nationalism grew, individual nations sought to grow, bringing in other, smaller states that shared similar characteristics such as language and cultural beliefs. Unfortunately, a major side effect of these growing nationalistic beliefs was often conflict and outright **war**.

In Europe, imperialism led countries to spread their influence into Africa and Asia. **Africa** was eventually divided among several European countries that wanted certain raw materials. **Asia** also came under European control, with the exception of China, Japan, and Siam (now Thailand). In the US, **Manifest Destiny** became the rallying cry as the country expanded west. Italy and Germany formed larger nations from a variety of smaller states.

Review Video: Historical Nationalism
Visit mometrix.com/academy and enter code: 510185

Review Video: Nationalism
Visit mometrix.com/academy and enter code: 865693

Events of World War I in the European Theater

WWI began in 1914 with the assassination of **Archduke Franz Ferdinand**, heir to the throne of Austria-Hungary, by a Serbian national. This led to a conflict between Austria-Hungary and Serbia that quickly escalated into the First World War. Europe split into the **Allies**—Britain, France, and Russia, and later Italy, Japan, and the US, against the **Central Powers**—Austria-Hungary, Germany, the Ottoman Empire, and Bulgaria. As the war spread, countries beyond Europe became involved. The war left Europe deeply in debt, and particularly devastated the German economy. The ensuing **Great Depression** made matters worse, and economic devastation opened the door for communist, fascist, and socialist governments to gain power.

Combat in World War I

Despite the fact that almost every nation in Europe had entered into World War I, most Europeans thought the conflict would be brief. Instead, advances in **weapons technology** made the war bloody and excruciatingly slow. Fighting during WWI largely took place in a series of **trenches** built along the Eastern and Western Fronts. These trenches added up to more than 24,000 miles. This produced fronts that stretched over 400 miles, from the coast of Belgium to the border of Switzerland. The Allies made use of straightforward open-air trenches with a front line, supporting lines, and communications lines. By contrast, the German trenches sometimes included well-equipped underground living quarters.

Contributions of the American Public and Public Opinion of the War

The **18th amendment** to the Constitution, otherwise known as the **Volstead Act**, outlawed alcohol in 1920. This amendment was purported to conserve food, though it was really an attempt to influence public morality. Through the **Food Administration**, President Wilson encouraged people to plant "victory gardens," and to skip meat one day a week. The war was also supported through the **Espionage and Sedition Acts of 1917-8**, which made it illegal to say negative things about the war or to interfere with the sale of war bonds. In **Schenck v. US** (1919), the arrest of the Socialist leader Charles Schenck for criticizing the war was upheld by the Supreme Court, which asserted that First Amendment rights were only exercisable when they did not present a clear and present danger to the nation. In **Abrams v. US** (1919), a Russian immigrant critical of the US actions in Russia was also declared to be a clear and present danger.

Treaty of Versailles

As the First World War wound down, a disgruntled German populace ousted the emperor and installed a moderate socialist government. This government, known as the **Weimar Republic**, would last until 1933. At the **Paris Peace Conference**, the victors of the war (the US, Britain, France, and Italy) exacted some revenge on Germany. The **Treaty of Versailles** penalized Germany economically and territorially; Alsace-Lorraine became independent, and the German military was dismantled. The Treaty of Versailles would need to be modified by two subsequent agreements: the **Treaty of Locarno,** which outlined a more reasonable reparations plan for Germany, and the **Kellogg-Briand Pact,** which asserted that diplomacy rather than force would be used to resolve conflicts.

Bolshevik Revolution

Factors Leading to the Bolshevik Revolution of 1917

Throughout its modern history, Russia had lagged behind other countries in development. The continued existence of a feudal system, combined with harsh conditions and the overall size of the country, led to massive food shortages and increasingly harsh conditions for the majority of the population. The tyrannical rule of the czars only made this worse, as did repeated losses in various military conflicts. Increasing poverty, decreasing supplies, and the czar's violation of the **October Manifesto,** which had given some political power and civil rights to the people, finally came to a head with the **Bolshevik Revolution**.

Events of the Bolshevik Revolution

A **workers' strike in Petrograd** in 1917 set the revolutionary wheels in motion when the army sided with the workers. While parliament set up a provisional government made up of nobles, the workers and military joined to form their own governmental system known as **soviets**, which consisted of local councils elected by the people. The ensuing chaos opened the doors for formerly exiled leaders Vladimir Lenin, Joseph Stalin, and Leon Trotsky to move in and gain popular support as well as the support of the Red Guard. Overthrowing parliament, they took power, creating a **communist** state in Russia. This development led to the spread of communism throughout Eastern Europe and elsewhere, greatly affecting diplomatic policies throughout the world for several decades.

Communism vs. Socialism

At their roots, socialism and communism both focus on public ownership and distribution of goods and services. However, **communism** works toward revolution by drawing on what it sees to be inevitable class antagonism, eventually overthrowing the upper classes and the systems of capitalism. **Socialism** makes use of democratic procedures, building on the existing order. This was particularly true of the utopian socialists, who saw industrial capitalism as oppressive, not allowing workers to prosper. While socialism struggled between the World Wars, communism took hold, especially in Eastern Europe. After WWII, **democratic socialism** became more common. Later,

capitalism took a stronger hold again, and today most industrialized countries in the western world function under an economy that mixes elements of capitalism and socialism.

> **Review Video: Communism vs. Socialism**
> Visit mometrix.com/academy and enter code: 917677

Conditions That Led to the Rise of the Nazi Party in Germany

The **Great Depression** had a particularly devastating effect on Germany's economy, especially after the US was no longer able to supply reconstruction loans to help the country regain its footing. With unemployment rising rapidly, dissatisfaction with the government grew. Fascist and Communist parties rose, promising change and improvement.

Led by **Adolf Hitler**, the fascist **Nazi Party** eventually gained power in Parliament based on these promises and the votes of desperate German workers. When Hitler became chancellor, he launched numerous expansionist policies, violating the peace treaties that had ended WWI. His military buildup and conquering of neighboring countries sparked the aggression that soon led to WWII.

Belief System of the Nazi Party

Led by **Adolf Hitler**, the Nazi party championed the **Aryan race** as superior to all others, especially the "insidious" Jews. Hitler suggested that the noble ambitions of the true German people required ***lebensraum***, or living space. In other words, Germany needed more territory. In its early days, the Nazi party was part of the German republican system; Nazi candidates ran for office and served in the **Reichstag** (German parliament). As Germany suffered through a terrible economic depression in the early 1930s, however, the people became impatient. In 1933, the Reichstag was set on fire, and the Nazis used the opportunity to claim total control of the government. Hitler had already been appointed Chancellor in January 1933. He was able to quickly improve the German economy, mostly through the expansion of the weapon-building industry. At the same time, the new government began to quietly round up Jews, Gypsies, and homosexuals.

Beginning and Initial Years of World War II in Europe

Still shell-shocked from the First World War, the nations of western Europe were slow to respond to the growing menace of **Nazi Germany**. In general, they pursued a policy of appeasement and isolation. The British prime minister **Neville Chamberlain** was especially committed to using diplomacy over war. Then, in 1936, Hitler sent troops to occupy the **Rhineland**, a strip of territory on the German border. At around the same time, **Mussolini** invaded Ethiopia; the two aggressors, Germany and Italy, entered into an agreement making them the **Axis Powers**. In 1938, Germany annexed Austria and indicated that it was about to attack Czechoslovakia. In response to these actions, Chamberlain brought together Mussolini and Hitler for the **Munich Conference of 1938**. These talks would only briefly suspend German aggression.

After **Chamberlain** had tried to forestall German aggression at the **Munich Conference of 1938**, Germany nevertheless invaded Czechoslovakia in 1939. It was also during this year that Hitler signed a secret agreement with **Stalin** pledging not to attack Russia so long as Russia stayed out of German affairs. Hitler then declared war on and conquered Poland. At this step, Great Britain and France were finally forced to declare war upon Germany. Germany at this point was a dominating military adversary. The **Axis powers** conquered almost the entire European continent, including France, over the course of 1940.

Importance of the German Blitzkrieg to the Progression of World War II

The blitzkrieg, or "lightning war," consisted of fast, powerful surprise attacks that disrupted communications, made it difficult if not impossible for the victims to retaliate, and demoralized Germany's foes. The "blitz," or the aerial bombing of England in 1940, was one example, with bombings occurring in London and other cities 57 nights in a row. The **Battle of Britain** in 1940 also brought intense raids by Germany's air force, the **Luftwaffe**, mostly targeting ports and British air force bases. Eventually, Britain's Royal Air Force blocked the Luftwaffe, ending Germany's hopes for conquering Britain.

Battle of the Bulge

Following the **D-Day Invasion**, Allied forces gained considerable ground and began a major campaign to push through Europe. In December of 1944, Hitler launched a counteroffensive, attempting to retake Antwerp, an important port. The ensuing battle became the largest land battle on the war's Western Front and was known as the Battle of the Ardennes, or the **Battle of the Bulge**. The battle lasted from December 16, 1944, to January 25, 1945. The Germans pushed forward, making inroads into Allied lines, but in the end, the Allies brought the advance to a halt. The Germans were pushed back, with massive losses on both sides. However, those losses proved crippling to the German army. Surrounded and with the war lost, Hitler committed suicide in his bunker in Berlin in April 1945, and the remaining German forces surrendered shortly afterward.

Holocaust

As Germany sank deeper and deeper into dire economic straits, the tendency was to look for a person or group of people to blame for the problems of the country. With distrust of the Jewish people already ingrained, it was easy for German authorities to set up the **Jews** as scapegoats for Germany's problems. Under the rule of Hitler and the Nazi party, the "Final Solution" for the supposed Jewish problem was devised. Millions of Jews, as well as Gypsies, homosexuals, communists, Catholics, the mentally ill, and others, simply named as criminals, were transported to concentration camps during the course of the war. At least six million were slaughtered in death camps such as **Auschwitz**, where horrible conditions and torture of prisoners were commonplace. The Allies were aware of rumors of mass slaughter throughout the war, but many discounted the reports. Only when troops went in to liberate the prisoners was the true horror of the concentration camps brought to light. The **Holocaust** resulted in massive loss of human life, but also in the loss and destruction of cultures. Because the genocide focused on specific ethnic groups, many traditions, histories, knowledge, and other cultural elements were lost, particularly among the Jewish and Gypsy populations. After World War II, the United Nations recognized **genocide** as a "crime against humanity." The UN passed the **Universal Declaration of Human Rights** in 1948 in order to further specify what rights the organization protected. Nazi war criminals faced justice during the **Nuremberg Trials**. There, individuals, rather than their governments, were held accountable for war crimes.

Review Video: The Holocaust
Visit mometrix.com/academy and enter code: 350695

Pacific Arena in WWII

The **Japanese**, like the Germans, became seduced by the notion of their own racial superiority during the 1930s. As in Germany, this inevitably led to a lust for territorial expansion. By 1941, Japan had conquered Korea, Manchuria, and parts of China. Japan was also threatening to invade American interests in the Philippines. The United States imposed **economic sanctions** on Japan, making it difficult for the Japanese war industry to function. In response, the Japanese launched a surprise attack on the United States by bombing the US naval base of **Pearl Harbor**. After the attack on Pearl Harbor, the United States declared war upon Japan (and Germany, in turn, declared war on the United States). The Japanese made huge territorial gains before the US turned the tide at the **Battles of Midway and Guadalcanal**. The war in the Pacific would take much longer than the war in Europe due to the island-hopping nature of the fight. The unwillingness of the Japanese to surrender made it almost impossible for America to entirely vanquish them without enormous loss of life. So, the United States decided to drop atomic bombs on **Hiroshima** and **Nagasaki** to force Japan to surrender and finally end the war in the Pacific in August 1945.

India and Pakistan After WWII

In 1947, after years of peaceful protests led by **Mahatma Gandhi**, India was given its independence and partitioned into two states, **India** and **Pakistan**. The following year, Gandhi would be assassinated in India. In 1965, border disputes would flare into the **Indo-Pakistani War**. In 1971, Pakistan would fend off attacks from Bengali rebels, who sought to achieve independence. The next year, however, **Bangladesh** would be established as an independent state. In 1984, India had its own internal problems; after the Indian army occupied the **Golden Temple** sacred to the Sikhs, the Indian leader **Indira Gandhi** was assassinated by her Sikh bodyguards. **Anti-Sikh riots** resulted, and much blood was shed.

World War II and the Ensuing Diplomatic Climate that Led to the Cold War

With millions of military and civilian deaths and over 12 million persons displaced, **WWII** left large regions of Europe and Asia in disarray. **Communist** governments moved in with promises of renewed prosperity and economic stability. The **Soviet Union** backed communist regimes in much of Eastern Europe. In China, **Mao Zedong** led communist forces in the overthrow of the Chinese Nationalist Party and instituted a communist government in 1949. While the new communist governments restored a measure of stability to much of Eastern Europe, it brought its own problems, with dictatorial governments and an oppressive police force. The spread of communism also led to several years of tension between communist countries and the democratic West, as the West fought to slow the spread of oppressive regimes throughout the world. With both sides in possession of nuclear weapons, tensions rose. Each side feared the other would resort to nuclear attack. This standoff lasted until 1989, when the **Berlin Wall** fell. The Soviet Union was dissolved two years later.

Truman Doctrine, Marshall Plan, NATO, and Warsaw Pact

In order to stop the spread of communism in Europe and elsewhere, President Truman asserted his policy of "containment" in the so-called **Truman Doctrine**. This meant that the US would support anticommunist governments throughout the world. The **Marshall Plan** advanced this policy by supplying aid to war-ravaged countries in Western Europe. When the **Eastern Bloc countries** prevented aid from reaching West Berlin, the US, England, and France organized the **Berlin Airlift** to overcome this obstacle. In 1949, the Western European and North American nations entered into a mutual defense treaty, NATO (North Atlantic Treaty Organization). As a response, the Eastern Bloc nations joined with the Soviet Union in the **Warsaw Pact**.

Origins of the United Nations

The United Nations (**UN**) came into being toward the end of World War II. A successor to the less-than-successful League of Nations formed after World War I, the UN built and improved on those ideas. Since its inception, the UN has worked to bring the countries of the world together for **diplomatic solutions** to international problems, including sanctions and other restrictions. It has also initiated military action, calling for peacekeeping troops from member countries to move against countries violating UN policies. The **Korean War** was the first example of UN involvement in an international conflict.

Effects of Decolonization on the Post-War Period

A rise of nationalism among European colonies led to many of them declaring independence. **India** and **Pakistan** became independent of Britain in 1947, and numerous African and Asian colonies declared independence as well. This period of **decolonization** lasted into the 1960s. Some colonies moved successfully into independence, but many, especially in Africa and Asia, struggled to create stable governments and economies and suffered from ethnic and religious conflicts, some of which continue today.

Factors and Shifts in Power that Led to the Korean War

In 1910, Japan annexed Korea and maintained this control until 1945. After WWII, Soviet and US troops occupied Korea, with the **Soviet Union** controlling North Korea and the **US** controlling South Korea. In 1947, the UN ordered elections in Korea to unify the country, but the Soviet Union refused to allow them to take place in North Korea, instead setting up a communist government. In 1950, the US withdrew troops, and the North Korean troops moved to invade South Korea. The **Korean War** was the first war in which the UN—or any international organization—played a major role. The US, Australia, Canada, France, Netherlands, Great Britain, Turkey, China, the USSR, and other countries sent troops at various times, for both sides, throughout the war. In 1953, the war ended in a truce, but no peace agreement was ever achieved, and Korea remains divided.

Events that Led to the Vietnam War

Vietnam had previously been part of a French colony called French Indochina. The **Vietnam War** began with the **First Indochina War** from 1946 to 1954, in which France battled with the Democratic Republic of Vietnam, ruled by Ho Chi Minh.

In 1954, a siege at Dien Bien Phu ended in a Vietnamese victory. Vietnam was then divided into North and South, much like Korea. Communist forces controlled the North, and the South was controlled by South Vietnamese forces, supported by the US. Conflict ensued, leading to another war. US troops eventually led the fight, in support of South Vietnam. The war became a major political issue in the US, with many citizens protesting American involvement. In 1975, South Vietnam surrendered, and Vietnam became the **Socialist Republic of Vietnam**.

Middle East from 1947 to 1977

After WWII, the United Nations announced that **Palestine** would be partitioned in order to make room for a new Jewish state. **Israel** was created in 1948. In 1951, the Iranian leader **Mossadegh** nationalized the oil interests, making his government extremely wealthy and powerful. This move would be emulated by future leaders. In 1967, in the **Six-Day War**, Israel routed a coalition of Arab nations, seizing the West Bank, Sinai, and Jerusalem. In 1972, Palestinian terrorists murdered 12 Israeli athletes at the Olympics in Munich. In 1973, the oil-producing Arab nations placed an embargo on shipments to the West, causing major energy crises in the US and Europe. Also, in 1973, Israelis and Arabs battled again in the **Yom Kippur War**. In 1977, Egyptian leader **Anwar Sadat** became the first Arab leader to visit Israel.

Middle East from 1978 to 1985

In 1978, American President **Jimmy Carter** hosted successful peace talks between Egypt and Israel at **Camp David**. The next year, however, a fundamentalist Islamist regime would take power in Iran, and many Americans would be taken hostage, only released upon the election of **Ronald Reagan**. Between 1980 and 1988, Iran and Iraq engaged in a bloody and brutal war, begun when the Iraqi leader **Saddam Hussein** seized territory in eastern Iran. Also, during this period, Afghan rebels were engaged in a prolonged, ultimately successful fight for independence from the Soviets. In 1982, Israel attacked Lebanon, which was harboring the Palestinian leader **Yasser Arafat**. Lebanon would be forced to oust Arafat the next year. Israel would continue attacking Arafat and the **Palestinian Liberation Organization**, and the PLO would continue to sponsor terrorist activities against Israel.

End of the Cold War

Over time, the leaders of the Soviet Union and United States began to realize the total annihilation that would ensue if nuclear war was declared, and it was agreed that both sides would **disarm**. The two treaties that were signed during the 1970s are known as the **Strategic Arms Limitation Talks (SALT) I and II**. When **Mikhail Gorbachev** came into power in the USSR in 1985, he established a policy of **glasnost**, or "openness." In response to US President Ronald Reagan's military build-up using the might of the US economy, Gorbachev understood that the Soviet Union could not economically compete militarily under a communist system and overcome the military might of the United States. He thus advocated **perestroika**, a gradual metamorphosis of the Soviet economy. In 1991, these reforms culminated in the disintegration of the ruling Communist party, and the **disbanding of the Soviet Union**. This occurred two years after the **Berlin Wall**, which for more than forty years had separated communist and anticommunist Germany, was finally torn down.

Globalism

In the modern era, globalism has emerged as a popular political ideology. **Globalism** is based on the idea that all people and all nations are **interdependent**. Each nation is dependent on one or more other nations for production of and markets for goods, and for income generation. Today's ease of international travel and communication, including technological advances such as the airplane, has heightened this sense of interdependence. The global economy and the general idea of globalism have shaped many economic and political choices since the beginning of the 20th century. Many of today's issues, including environmental awareness, economic struggles, and continued warfare, often require the cooperation of many countries if they are to be dealt with effectively.

Effect of Globalization on the Way Countries Interact With Each Other

Countries worldwide often seek the same resources, leading to high demand, particularly for **nonrenewable resources**. This can result in heavy fluctuations in price. One major example is the demand for petroleum products such as oil and natural gas. Increased travel and communication make it possible to deal with diseases in remote locations; however, this also allows diseases to be spread via travelers.

A major factor contributing to increased globalization over the past few decades has been the **internet**. By allowing instantaneous communication with anyone nearly anywhere on the globe, the internet has led to interaction between far-flung individuals and countries, and an ever-increasing awareness of events all over the world.

Review Video: Globalization
Visit mometrix.com/academy and enter code: 551962

Role of the Middle East in International Relations and Economics

The location on the globe, with ease of access to Europe and Asia, and its preponderance of oil deposits, makes the **Middle Eastern countries** crucial in many international issues, both diplomatic and economic. Because of its central location, the Middle East has been a hotbed for violence since before the beginning of recorded history. Conflicts over land, resources, and religious and political power continue in the area today, spurred by conflict over control of the area's vast oil fields as well as over territories that have been disputed for thousands of years.

Middle East from 1987 to 2003

In 1987, Syrian troops entered Lebanon and stopped the civil war. Also, during this year, 402 pilgrims died during riots in the Saudi Arabian sacred city of Mecca. In 1988, the Palestinian resistance (known as the Intifada) began in earnest against Israel. Iraq invaded Kuwait in 1990, and after UN sanctions were levied, the US invaded in 1991. The Iraqi soldiers set fire to thousands of Kuwaiti oil wells while retreating. In 1992, Arafat and Israeli PM Yitzhak Rabin shook hands in Washington, and Arafat would soon return to Gaza after years of exile. In 1995, the Israelis and Palestinians signed an agreement giving the Palestinians autonomy in the West Bank and Gaza areas. Despite continuing violence, another agreement was reached in 1998, this one stating that the Palestinians would be granted land in exchange for keeping the peace. Violence continued, however, and in 2003, Israel began construction of a barrier between itself and the Palestinian territories.

War on Terror

Following the terrorist attacks on the United States on September 11, 2001, the United States invaded Afghanistan, marking the start of the Global War on Terrorism. This was a global campaign led by the Americans to oust Islamic extremist terrorist groups mainly situated in the Middle East. On the side of the Americans was a large coalition of other countries, many of whom were members of NATO. American allies that fought in the War on Terror included the United Kingdom, Australia, Canada, Denmark, France, Italy, the Netherlands, New Zealand, and Norway. Major wars occurred in Afghanistan and Iraq against al-Qaeda, the Taliban, and their allies.

While stopping terrorism was the main stated goal of the War on Terror, the American government invaded Iraq under the claims that Saddam Hussein's government had weapons of mass destruction, but these claims were found to be false. The goal of removing extremist groups from the region has also not been entirely successful, as the Taliban took control of Afghanistan in 2021, and militant groups continue to have heavy influence in the region.

New Europe after 1991 through 1998

In 1991, **Gorbachev** resigned as the last president of the USSR, and a number of the Soviet provinces, including Lithuania and Latvia, declared independence. The **Maastricht Treaty**, formally announcing the creation of the European Union, was signed in 1992, and the next year a unified European stock market opened. In the **"Velvet" Revolution of 1993**, Slovakia separated from Czechoslovakia, which became the Czech Republic. Meanwhile, the former USSR was enduring civil strife until **Boris Yeltsin** seized power in 1993. In 1994, Russian troops attacked **Chechnya**, which was trying to achieve independence. In 1998, President Clinton helped broker a peace agreement between the **British** and **North Irish rebels**.

New Europe After 1999

In 1999, the Czech Republic, Poland, and Hungary all joined **NATO**, further eliminating the old divides between western and eastern Europe. The conflict in Chechnya increased during this year, and Yeltsin was succeeded as Russian leader by the former KGB agent Vladimir Putin. An **International Criminal Court** was created in the Hague (Netherlands) in 2002, despite the vehement opposition of the United States. In the late '90s, many of the western European governments had become quasi-socialist, and they spent much of their time debating the immense increase in **immigration**. Meanwhile, the former Soviet states have had a rough transition from command to market economies, and are still somewhat economically depressed.

THE RUSSO-UKRAINIAN WAR

The Russo-Ukrainian war began in February of 2014 when Russia annexed the Crimea region of Ukraine following Ukraine's Revolution of Dignity, in which the pro-Russian president of Ukraine was ousted. This resulted in pro-Russian unrest in the Donbas region of Ukraine. A war eventually broke out between Ukraine and Russian-backed separatists in the region. This conflict is referred to as the Donbas War.

In 2022, the war was escalated by Russia's invasion of Ukraine, sparking the biggest conflict in Europe since WWII. Russia's actions in starting the invasion have been internationally condemned. The Ukrainians have since been fighting a costly war to maintain their independence, with casualties estimated to be in the tens of thousands. Russia has been accused of many war crimes, including deliberately targeting large numbers of civilians throughout the course of the war.

HUMAN-INDUCED GLOBAL CLIMATE CHANGE AND FURTHER CLIMATE CHANGE

Today, the climate change debate mostly focuses on whether it is specifically **human activities** that have wrought **changes in our world climate**; in other words, is mankind directly responsible for causing the change in global temperature and thus directly responsible for implementing choices to counteract the impact of its actions. For example, the United Nations Intergovernmental Panel on Climate Change, a multinational group of the world's leading environmental scientists, has documented increases in the average tidal levels, increasing temperatures at ground level, concentrations of greenhouse gases in the atmosphere, glaciers whose ice is melting, explorations of the Arctic ice core, and so forth. Based on this data, this panel has made predictions of variations in patterns of weather and temperatures in the near future. They believe these variations to be directly caused by emissions from human use of fossil fuels. These foremost scientists state that the climate likely will change dramatically within 50-100 years, almost completely due to human actions and their impact on the natural environment.

MAJOR OCCURRENCES OF GENOCIDE IN MODERN HISTORY

Five major occurrences of genocide in modern history other than the Holocaust are:

- **Armenian genocide**—from 1914 to 1918, the Young Turks, heirs to the Ottoman Empire, slaughtered between 800,000 and 1.5 million Armenians. This constituted approximately half of the Armenian population at the time.
- **Holodomor**—from 1932 to 1933, the people of Ukraine suffered the effects of a famine created by Joseph Stalin's collectivization of agriculture. Millions of Ukranians starved to death due to a lack of access to food.
- **Cambodian genocide**—from 1975 to 1979, the Khmer Rouge, a communist group, inflicted violence on the people of Cambodia. Between 1.5 million and 3 million Cambodians were killed. The Khmer Rouge were removed from power when the Vietnamese military took the capital of Cambodia.
- **Rwandan genocide**—in 1994, hundreds of thousands of Tutsis and Hutu sympathizers were slaughtered during the Rwandan Civil War. The UN did not act or authorize intervention during these atrocities.
- **Darfur genocide**—In 2003, militias tasked with combating rebel activity in Darfur kept the people of Darfur from accessing food and resources. This resulted in the death of hundreds of thousands of people in Darfur.

Chapter Quiz

Ready to see how well you retained what you just read? Scan the QR code to go directly to the chapter quiz interface for this study guide. If you're using a computer, simply visit the online resources page at **mometrix.com/resources719/praxsocst** and click the Chapter Quizzes link.

Geography

Transform passive reading into active learning! After immersing yourself in this chapter, put your comprehension to the test by taking a quiz. The insights you gained will stay with you longer this way. Scan the QR code to go directly to the chapter quiz interface for this study guide. If you're using a computer, simply visit the online resources page at **mometrix.com/resources719/praxsocst** and click the Chapter Quizzes link.

Geography is the study of Earth. Geographers study **physical characteristics** of Earth as well as man-made borders and boundaries. They also study the **distribution of life** on the planet, such as where certain species of animals can be found or how different forms of life interact. Major elements of the study of geography include:

- Locations
- Regional characteristics
- Spatial relations
- Natural and man-made forces that change elements of Earth

These elements are studied from regional, topical, physical, and human perspectives. Geography also focuses on the origins of Earth, as well as the history and backgrounds of different human populations.

Physical vs. Cultural Geography

Physical geography is the study of the physical characteristics of Earth: how they relate to each other, how they were formed, and how they develop. These characteristics include climate, land, and water, and also how they affect human population in various areas. Different landforms, in combination with various climates and other conditions, determine the characteristics of various cultures.

Cultural geography is the study of how the various aspects of physical geography affect individual cultures. Cultural geography also compares various cultures: how their lifestyles and customs are affected by their geographical location, climate, and other factors, as well as how they interact with their environment.

Review Video: Regional Geography
Visit mometrix.com/academy and enter code: 350378

Divisions of Geographical Study and Tools Used

The four divisions of geographical study and tools used are:

- **Topical**—the study of a single feature of Earth or one specific human activity that occurs worldwide.
- **Physical**—the various physical features of Earth, how they are created, the forces that change them, and how they are related to each other and to various human activities.
- **Regional**—specific characteristics of individual places and regions.
- **Human**—how human activity affects the environment. This includes the study of political, historical, social, and cultural activities.

Tools used in geographical study include special research methods like mapping, field studies, statistics, interviews, mathematics, and the use of various scientific instruments.

Important Ancient Geographers

The following are three important ancient geographers and their contributions to the study of geography:

- **Eratosthenes** lived in ancient Greek times and mathematically calculated the circumference of Earth and the tilt of Earth's axis. He also created the first map of the world.
- **Strabo** wrote a description of the ancient world called *Geographica* in seventeen volumes.
- **Ptolemy**, primarily an astronomer, was an experienced mapmaker. He wrote a treatise entitled *Geography*, which was used by Christopher Columbus in his travels.

Ways Geographers Analyze Areas of Human Population

In cities, towns, or other areas where many people have settled, geographers focus on the **distribution** of populations, neighborhoods, industrial areas, transportation, and other elements important to the society in question. For example, they would map out the locations of hospitals, airports, factories, police stations, schools, and housing groups. They would also make note of how these facilities are distributed in relation to the areas of habitation, such as the number of schools in a certain neighborhood or how many grocery stores are located in a specific suburban area. Another area of study and discussion is the distribution of **towns** themselves, from widely spaced rural towns to large cities that merge into each other to form a megalopolis.

Role of a Cartographer

A cartographer is a mapmaker. Mapmakers produce detailed illustrations of geographic areas to record where various features are located within that area. These illustrations can be compiled into maps, charts, graphs, and even globes. When constructing maps, **cartographers** must take into account the problem of **distortion**. Because Earth is round, a flat map does not accurately represent the correct proportions, especially if a very large geographical area is being depicted. Maps must be designed in such a way as to minimize this distortion and maximize accuracy. Accurately representing Earth's features on a flat surface is achieved through **projection**.

Types of Projection Used in Creating World Maps

The three major types of projection used in creating world maps are:

- **Cylindrical projection**—this is created by wrapping the globe of Earth in a cylindrical piece of paper, then using a light to project the globe onto the paper. The largest distortion occurs at the outermost edges.
- **Conical projection**—the paper is shaped like a cone and contacts the globe only at the cone's base. This type of projection is most useful for middle latitudes.
- **Flat-Plane projections**—also known as a gnomonic projection, this type of map is projected onto a flat piece of paper that only touches the globe at a single point. Flat-plane projections make it possible to map out Great-Circle routes, or the shortest route between one point and another on the globe, as a straight line.

Specific Types of Map Projections

Four specific types of map projections that are commonly used today are:

- **Winkel Tripel projection**—The Winkel Tripel projection balances size and shape, greatly reducing distortion. In 1998, the National Geographic Society accepted the Winkel Tripel projection as a standard, though other map forms have remained popular.
- **Robinson projection**—east and west sections of the map are less distorted, but continental shapes are somewhat inaccurate.
- **Goode homolosine projection**—sizes and shapes are accurate, but distances are not. This projection basically represents a globe that has been cut into connected sections so that it can lie flat.
- **Mercator projection**—though distortion is high, particularly in areas farther from the equator, this cylindrical projection is commonly used by seafarers.

Major Elements of Any Map

The five major elements of any map are:

- **Title**—this tells basic information about the map, such as the area represented.
- **Legend**—also known as the key, the legend explains what symbols used on a particular map represent, such as symbols for major landmarks.
- **Grid**—this most commonly represents the geographic grid system, or latitude and longitude marks used to precisely locate specific locations.
- **Directions**—a compass rose or other symbol is used to indicate the cardinal directions.
- **Scale**—this shows the relation between a certain distance on the map and the actual distance. For example, one inch might represent one mile, or ten miles, or even more, depending on the size of the map.

Review Video: Elements of a Map
Visit mometrix.com/academy and enter code: 437727

Equal-Area Maps vs. Conformal Maps

An equal-area map is designed such that the proportional sizes of various areas are accurate. For example, if one landmass is one-fifth the size of another, the lines on the map will be shifted to accommodate for distortion so that the proportional size is accurate. In many maps, areas farther from the equator are greatly distorted; this type of map compensates for this phenomenon. A **conformal map** focuses on representing the correct shape of geographical areas, with less concern for comparative size.

Consistent Scale Maps and Thematic Maps

With a consistent scale map, the same scale, such as one inch being equal to ten miles, is used throughout the entire map. This is most often used for maps of smaller areas, as maps that cover larger areas, such as the full globe, must make allowances for distortion. Maps of very large areas often make use of more than one scale, with scales closer to the center representing a larger area than those at the edges.

A **thematic map** is constructed to show very specific information about a chosen theme. For example, a thematic map might represent political information, such as how votes were distributed in an election, or could show population distribution or climatic features.

RELIEF MAPS

A relief map is constructed to show details of various **elevations** across the area of the map. Higher elevations are represented by different colors than lower elevations. **Relief maps** often also show additional details, such as the overall ruggedness or smoothness of an area. Mountains would be represented as ridged and rugged, while deserts would be shown as smooth.

Elevation in relief maps can also be represented by contour lines, or lines that connect points of the same elevation. Some relief maps even feature textures, reconstructing details in a sort of miniature model.

GEOGRAPHICAL FEATURES

- **Mountains** are elevated areas that measure 2,000 feet or more above sea level. Often steep and rugged, they usually occur in groups called chains or ranges. Six of the seven continents on Earth contain at least one range.
- **Hills** are of lower elevation than mountains, at about 500-2,000 feet. Hills are usually more rounded and are found throughout every continent.
- **Plains** are large, flat areas and are usually very fertile. The majority of Earth's population is supported by crops grown on vast plains.
- **Valleys** lie between hills and mountains. Depending on their location, their specific features can vary greatly, from fertile and habitable to rugged and inhospitable.
- **Plateaus** are elevated, but flat on top. Some plateaus are extremely dry, such as the Kenya Plateau, because surrounding mountains prevent them from receiving moisture.
- **Deserts** receive less than ten inches of rain per year. They are usually large areas, such as the Sahara Desert in Africa or the Australian Outback.
- **Deltas** occur at river mouths. Because the rivers carry sediment to the deltas, these areas are often very fertile.
- **Mesas** are flat, steep-sided mountains or hills. The term is sometimes used to refer to plateaus.
- **Basins** are areas of low elevation where rivers drain.
- **Foothills** are the transitional area between plains and mountains, usually consisting of hills that gradually increase in size as they approach a mountain range.
- **Marshes** and **swamps** are also lowlands, but they are very wet and largely covered in vegetation such as reeds and rushes.

GEOGRAPHICAL TERMS REFERRING TO BODIES OF WATER

- The **ocean** refers to the salt water that covers about two-thirds of Earth's surface.
- **Ocean basins** are named portions of the ocean. The five major ocean basins are the Atlantic, Pacific, Indian, Southern, and Arctic.
- **Seas** are generally also salt water, but are smaller than ocean basins and surrounded by land. Examples include the Mediterranean Sea, the Caribbean Sea, and the Caspian Sea.
- **Lakes** are bodies of fresh water found inland. Sixty percent of all lakes are located in Canada.
- **Rivers** are moving bodies of water that flow from higher elevations to lower. They usually start as rivulets or streams and grow until they finally empty into a sea or the ocean.
- **Canals**, such as the Panama Canal and the Suez Canal, are man-made waterways connecting two large bodies of water.

How Communities Develop

Communities, or groups of people who settle together in a specific area, typically gather where certain conditions exist. These conditions include:

- Easy access to resources such as food, water, and raw materials
- Ability to easily transport raw materials and goods, such as access to a waterway
- Room to house a sufficient workforce

People also tend to form groups with others who are similar to them. In a typical **community**, people can be found who share values, a common language, and common or similar cultural characteristics and religious beliefs. These factors will determine the overall composition of a community as it develops.

Differences Between Cities in Various Areas of the World

Cities develop and grow as an area develops. Modern statistics show that over half of the world's people live in **cities**. That percentage is even higher in developed areas of the globe. Cities are currently growing more quickly in developing regions, and even established cities continue to experience growth throughout the world. In developing or developed areas, cities often are surrounded by a metropolitan area made up of both urban and suburban sections. In some places, cities have merged into each other and become a **megalopolis**—a single, huge city.

Cities develop differently in different areas of the world. The area available for cities to grow, as well as cultural and economic forces, drives how cities develop. For example, North American cities tend to cover wider areas. European cities tend to have better-developed transportation systems. In Latin America, the richest inhabitants can be found in the city centers, while in North America, wealthier inhabitants tend to live in suburban areas.

In other parts of the world, transportation and communication between cities are less developed. Technological innovations such as the cell phone have increased communication even in these areas. Urban areas must also maintain communication with rural areas in order to procure food, resources, and raw materials that cannot be produced within the city limits.

Weather vs. Climate

Weather and climate are physical systems that affect geography. Though they deal with similar information, the way this information is measured and compiled is different.

Weather involves daily conditions in the atmosphere that affect temperature, precipitation (rain, snow, hail, or sleet), wind speed, air pressure, and other factors. Weather focuses on the short-term—what the conditions will be today, tomorrow, or over the next few days.

In contrast, **climate** aggregates information about daily and seasonal weather conditions in a region over a long period of time. The climate takes into account average monthly and yearly temperatures, average precipitation over long periods of time, and the growing season of an area.

Climates are classified according to latitude, or how close they lie to Earth's equator. The three major divisions are:

- **Low Latitudes**, lying from 0 to approximately 23.5 degrees
- **Middle Latitudes**, found from approximately 23.5 to 66.5 degrees
- **High Latitudes**, found from approximately 66.5 degrees to the poles

Review Video: Climates
Visit mometrix.com/academy and enter code: 991320

Climates Found in the Low Latitudes

Rainforests, savannas, and deserts occur in low latitudes:

- **Rainforest** climates, near the equator, experience high average temperatures and humidity, as well as relatively high rainfall.
- **Savannas** are found on either side of the rainforest region. Mostly grasslands, they typically experience dry winters and wet summers.
- Beyond the savannas lie the **desert** regions, with hot, dry climates, sparse rainfall, and temperature fluctuations of up to fifty degrees from day to night.

Climate Regions Found in the Middle Latitudes

The climate regions found in the middle latitudes are:

- **Mediterranean**—the Mediterranean climate occurs between 30- and 40-degrees latitude, both north and south, on the western coasts of continents. Characteristics include a year-long growing season; hot, dry summers followed by mild winters; and sparse rainfall that occurs mostly during the winter months.
- **Humid-subtropical**—humid-subtropical regions are located in southeastern coastal areas. Winds that blow in over warm ocean currents produce long summers, mild winters, and a long growing season. These areas are highly productive and support a larger part of Earth's population than any other climate.
- **Humid-continental**—the humid continental climate produces the familiar four seasons typical of a good portion of the US. Some of the most productive farmlands in the world lie in these climates. Winters are cold, and summers are hot and humid.

Marine, Steppe, and Desert Climates

The climate regions found in the middle latitudes are:

- **Marine**—marine climates are found near water or on islands. Ocean winds help make these areas mild and rainy. Summers are cooler than humid-subtropical summers, but winters also bring milder temperatures due to the warmth of the ocean winds.
- **Steppe**—steppe climates, or prairie climates, are found far inland on large continents. Summers are hot and winters are cold, but rainfall is sparser than in continental climates.
- **Desert**—desert climates occur where steppe climates receive even less rainfall. Examples include the Gobi Desert in Asia as well as desert areas of Australia and the southwestern US.

Climates Found in the High Latitudes

The high latitudes consist of two major climate areas, the tundra and taiga:

- **Tundra** means "marshy plain." The ground is frozen throughout long, cold winters, but there is little snowfall. During the short summers, it becomes wet and marshy. Tundras are not amenable to crops, but many plants and animals have adapted to the conditions.
- **Taigas** lie south of tundra regions and include the largest forest areas in the world, as well as swamps and marshes. Large mineral deposits exist here, as well as many animals valued for their fur. In the winter, taiga regions are colder than the tundra, and summers are hotter. The growing season is short.

A **vertical climate** exists in high mountain ranges. Increasing elevation leads to varying temperatures, growing conditions, types of vegetation and animals, and occurrence of human habitation, often encompassing elements of various other climate regions.

Factors Affecting Climate

Because Earth is tilted, its **rotation** brings about changes in **seasons**. Regions closer to the equator, and those nearest the poles, experience very little change in seasonal temperatures. Mid-range latitudes are most likely to experience distinct seasons. Large bodies of water also affect climate. Ocean currents and wind patterns can change the climate for an area that lies in a typically cold latitude, such as England, to a much more temperate climate. Mountains can affect both short-term weather and long-term climates. Some deserts occur because precipitation is stopped by the wall of a mountain range.

Over time, established **climate patterns** can shift and change. While the issue is hotly debated, it has been theorized that human activity has also led to climate change.

Effect of Human Systems

Human Systems that Geographers Incorporate into the Study of Earth

Human systems affect geography in the way in which they settle, form groups that grow into large-scale habitations, and even create permanent changes in the landscape. **Geographers** study movements of people, how they distribute goods among each other and to other settlements or cultures, and how ideas grow and spread. Migrations, wars, forced relocations, and trade can all spread cultural ideas, language, goods, and other practices to widespread areas. Throughout history, cultures have been changed due to a wide range of events, including major migrations and the conquering of one people by another. In addition, **human systems** can lead to various conflicts or alliances to control access to and the use of natural resources.

Human Systems that Form the Basis of Cultures in North America

North America consists of 23 countries, including (in decreasing population order) the United States of America, Mexico, Canada, Guatemala, Cuba, Haiti, and the Dominican Republic. The US and Canada support similarly diverse cultures, as both were formed from groups of native races and large numbers of immigrants. Many **North American cultures** come from a mixture of indigenous and colonial European influences. Agriculture is important to North American countries, while service industries and technology also play a large part in the economy. On average, North America supports a high standard of living and a high level of development and supports trade with countries throughout the world.

Human Systems that Shape South America

Home to twelve sovereign states, including Brazil (largest in area and population), Colombia, Argentina, Venezuela, and Peru; two independent territories; and one internal territory, **South America** is largely defined by its prevailing languages. The majority of countries in South America speak Spanish or Portuguese. Most of South America has experienced a similar history, having been originally dominated by Native cultures and then conquered by European nations. The countries of South America have since gained independence, but there is a wide disparity between various countries' economic and political factors. Most South American countries rely on only one or two exports, usually agricultural, with suitable lands often controlled by rich families. Most societies in South America feature major separations between classes, both economically and socially. Challenges faced by developing South American countries include geographical limitations, economic issues, and sustainable development, including the need to preserve the existing rainforests.

Human Systems Influencing Europe

Europe contains a wide variety of cultures, ethnic groups, physical geographical features, climates, and resources, all of which have influenced the distribution of its varied population. **Europe**, in general, is industrialized and developed, with cultural differences giving each individual country its own unique characteristics. Greek and Roman influences played a major role in European culture, as did Christianity. European countries spread their beliefs and cultural elements throughout the world by means of migration and colonization. They have had a significant influence on nearly every other continent in the world. While Western Europe has been largely democratic, Eastern Europe functioned under communist rule for many years. The formation of the European Union (EU) in 1993 has increased stability and positive diplomatic relations among European nations. Like other industrialized regions, Europe is now focusing on various environmental issues.

Human Systems that Have Shaped Russia

After numerous conflicts, Russia became a Communist state, known as the **USSR**. With the collapse of the USSR in 1991, the country has struggled in its transition to a market-driven economy. Attempts to build a workable system have led to the destruction of natural resources as well as problems with nuclear power, including accidents such as Chernobyl. To complete the transition to a market economy, Russia would need to improve its transportation and communication systems and find a way to more efficiently use its natural resources.

The population of Russia is not distributed evenly, with three-quarters of the population living west of the Ural Mountains. The people of Russia encompass over a hundred different ethnic groups. Over eighty percent of the population is ethnically Russian, and Russian is the official language of the country.

Human Systems that Have Shaped North Africa and Southwest and Central Asia

The largely desert climate of these areas has led most population centers to rise around sources of **water**, such as the Nile River. This area is the home of the **earliest known civilizations** and the origin of Christianity, Judaism, and Islam. After serving as the site of huge, independent civilizations in ancient times, North Africa and Southwest and Central Asia were largely parceled out as **European colonies** during the 18th and 19th centuries. The beginning of the 20th century saw many of these countries gain their independence. **Islam** has served as a unifying force for large portions of these areas, and many of the inhabitants speak Arabic. In spite of the arid climate, agriculture is a large business, but the most valuable resource is **oil**. Centuries of conflict throughout this area have led to ongoing political problems. These political problems have also contributed to environmental issues.

Human Systems that Shape and Influence the Culture of Sub-Saharan Africa

South of the Sahara Desert, **Africa** is divided into a number of culturally diverse nations. The inhabitants are unevenly distributed due to geographical limitations that prevent settlement in vast areas. **AIDS** has become a major plague throughout this part of Africa, killing millions, largely due to restrictive beliefs that prevent education about the disease, as well as abject poverty and unsettled political situations that make it impossible to manage the pandemic. The population of this area of Africa is widely diverse due to extensive **migration**. Many of the people still rely on **subsistence farming** for their welfare. Starvation and poverty are rampant due to drought and political instability. Some areas are far more stable than others due to the greater availability of resources. These areas have been able to begin the process of **industrialization**.

Human Systems that Determine the Cultural Makeup of South Asia

South Asia is home to one of the first human civilizations, which grew up in the **Indus River Valley**. With a great deal of disparity between rural and urban life, South Asia has much to do to improve the quality of life for its lower classes. Two major religions, **Hinduism** and **Buddhism**, have their origins in this region. Parts of South Asia, most notably India, were subject to **British rule** for several decades and are still working to improve independent governments and social systems. Overall, South Asia is very culturally diverse, with a wide mix of religions and languages throughout. Many individuals are **farmers**, but a growing number have found prosperity in the spread of **high-tech industries**. Industrialization is growing in South Asia but continues to face environmental, social, religious, and economic challenges.

Human Systems Shaping the Culture of East Asia

Governments in East Asia are varied, ranging from communist to democratic governments, with some governments that mix both approaches. **Isolationism** throughout the area limited the countries' contact with other nations until the early 20th century. The unevenly distributed population of East Asia consists of over one and a half billion people with widely diverse ethnic backgrounds, religions, and languages. More residents live in **urban** areas than in **rural** areas, creating shortages of farmworkers at times. Japan, Taiwan, and South Korea are overall more urban, while China and Mongolia are more rural. Japan stands as the most industrial country in East Asia. Some areas of East Asia are suffering from major environmental issues. Japan has dealt with many of these problems and now has some of the strictest environmental laws in the world.

Human Systems that Have Influenced Southeast Asia

Much of Southeast Asia was **colonized** by European countries during the 18th and 19th centuries, with the exception of Siam, now known as Thailand. All Southeast Asian countries are now independent, but the 20th century saw numerous conflicts between **communist** and **democratic** forces.

Southeast Asia has been heavily influenced by both Buddhist and Muslim religions. Industrialization is growing, with the population moving in large numbers from rural to urban areas. Some have moved to avoid conflict, oppression, and poverty.

Natural disasters, including volcanoes, typhoons, and flash flooding, are fairly common in Southeast Asia, creating extensive economic damage and societal disruption.

Human Systems that Affect the Development and Culture of Australia, Oceana, and Antarctica

South Pacific cultures originally migrated from Southeast Asia, creating hunter-gatherer or sometimes settled agricultural communities. **European** countries moved in during later centuries, seeking the plentiful natural resources of the area. Today, some South Pacific islands remain under the control of foreign governments, and culture in these areas mixes modern, industrialized society with indigenous culture. Population is unevenly distributed, largely due to the inhabitability of many parts of the South Pacific, such as the extremely hot desert areas of Australia. **Agriculture** still drives much of the economy, with **tourism** growing. **Antarctica** remains the only continent that has not been claimed by any country. There are no permanent human habitations in Antarctica, but scientists and explorers visit the area on a temporary basis.

Human-Environment Interaction

Geography also studies the ways people interact with, use, and change their **environment**. The effects, reasons, and consequences of these changes are studied, as are the ways the environment limits or influences human behavior. This kind of study can help determine the best course of action when a nation or group of people is considering making changes to the environment, such as building a dam or removing natural landscape to build or expand roads. Study of the **consequences** can help determine if these actions are manageable and how long-term, detrimental results can be mitigated.

Physical Geography and Climates

Physical Geography and Climate of North America

Together, the US and Canada make up the majority of North America and both have a similar distribution of geographical features: mountain ranges in both the east and the west, stretches of fertile plains through the center, and lakes and waterways. Both areas were shaped by **glaciers**, which also deposited highly fertile soil. Because they are so large, Canada and the US experience several varieties of **climate**, including continental climates with four seasons in median areas, tropical climates in the southern part of the US, and arctic climes in the far north. The remaining area of North America includes Mexico, Central America, the Caribbean Isles, and Greenland.

Physical Geography and Climate of South America

South America contains a wide variety of geographical features, including high **mountains** such as the Andes, wide **plains**, and high-altitude **plateaus**. The region contains numerous natural resources, but many of them have remained unused due to various obstacles, including political issues, geographic barriers, and lack of sufficient economic power. Climate zones in South America are largely **tropical**, with rainforests and savannas, but vertical climate zones and grasslands also exist in some places.

Physical Geography and Climate of Europe

Europe spans a wide area with a variety of climate zones. In the east and south are **mountain** ranges, while the north is dominated by a **plains** region. The long coastline and the island nature of some countries, such as Britain, mean the climate is often warmer than other lands at similar latitudes, as the area is warmed by **ocean currents**. Many areas of western Europe have a moderate climate, while areas of the south are dominated by the classic Mediterranean climate. Europe carries a high level of natural resources. Numerous waterways help connect the inner regions with the coastal areas. Much of Europe is **industrialized**, and **agriculture** has been developed for thousands of years.

Physical Geography and Climate of Russia

Russia's area encompasses part of Asia and Europe. From the standpoint of square footage alone, **Russia** is the largest country in the world. Due to its size, Russia encompasses a wide variety of climatic regions, including **plains**, **plateaus**, **mountains**, and **tundra**.

Russia's **climate** can be quite harsh, with rivers that are frozen most of the year, making transportation of the country's rich natural resources more difficult. Siberia, in northern Russia, is dominated by **permafrost**. Native peoples in this area still follow a hunting and gathering lifestyle, living in portable yurts and subsisting largely on herds of reindeer or caribou. Other areas include taiga with extensive, dense woods in north-central Russia and more temperate steppes and grasslands in the southwest.

Physical Geography and Climate of North Africa, Southwest, and Central Asia

This area of the world is complex in its geographical structure and climate, incorporating seas, peninsulas, rivers, mountains, and numerous other features. **Earthquakes** are common, with tectonic plates in the area remaining active. Much of the world's **oil** lies in this area. The tendency of the large rivers of North Africa, especially the Nile, to follow a set pattern of **drought** and extreme **fertility**, led people to settle there from prehistoric times. As technology has advanced, people have tamed this river, making its activity more predictable and the land around it more productive. The extremely arid nature of many other parts of this area has also led to **human intervention** such as irrigation to increase agricultural production.

Physical Geography and Climate of the Southern Portion of Africa

South of the Sahara Desert, the high elevations and other geographical characteristics have made it very difficult for human travel or settlement to occur. The geography of the area is dominated by a series of **plateaus**. There are also mountain ranges and a large rift valley in the eastern part of the country. Contrasting the wide desert areas, sub-Saharan Africa contains numerous lakes, rivers, and world-famous waterfalls. The area has **tropical** climates, including rainforests, savannas, steppes, and desert areas. The main natural resources are minerals, including gems and water.

Physical Geography and Climate of South Asia

The longest **alluvial plain**, a plain caused by shifting floodplains of major rivers and river systems over time, exists in South Asia. South Asia boasts three major **river systems** in the Ganges, Indus, and Brahmaputra. It also has large deposits of **minerals**, including iron ore that is in great demand internationally. South Asia holds mountains, plains, plateaus, and numerous islands. The climates range from tropical to highlands and desert areas. South Asia also experiences monsoon winds that cause a long rainy season. Variations in climate, elevation, and human activity influence agricultural production.

Geography and Climate of East Asia

East Asia includes North and South Korea, Mongolia, China, Japan, and Taiwan. Mineral resources are plentiful but not evenly distributed throughout. The coastlines are long, and while the population is large, farmlands are sparse. As a result, the surrounding ocean has become a major source of sustenance. East Asia is large enough to encompass several climate regions. **Ocean currents** provide milder climates to coastal areas, while **monsoons** provide the majority of the rainfall for the region. **Typhoons** are somewhat common, as are **earthquakes**, **volcanoes**, and **tsunamis**. The latter occur because of the tectonic plates that meet beneath the continent and remain somewhat active.

Geography and Climate of Southeast Asia

Southeast Asia lies largely on the **equator**, and roughly half of the countries of the region are island nations. These countries include Indonesia, the Philippines, Vietnam, Thailand, Myanmar, and Malaysia (which is partially on the mainland and partially an island country). The island nations of Southeast Asia feature mountains that are considered part of the **Ring of Fire**, an area where tectonic plates remain active, leading to extensive volcanic activity as well as earthquakes and tsunamis. Southeast Asia boasts many rivers and abundant natural resources, including gems, fossil fuels, and minerals. There are basically two seasons: wet and dry. The wet season arrives with the **monsoons**. In general, Southeast Asia consists of **tropical rainforest climates**, but there are some mountain areas and tropical savannas.

Geography and Climate of Australia, Oceania, and Antarctica

In the far southern hemisphere of the globe, Australia and Oceania present their own climatic combinations. **Australia**, the only island on Earth that is also a continent, has extensive deserts as well as mountains and lowlands. The economy is driven by agriculture, including ranches and farms, and minerals. While the steppes bordering extremely arid inland areas are suitable for livestock, only the coastal areas receive sufficient rainfall for crops without using irrigation. **Oceania** refers to over 10,000 Pacific islands created by volcanic activity. Most of these have tropical climates with wet and dry seasons. **New Zealand**, Australia's nearest neighbor, boasts rich forests, mountain ranges, and relatively moderate temperatures, including rainfall throughout the year. **Antarctica** is covered with ice. Its major resource consists of scientific information. It supports some wildlife, such as penguins, and little vegetation, primarily mosses or lichens.

Theory of Plate Tectonics

According to the geological theory of plate tectonics, Earth's crust is made up of ten major and several minor **tectonic plates**. These plates are the solid areas of the crust. They float on top of Earth's mantle, which is made up of molten rock. Because the plates float on this liquid component of Earth's crust, they move, creating major changes in Earth's surface. These changes can happen very slowly over a long time period, such as in continental drift, or rapidly, such as when earthquakes occur. **Interaction** between the different continental plates can create mountain ranges, volcanic activity, major earthquakes, and deep rifts.

Types of Plate Boundaries

Plate tectonics defines three types of plate boundaries, determined by how the edges of the plates interact. These **plate boundaries** are:

- **Convergent boundaries**—the bordering plates move toward one another. When they collide directly, this is known as continental collision, which can create very large, high mountain ranges such as the Himalayas and the Andes. If one plate slides under the other, this is called subduction. Subduction can lead to intense volcanic activity. One example is the Ring of Fire that lies along the northern Pacific coastlines.
- **Divergent boundaries**—plates move away from each other. This movement leads to rifts such as the Mid-Atlantic Ridge and East Africa's Great Rift Valley.
- **Transform boundaries**—plate boundaries slide in opposite directions against each other. Intense pressure builds up along transform boundaries as the plates grind along each other's edges, leading to earthquakes. Many major fault lines, including the San Andreas Fault, lie along transform boundaries.

Erosion, Weathering, Transportation, and Deposition

Erosion involves movement of any loose material on Earth's surface. This can include soil, sand, or rock fragments. These loose fragments can be displaced by natural forces such as wind, water, ice, plant cover, and human factors. **Mechanical erosion** occurs due to natural forces. **Chemical erosion** occurs as a result of human intervention and activities. **Weathering** occurs when atmospheric elements affect Earth's surface. Water, heat, ice, and pressure all lead to weathering. **Transportation** refers to loose material being moved by wind, water, or ice. Glacial movement, for example, carries everything from pebbles to boulders, sometimes over long distances. **Deposition** is the result of transportation. When material is transported, it is eventually deposited, and builds up to create formations like moraines and sand dunes.

Effects of Human Interaction and Conflict on Geographical Boundaries

Human societies and their interaction have led to divisions of territories into **countries** and various other subdivisions. While these divisions are at their root artificial, they are important to geographers in discussing various populations' interactions.

Geographical divisions often occur through conflict between different human populations. The reasons behind these divisions include:

- Control of resources
- Control of important trade routes
- Control of populations

Conflict often occurs due to religious, political, language, or race differences. Natural resources are finite and so often lead to conflict over how they are distributed among populations.

State Sovereignty

State sovereignty recognizes the division of geographical areas into areas controlled by various governments or groups of people. These groups control not only the territory but also all its natural resources and the inhabitants of the area. The entire planet Earth is divided into **political** or **administratively sovereign areas** recognized to be controlled by a particular government, with the exception of the continent of Antarctica.

Alliances

Alliances form between different countries based on similar interests, political goals, cultural values, or military issues. Six existing **international alliances** include:

- North Atlantic Treaty Organization (NATO)
- Common Market
- European Union (EU)
- United Nations (UN)
- Caribbean Community
- Council of Arab Economic Unity

In addition, very large **companies** and **multi-national corporations** can create alliances and various kinds of competition based on the need to control resources, production, and the overall marketplace.

Ways Agricultural Revolution Changed Society

The agricultural revolution began approximately 6,000 years ago when the **plow** was invented in **Mesopotamia**. Using a plow drawn by animals, people were able to cultivate crops in large quantities rather than gathering available seeds and grains and planting them by hand. Because large-scale agriculture was labor-intensive, this led to the development of stable communities where people gathered to make farming possible. As **stable farming communities** replaced groups of nomadic hunter-gatherers, human society underwent profound changes. Societies became dependent on limited numbers of crops as well as subject to the vagaries of weather. Trading livestock and surplus agricultural output led to the growth of large-scale **commerce** and **trade routes**.

Ways Human Populations Modify Their Surrounding Environment

The agricultural revolution led human societies to begin changing their surroundings to accommodate their needs for shelter and room to cultivate food and to provide for domestic animals. Clearing ground for crops, redirecting waterways for irrigation purposes, and building permanent settlements all create major changes in the **environment**. Large-scale agriculture can lead to loose topsoil and damaging erosion. Building large cities leads to degraded air quality, water pollution from energy consumption, and many other side effects that can severely damage the environment. Recently, many countries have taken action by passing laws to **reduce human impact** on the environment and reduce the potentially damaging side effects. This is called **environmental policy**.

Ecology

Ecology is the study of the way living creatures interact with their environment. **Biogeography** explores the way physical features of Earth affect living creatures.

Ecology bases its studies on three different levels of the environment:

- **Ecosystem**—this is a specific physical environment and all the organisms that live there.
- **Biome**—this is a group of ecosystems, usually consisting of a large area with similar flora and fauna as well as similar climate and soil. Examples of biomes include deserts, tropical rain forests, taigas, and tundra.
- **Habitat**—this is an area in which a specific species usually lives. The habitat includes the necessary soil, water, and resources for that particular species, as well as predators and other species that compete for the same resources.

Types of Interactions Occurring Between Species in an Individual Habitat

Different interactions occur among species and members of single species within a habitat. These **interactions** fall into three categories:

- **Competition** — competition occurs when different animals, either of the same species or of different species, compete for the same resources. Robins can compete with other robins for available food, but other insectivores also compete for these same resources.
- **Predation**— predation occurs when one species depends on the other species for food, such as a fox who subsists on small mammals.
- **Symbiosis** — symbiosis occurs when two different species exist in the same environment without negatively affecting each other. Some symbiotic relationships are beneficial to one or both organisms without harm occurring to either.

Importance of an Organism's Ability to Adapt

If a species is relocated from one habitat to another, it must **adapt** in order to survive. Some species are more capable of adapting than others. Those that cannot adapt will not survive. There are different ways a creature can adapt, including behavior modification and structural or physiological changes. Adaptation is also vital if an organism's environment changes around it. Although the creature has not been relocated, it finds itself in a new environment that requires changes in order to survive. The more readily an organism can adapt, the more likely it is to survive. The almost infinite ability of **humans** to adapt is a major reason why they are able to survive in almost any habitat in any area of the world.

BIODIVERSITY

Biodiversity refers to the variety of habitats that exist on the planet, as well as the variety of organisms that can exist within these habitats. A greater level of **biodiversity** makes it more likely that an individual habitat will flourish along with the species that depend upon it. Changes in habitat, including climate change, human intervention, or other factors, can reduce biodiversity by causing the extinction of certain species.

Chapter Quiz

Ready to see how well you retained what you just read? Scan the QR code to go directly to the chapter quiz interface for this study guide. If you're using a computer, simply visit the online resources page at **mometrix.com/resources719/praxsocst** and click the Chapter Quizzes link.

Civics

Transform passive reading into active learning! After immersing yourself in this chapter, put your comprehension to the test by taking a quiz. The insights you gained will stay with you longer this way. Scan the QR code to go directly to the chapter quiz interface for this study guide. If you're using a computer, simply visit the online resources page at **mometrix.com/resources719/praxsocst** and click the Chapter Quizzes link.

Political Science and Its Ties to Other Major Disciplines

Political science focuses on studying different governments and how they compare to each other, general political theory, ways political theory is put into action, how nations and governments interact with each other, and a general study of governmental structure and function. Other elements of **political science** include the study of elections, governmental administration at various levels, development and action of political parties, and how values such as freedom, power, justice, and equality are expressed in different political cultures. Political science also encompasses elements of other disciplines, including:

- **History**—how historical events have shaped political thought and process
- **Sociology**—the effects of various stages of social development on the growth and development of government and politics
- **Anthropology**—the effects of governmental process on the culture of an individual group and its relationships with other groups
- **Economics**—how government policies regulate the distribution of products and how they can control and/or influence the economy in general

General Political Theory

Based on general political theory, the four major purposes of any given government are:

- **Ensuring national security**—the government protects against international, domestic, and terrorist attacks and also ensures ongoing security through negotiating and establishing relationships with other governments.
- **Providing public services**—the government should "promote the general welfare," as stated in the Preamble to the US Constitution, by providing whatever is needed to its citizens.
- **Ensuring social order**—the government supplies means of settling conflicts among citizens as well as making laws to govern the nation, state, or city.
- **Making decisions regarding the economy**—laws help form the economic policy of the country, regarding both domestic and international trade and related issues. The government also has the ability to distribute goods and wealth to some extent among its citizens.

MAIN THEORIES REGARDING THE ORIGIN OF THE STATE

There are four main theories regarding the origin of the state:

- **Evolutionary**—the state evolved from the family, with the head of state the equivalent of the family's patriarch or matriarch.
- **Force**—one person or group of people brought everyone in an area under their control, forming the first government.
- **Divine Right**—certain people were chosen by the prevailing deity to be the rulers of the nation, which is itself created by the deity or deities.
- **Social Contract**—there is no natural order. The people allow themselves to be governed to maintain social order, while the state, in turn, promises to protect the people they govern. If the government fails to protect its people, the people have the right to seek new leaders.

PUBLIC POLICY

Public policy is the study of how the various levels of government formulate and implement policies. **Public policy** also refers to the set of policies that a government adopts and implements, including laws, plans, actions, and behaviors, for the purpose of governing society. Public policy is developed and adapted through the process of **policy analysis**. Public policy analysis is the systematic evaluation of alternative means of reaching social goals. Public policy is divided into various policy areas, including domestic policy, foreign policy, healthcare policy, education policy, criminal policy, national defense policy, and energy policy.

INFLUENCES OF PHILOSOPHERS ON POLITICAL STUDY

Ancient Greek philosophers **Aristotle** and **Plato** believed political science would lead to order in political matters and that this scientifically organized order would create stable, just societies.

- **Thomas Aquinas** adapted the ideas of Aristotle to a Christian perspective. His ideas stated that individuals should have certain rights but also certain duties, and that these rights and duties should determine the type and extent of government rule. In stating that laws should limit the role of government, he laid the groundwork for ideas that would eventually become modern constitutionalism.
- **Niccolò Machiavelli**, author of *The Prince*, was a proponent of politics based on power. He is often considered the founder of modern political science.
- **Thomas Hobbes**, author of *Leviathan* (1651), believed that individuals' lives were focused solely on a quest for power and that the state must work to control this urge. Hobbes felt that people were completely unable to live harmoniously without the intervention of a powerful, undivided government.

CONTRIBUTIONS OF JOHN LOCKE, MONTESQUIEU, AND ROUSSEAU TO POLITICAL SCIENCE

John Locke published *Two Treatises of Government* in 1689. This work argued against the ideas of Thomas Hobbes. He put forth the theory of *tabula rasa*—that people are born with minds like blank slates. Individual minds are molded by experience, not innate knowledge or intuition. He also believed that all men should be independent and equal. Many of Locke's ideas found their way into the Constitution of the United States.

The two French philosophers, **Montesquieu** and **Rousseau**, heavily influenced the French Revolution (1789-1799). They believed government policies and ideas should change to alleviate existing problems, an idea referred to as "liberalism." Rousseau, in particular, directly influenced the Revolution with writings such as *The Social Contract* (1762) and *Declaration of the Rights of Man and of the Citizen* (1789). Other ideas Rousseau and Montesquieu espoused included:

- Individual freedom and community welfare are of equal importance
- Man's innate goodness leads to natural harmony
- Reason develops with the rise of civilized society
- Individual citizens carry certain obligations to the existing government

Political Ideologies of Famous Philosophers

David Hume and **Jeremy Bentham** believed politics should have as its main goal maintaining "the greatest happiness for the greatest number." Hume also believed in empiricism, or that ideas should not be believed until the proof has been observed. He was a natural skeptic and always sought out the truth of matters rather than believing what he was told.

John Stuart Mill, a British philosopher and economist, made significant contributions to the fields of social and economic theory. A majorly influential thinker in the realm of classical liberalism, Mill believed in progressive policies such as women's suffrage, emancipation, and the development of labor unions and farming cooperatives. His ideas on free speech and the harm principle were the basis for the "clear and present danger" test outlined by Oliver Wendell Holmes Jr. when determining if speech is protected by the First Amendment of the US Constitution.

Johann Fichte and **Georg Hegel**, German philosophers in the late 18th and early 19th centuries, supported a form of liberalism grounded largely in socialism and a sense of nationalism.

Main Political Orientations

The four main political orientations are:

- **Liberal**—liberals believe that government should work to increase equality, even at the expense of some freedoms. Government should assist those in need, focusing on enforced social justice and free basic services for everyone.
- **Conservative**—a conservative believes that government should be limited in most cases. The government should allow its citizens to help one another and solve their own problems rather than enforcing solutions. Business should not be overregulated, allowing a free market.
- **Moderate**—this ideology incorporates some liberal and some conservative values, generally falling somewhere between in overall belief.
- **Libertarian**—libertarians believe that the government's role should be limited to protecting the life and liberty of citizens. Government should not be involved in any citizen's life unless that citizen is encroaching upon the rights of another.

Major Principles of Government as Outlined in the United States Constitution

The six major principles of government as outlined in the United States Constitution are:

- **Federalism**—the power of the government does not belong entirely to the national government but is divided between federal and state governments.
- **Popular sovereignty**—the government is determined by the people and gains its authority and power from the people.
- **Separation of powers**—the government is divided into three branches (executive, legislative, and judicial) with each having its own set of powers.

- **Judicial review**—courts at all levels of government can declare laws invalid if they contradict the constitutions of individual states, or the US Constitution, with the Supreme Court serving as the final judicial authority on decisions of this kind.
- **Checks and balances**—no single branch can act without input from another, and each branch has the power to "check" any other, as well as balance other branches' powers.
- **Limited government**—governmental powers are limited, and certain individual rights are defined as inviolable by the government.

Types of Powers Delegated to the National Government by the US Constitution

The structure of the US government divides power between national and state governments. Powers delegated to the federal government by the Constitution are:

- **Expressed powers**—powers directly defined in the Constitution, including power to declare war, regulate commerce, make money, and collect taxes
- **Implied powers**—powers the national government must have in order to carry out the expressed powers
- **Inherent powers**—powers inherent to any government, not expressly defined in the Constitution

Some of these powers, such as collection and levying of taxes, are also granted to the individual state governments.

Primary Positions of Federalism and Development through the Years in the US

The way federalism should be practiced has been the subject of debate since the writing of the Constitution. There were—and still are—two main factions regarding this issue:

- **States' rights**—those favoring the states' rights position feel that the state governments should take the lead in performing local actions to manage various problems.
- **Nationalist**—those favoring a nationalist position feel the national government should take the lead to deal with those same matters.

The flexibility of the Constitution has allowed the US government to shift and adapt as the needs of the country have changed. Power has often shifted from the state governments to the national government and back again, and both levels of government have developed various ways to influence each other.

Effects of Federalism on Policy-Making and the Balance of Politics in the US

Federalism has three major effects on **public policy** in the US:

- Determining whether the local, state, or national government originates policy
- Affecting how policies are made
- Ensuring policy-making functions under a set of limitations

Federalism also influences the **political balance of power** in the US by:

- Making it difficult, if not impossible, for a single political party to seize total power
- Ensuring that individuals can participate in the political system at various levels
- Making it possible for individuals working within the system to be able to affect policy at some level, whether local or more widespread

Three Branches of the US Federal Government

The following are the three branches of the US Federal government and the individuals that belong to each branch:

- **Legislative Branch**—this consists of the two houses of Congress: the House of Representatives and the Senate. All members of the Legislative Branch are elected officials.
- **Executive Branch**—this branch is made up of the president, vice president, presidential advisors, and other various cabinet members. Advisors and cabinet members are appointed by the president, but they must be approved by Congress.
- **Judicial Branch**—the federal court system, headed by the Supreme Court.

Review Video: What Does the Executive Branch Do?
Visit mometrix.com/academy and enter code: 210629

Review Video: What Does the Judicial Branch Do?
Visit mometrix.com/academy and enter code: 278093

Review Video: What Does the Legislative Branch Do?
Visit mometrix.com/academy and enter code: 405303

Major Responsibilities of the Three Branches of the Federal Government

The three branches of the federal government each have specific roles and responsibilities:

- The **Legislative Branch** is largely concerned with lawmaking. All laws must be approved by Congress before they go into effect. They are also responsible for regulating money and trade, approving presidential appointments, and establishing organizations like the postal service and federal courts. Congress can also propose amendments to the Constitution, and can impeach, or bring charges against, the president. Only Congress can declare war.
- The **Executive Branch** carries out laws, treaties, and war declarations enacted by Congress. The president can also veto bills approved by Congress, and serves as commander in chief of the US military. The president appoints cabinet members, ambassadors to foreign countries, and federal judges.

- The **Judicial Branch** makes decisions on challenges as to whether laws passed by Congress meet the requirements of the US Constitution. The Supreme Court may also choose to review decisions made by lower courts to determine their constitutionality.

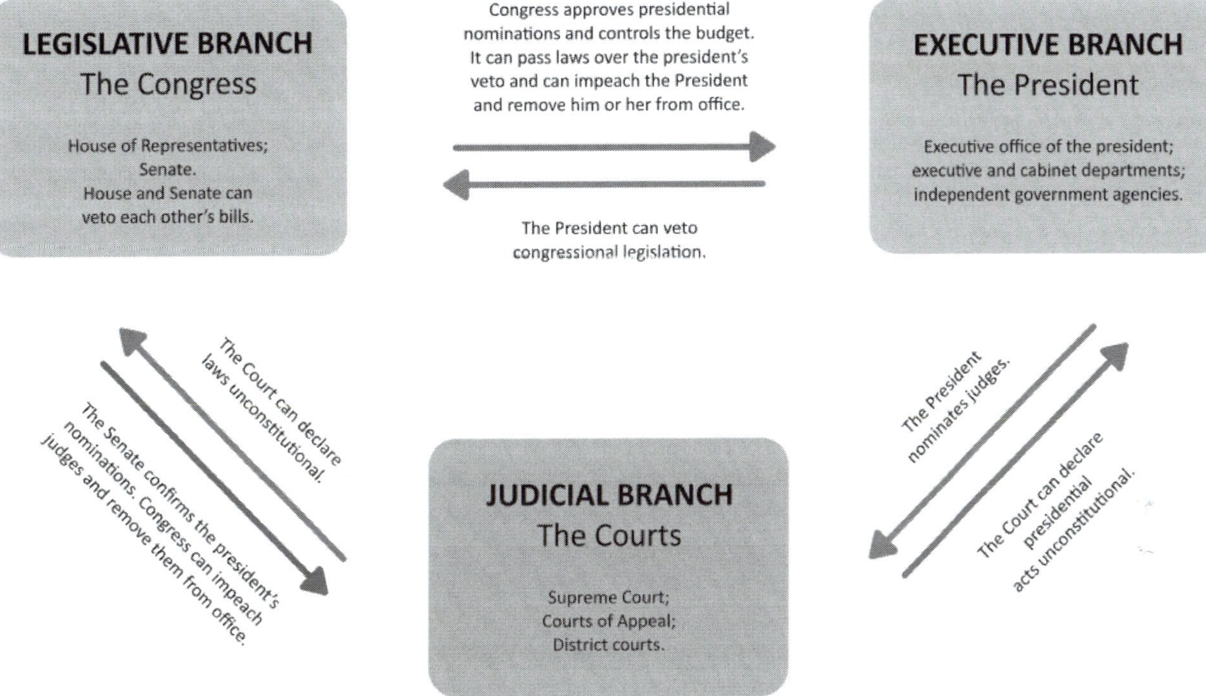

US Citizenship

Qualifications of a US citizen/How Citizenship May Be Lost

Anyone born in the US, born abroad to a US citizen, or who has gone through a process of naturalization is considered a **citizen** of the United States. It is possible to lose US citizenship as a result of conviction of certain crimes such as treason. Citizenship may also be lost if a citizen pledges an oath to another country or serves in the military of a country engaged in hostilities with the US. A US citizen can also choose to hold dual citizenship, work as an expatriate in another country without losing US citizenship, or even to renounce citizenship if he or she so chooses.

Rights, Duties, and Responsibilities Granted to or Expected from Citizens

Citizens are granted certain rights under the US government. The most important of these are defined in the **Bill of Rights**, and include freedom of speech, religion, assembly, and a variety of other rights the government is not allowed to remove. A US citizen also has a number of **duties**:

- Paying taxes
- Loyalty to the government (though the US does not prosecute those who criticize or seek to change the government)
- Support and defense of the Constitution
- Serving in the Armed Forces when required by law
- Obeying laws as set forth by the various levels of government.

Responsibilities of a US citizen include:

- Voting in elections
- Respecting one another's rights and not infringing on them

- Staying informed about various political and national issues
- Respecting one another's beliefs

BILL OF RIGHTS

IMPORTANCE OF THE BILL OF RIGHTS

The first ten amendments of the US Constitution are known as the **Bill of Rights**. These amendments prevent the government from infringing upon certain freedoms that the Founding Fathers felt were natural rights that already belonged to all people. These rights included freedom of speech, freedom of religion, freedom of assembly, and the right to bear arms. Many of the rights were formulated in direct response to the way the colonists felt they had been mistreated by the British government.

RIGHTS GRANTED IN THE BILL OF RIGHTS

The first ten amendments were passed by Congress in 1789. Three-fourths of the existing thirteen states had ratified them by December of 1791, making them official additions to the Constitution. The rights granted in the Bill of Rights are:

- **First Amendment**—freedom of religion, speech, freedom of the press, and the right to assemble and to petition the government
- **Second Amendment**—the right to bear arms
- **Third Amendment**—Congress cannot force individuals to house troops
- **Fourth Amendment**—protection from unreasonable search and seizure
- **Fifth Amendment**—no individual is required to testify against himself, and no individual may be tried twice for the same crime
- **Sixth Amendment**—the right to criminal trial by jury and the right to legal counsel
- **Seventh Amendment**—the right to civil trial by jury
- **Eighth Amendment**—protection from excessive bail or cruel and unusual punishment
- **Ninth Amendment**—prevents rights not explicitly named in the Constitution from being taken away because they are not named
- **Tenth Amendment**—any rights not directly delegated to the national government, or not directly prohibited by the government from the states, belong to the states or to the people

Review Video: Bill of Rights
Visit mometrix.com/academy and enter code: 585149

SITUATIONS WHERE THE GOVERNMENT RESTRICTS THE FIRST AMENDMENT FREEDOMS

In some cases, the government restricts certain elements of First Amendment rights. Some examples include:

- **Freedom of religion**—when a religion espouses illegal activities, the government often restricts these forms of religious expression. Examples include polygamy, animal sacrifice, and use of illicit drugs or illegal substances.
- **Freedom of speech**—this can be restricted if exercise of free speech endangers other people.
- **Freedom of the press**—laws prevent the press from publishing falsehoods.

In **emergency situations** such as wartime, stricter restrictions are sometimes placed on these rights, especially rights to free speech and assembly, and freedom of the press, in order to protect national security.

Constitution's Address of the Rights of Those Accused of Crimes

The US Constitution makes allowances for the **rights of criminals**, or anyone who has transgressed established laws. There must be laws to protect citizens from criminals, but those accused of crimes must also be protected and their basic rights as individuals preserved. In addition, the Constitution protects individuals from the power of authorities to prevent police forces and other enforcement organizations from becoming oppressive. The fourth, fifth, sixth, and eighth amendments specifically address these rights.

Supreme Court's Provision of Equal Protection for All Individuals

When the Founding Fathers wrote in the Declaration of Independence that "all men are created equal," they actually were referring to men, and, in fact, defined citizens as white men who owned land. However, as the country has developed and changed, the definition has expanded to more wholly include all people.

"**Equality**" does not mean all people are inherently the same, but it does mean they all should be granted the same rights and should be treated the same by the government. Amendments to the Constitution have granted citizenship and voting rights to all Americans regardless of race or gender. The Supreme Court evaluates various laws and court decisions to determine if they properly represent the idea of **equal protection**. One sample case was Brown v. Board of Education in 1954, which declared separate-but-equal treatment to be unconstitutional.

Protests

A protest is an expression of opposition to, and sometimes of support of, events or circumstances. **Protests** represent a means for individuals to publicly make their views heard in an effort to influence public opinion or government policy, or as a means to enact **change**. Protests generally result when self-expression of opposing views is restricted by government policy, political or economic circumstances, religion, social structures, or the media, and people react by declaring their views through cultural mechanisms or on the streets. There are numerous forms of protest, including boycotts, civil disobedience, demonstrations, non-violent protests, picketing, protest marches, protest songs, riots, sit-ins, teach-ins, strikes, and others.

Civil Liberty Challenges Addressed in Current Political Discussions

The **civil rights movements** of the 1960s and the ongoing struggle for the rights of women and other minorities have sparked **challenges to existing law**. In addition, debate has raged over how much information the government should be required to divulge to the public. Major issues in the 21st century political climate include:

- Continued debate over women's rights, especially regarding equal pay for equal work
- Debate over affirmative action to encourage hiring of minorities
- Debate over civil rights of homosexuals, including marriage and military service
- Decisions as to whether minorities should be compensated for past discriminatory practices
- Balance between the public's right to know and the government's need to maintain national security
- Balance between the public's right to privacy and national security

Civil Liberties vs. Civil Rights

While the terms *civil liberties* and *civil rights* are often used interchangeably, in actuality, their definitions are slightly different. The two concepts work together, however, to define the basics of a free state:

- **"Civil liberties"** define the constitutional freedoms guaranteed to citizens. Examples include freedoms such as free speech, privacy, or free thought.
- **"Civil rights"** are guarantees of or protections of civil liberties. One comparison can be found in the case of freedom of religion. The civil liberty is that one has the freedom to practice the religion of his or her choice, whereas the civil right would protect that individual from being denied a job on the basis of their religion.

Suffrage, Franchise, and the Change of Voting Rights Over American History

Suffrage and franchise both refer to the right to **vote**. As the US developed as a nation, there was much debate over which individuals should hold this right. In the early years, only white male landowners were granted suffrage. By the 19th century, most states had franchised, or granted the right to vote, to all adult white males. The **Fifteenth Amendment** of 1870 granted suffrage to formerly enslaved men. The **Nineteenth Amendment** gave women the right to vote in 1920, and in 1971 the **Twenty-sixth Amendment** expanded voting rights to include any US citizen over the age of eighteen. However, those who have not been granted full citizenship and citizens who have committed certain crimes do not have voting rights.

Ways in Which the Voting Process Has Changed Over the Years

The first elections in the US were held by **public ballot**. However, election abuses soon became common, since public ballot made it easy to intimidate, threaten, or otherwise influence the votes of individuals or groups of individuals. New practices were put into play, including **registering voters** before elections took place and using a **secret or Australian ballot**. In 1892, the introduction of the **voting machine** further privatized the voting process, since it allowed complete privacy for voting. Today, debate continues about the accuracy of various voting methods, including high-tech voting machines and even low-tech punch cards.

Effect of Political Parties on the Functioning of an Individual Government

Different types and numbers of political parties can have a significant effect on how a government is run. If there is a **single party**, or a one-party system, the government is defined by that one party, and all policy is based on that party's beliefs. In a **two-party system**, two parties with different viewpoints compete for power and influence. The US is basically a two-party system, with checks and balances to make it difficult for one party to gain complete power over the other. There are also **multiparty systems**, with three or more parties. In multiparty systems, various parties will often come to agreements in order to form a majority and shift the balance of power.

Development of Political Parties in the US.

George Washington was adamantly against the establishment of **political parties**, based on the abuses perpetrated by such parties in Britain. However, political parties developed in US politics almost from the beginning. Major parties throughout US history have included:

- **Federalists and Democratic-Republicans**—these parties formed in the late 1700s and disagreed on the balance of power between national and state government.
- **Democrats and Whigs**—these developed in the 1830s, and many political topics of the time centered on national economic issues.
- **Democrats and Republicans**—the Republican Party developed before the Civil War, after the collapse of the Whig party, and the two parties debated issues centering on slavery and economic issues, such as taxation.

While third parties sometimes enter the picture in US politics, the government is basically a two-party system, dominated by the Democrats and Republicans.

Functions of Political Parties

Political parties form organizations at all levels of government. Activities of individual parties include:

- Recruiting and backing candidates for offices
- Discussing various issues with the public, increasing public awareness
- Working toward compromise on difficult issues
- Staffing government offices and providing administrative support

At the administrative level, parties work to ensure that viable candidates are available for elections and that offices and staff are in place to support candidates as they run for office and afterward, when they are elected.

Processes of Selecting Political Candidates

Historically, in the quest for political office, a potential candidate has followed one of the following four processes:

- **Nominating convention**—an official meeting of the members of a party for the express purpose of nominating candidates for upcoming elections. The Democratic National Convention and the Republican National Convention, convened to announce candidates for the presidency, are examples of this kind of gathering.
- **Caucus**—a meeting, usually attended by a party's leaders. Some states still use caucuses, but not all.
- **Primary election**—the most common method of choosing candidates today, the primary is a publicly held election to choose candidates.
- **Petition**—signatures gathered to place a candidate on the ballot. Petitions can also be used to place legislation on a ballot.

Ways the Average Citizen Participates in the Political Process

In addition to voting for elected officials, American citizens are able to participate in the political process through several other avenues. These include:

- Participating in local government
- Participating in caucuses for large elections

- Volunteering to help political parties
- Running for election to local, state, or national offices

Individuals can also donate money to political causes or support political groups that focus on specific causes such as abortion, wildlife conservation, or women's rights. These groups often make use of **representatives** who lobby legislators to act in support of their efforts.

Ways in Which Political Campaign Gains Funding

Political campaigns are very expensive. In addition to the basic necessities of a campaign office, including office supplies, office space, etc., a large quantity of the money that funds a political campaign goes toward **advertising**. Money to fund a political campaign can come from several sources, including:

- The candidate's personal funds
- Donations by individuals
- Special interest groups

The most significant source of campaign funding is **special interest groups**. Groups in favor of certain policies will donate money to candidates they believe will support those policies. Special interest groups also do their own advertising in support of candidates they endorse.

Presidential Elections

The President of the United States is elected **indirectly** by members of an **electoral college**. Members of the electoral college nearly always vote along the lines of the popular vote of their respective states. The winner of a presidential election is the candidate with at least 270 **Electoral College votes**. It is possible for a candidate to win the electoral vote and lose the popular vote. Incumbent Presidents and challengers typically prefer a balanced ticket, where the President and Vice President are elected together and generally balance one another with regard to geography, ideology, or experience working in government. The nominated Vice Presidential candidate is referred to as the President's **running mate**.

Importance of Free Press and the Media

The right to free speech guaranteed in the first amendment to the Constitution allows the media to report on **government and political activities** without fear of retribution. Because the media has access to information about the government, the government's policies and actions, and debates and discussions that occur in Congress, it can keep the public informed about the inner workings of the government. The media can also draw attention to injustices, imbalances of power, and other transgressions the government or government officials might commit. However, media outlets may, like special interest groups, align themselves with certain political viewpoints and skew their reports to fit that viewpoint. The rise of the **internet** has made media reporting even more complex, as news can be found from an infinite variety of sources, both reliable and unreliable.

Forms of Government

Anarchism, Communism, and Dictatorship

Anarchists believe that all government should be eliminated and that individuals should rule themselves. Historically, anarchists have used violence and assassination to further their beliefs.

Communism is based on class conflict, revolution, and a one-party state. Ideally, a communist government would involve a single government for the entire world. Communist government controls the production and flow of goods and services rather than leaving this to companies or individuals.

Dictatorship involves rule by a single individual. If rule is enforced by a small group, this is referred to as an oligarchy. Dictators tend to rule with a violent hand, using a highly repressive police force to ensure control over the populace.

Fascism and Monarchy

Fascism centers on a single leader and is, ideologically, an oppositional belief to communism. **Fascism** includes a single-party state and centralized control. The power of the fascist leader lies in the "cult of personality," and the fascist state often focuses on expansion and conquering of other nations. **Monarchy** was the major form of government for Europe through most of its history.

A monarchy is led by a king or a queen. This position is hereditary, and the rulers are not elected. In modern times, constitutional monarchy has developed, where the king and queen still exist, but most of the governmental decisions are made by democratic institutions such as a parliament.

Parliamentary and Democratic Systems

In a parliamentary system, government involves a legislature and a variety of political parties. The head of government, usually a prime minister, is typically the head of the dominant party. A head of state can be elected, or this position can be taken by a monarch, as in Great Britain's constitutional monarchy system.

In a **democratic system** of government, the people elect their government representatives. The word *democracy* is a Greek term that means "rule of the people." There are two forms of democracy: direct and indirect. In a direct democracy, each issue or election is decided by a vote where each individual is counted separately. An indirect democracy employs a legislature that votes on issues that affect large numbers of people whom the legislative members represent. Democracy can exist as a parliamentary system or a presidential system. The US is a presidential, indirect democracy.

Presidential System and Socialism

A presidential system, like a parliamentary system, has a legislature and political parties, but there is no difference between the head of state and the head of government. Instead of separating these functions, an elected president performs both. Election of the president can be direct or indirect, and the president may not necessarily belong to the largest political party. In **socialism**, the state controls the production of goods, though it does not necessarily own all means of production. The state also provides a variety of social services to citizens and helps guide the economy. A democratic form of government often exists in socialist countries.

Review Video: Communism vs. Socialism
Visit mometrix.com/academy and enter code: 917677

Totalitarian and Authoritarian Systems

A totalitarian system believes everything should be under the control of the government—from resource production, to the press, to religion, and other social institutions. All aspects of life under a totalitarian system must conform to the ideals of the government. **Authoritarian** governments practice widespread state authority but do not necessarily dismantle all public institutions. If a church, for example, exists as an organization but poses no threat to the authority of the state, an authoritarian government might leave it as it is. While all totalitarian governments are by definition authoritarian, a government can be authoritarian without becoming totalitarian.

Review Video: Totalitarianism vs. Authoritarianism
Visit mometrix.com/academy and enter code: 104046

Parliamentary and Democratic Systems

In a parliamentary system, government involves a legislature and a variety of political parties. The head of government, usually a prime minister, is typically the head of the dominant party. A head of state can be elected, or this position can be taken by a monarch, as in Great Britain's constitutional monarchy system.

In a **democratic system** of government, the people elect their government representatives. The word *democracy* is a Greek term that means "rule of the people." There are two forms of democracy: direct and indirect. In a direct democracy, each issue or election is decided by a vote where each individual is counted separately. An indirect democracy employs a legislature that votes on issues that affect large numbers of people whom the legislative members represent. Democracy can exist as a parliamentary system or a presidential system. The US is a presidential, indirect democracy.

Realism, Liberalism, Institutionalism, and Constructivism

The theory of realism states that nations are by nature aggressive and work in their own self-interest. Relations between nations are determined by military and economic strength. The nation is seen as the highest authority. **Liberalism** believes states can cooperate and that they act based on capability rather than power. This term was originally coined to describe Woodrow Wilson's theories on international cooperation. In **institutionalism**, institutions provide structure and incentive for cooperation among nations. Institutions are defined as a set of rules used to make international decisions. These institutions also help distribute power and determine how nations will interact. **Constructivism**, like liberalism, is based on international cooperation but recognizes that perceptions countries have of each other can affect their relations.

Effects of Foreign Policy on a Country's Position in World Affairs

Foreign policy is a set of goals, policies, and strategies that determine how an individual nation will interact with other countries. These strategies shift, sometimes quickly and drastically, according to actions or changes occurring in the other countries. However, a nation's **foreign policy** is often based on a certain set of ideals and national needs. Examples of US foreign policy include isolationism versus internationalism. In the 1800s, the US leaned more toward isolationism, exhibiting a reluctance to become involved in foreign affairs. The World Wars led to a period of internationalism, as the US entered these wars in support of other countries and joined the United Nations. Today's foreign policy tends more toward **interdependence**, or **globalism**, recognizing the widespread effects of issues like economic health.

Major Figures Involved in Determining and Enacting US Foreign Policy

US foreign policy is largely determined by Congress and the president, influenced by the secretary of state, secretary of defense, and the national security adviser. Executive officials carry out policies. The main departments in charge of these day-to-day issues are the **US Department of State**, also referred to as the State Department. The Department of State carries out policy, negotiates treaties, maintains diplomatic relations, assists citizens traveling in foreign countries, and ensures that the president is properly informed of any international issues. The **Department of Defense**, the largest executive department in the US, supervises the armed forces and provides assistance to the president in his role as commander-in-chief.

Major Types of International Organizations

Two types of international organizations are:

- **Intergovernmental organizations (IGOs)**. These organizations are made up of members from various national governments. The UN is an example of an intergovernmental organization. Treaties among the member nations determine the functions and powers of these groups.
- **Nongovernmental organizations (NGOs)**. An NGO lies outside the scope of any government and is usually supported through private donations. An example of an NGO is the International Red Cross, which works with governments all over the world when their countries are in crisis but is formally affiliated with no particular country or government.

Role of Diplomats in International Relations

Diplomats are individuals who reside in foreign countries in order to maintain communications between that country and their home country. They help negotiate trade agreements and environmental policies, as well as conveying official information to foreign governments. They also help to resolve conflicts between the countries, often working to sort out issues without making the conflicts official in any way. **Diplomats**, or **ambassadors**, are appointed in the US by the president. Appointments must be approved by Congress.

Role of the United Nations in International Relations and Diplomacy

The United Nations (**UN**) helps form international policies by hosting representatives of various countries who then provide input into policy decisions. Countries that are members of the UN must agree to abide by all final UN resolutions, but this is not always the case in practice, as dissent is not uncommon. If countries do not follow UN resolutions, the UN can decide on sanctions against those countries, often economic sanctions, such as trade restriction. The UN can also send military forces to problem areas, with "peacekeeping" troops brought in from member nations. An example of this function is the Korean War, the first war in which an international organization played a major role.

Chapter Quiz

Ready to see how well you retained what you just read? Scan the QR code to go directly to the chapter quiz interface for this study guide. If you're using a computer, simply visit the online resources page at **mometrix.com/resources719/praxsocst** and click the Chapter Quizzes link.

Economics

Transform passive reading into active learning! After immersing yourself in this chapter, put your comprehension to the test by taking a quiz. The insights you gained will stay with you longer this way. Scan the QR code to go directly to the chapter quiz interface for this study guide. If you're using a computer, simply visit the online resources page at **mometrix.com/resources719/praxsocst** and click the Chapter Quizzes link.

Economics is the study of the ways specific societies **allocate** resources to individuals and groups within that society. Also important are the choices society makes regarding what efforts or initiatives are funded and which are not. Since resources in any society are finite, allocation becomes a vivid reflection of that society's values. In general, the economic system that drives an individual society is based on:

- What goods are produced
- How those goods are produced
- Who acquires the goods or benefits from them

Economics consists of two main categories: **macroeconomics**, which studies larger systems, and **microeconomics**, which studies smaller systems.

Scarcity and Choice

Economics could rightfully be called the study of **scarcity**. Limited resources are available to satisfy the wants and needs of both individuals and states. Economics involves the **choices** made by an economy to satisfy these wants and needs. Every economy must choose what goods and services to produce, how to produce them, and for whom they are intended. Limitations of the factors of production—land, labor, and capital—sometimes make these choices difficult. When an economic choice is made, there is an "**opportunity cost**" implicit in the choice. The opportunity cost is what is given up by making a choice. If a country chooses to manufacture automobiles, it may not have the industrial capacity to produce tanks or aircraft. Thus, the economic choice to make automobiles involves the opportunity cost of not making tanks or aircraft. Individuals and countries continually make economic choices and sacrifice opportunist costs in the process. An individual may choose to attend a film rather than go out to dinner. Choices are driven by what people and countries feel is in their best interest.

Marginalism

Marginalism concerns itself with the economic worth of the last (or next) product or service provided. The cost of making the last product, the cost of hiring the last employee, and the cost of selling the last product, determine the **marginal cost** of that next good. Presumably, a company will continue to produce goods and services until it becomes unprofitable. Production will cease when the marginal return of a product does not yield a profit. From the consumer's viewpoint, the **marginal utility** of the purchase is the crucial factor. How much satisfaction does an individual get from each purchase? When this marginal utility decreases too much, the buyer will not buy the next unit. The idea of diminishing returns often determines how many units of a good or service a buyer will purchase. For example, after eating a piece of pie, the want-satisfying power of the next piece of pie is decreased. When this marginal utility reaches a certain point, the consumer will stop buying.

Costs

Costs and revenues are the two determinants of income, the most common measuring tools for assessing business success. Firms incur **fixed costs**, which are constant and do not depend on that amount of production. Examples would be physical plants and heavy equipment, which must be paid for even if production is zero. **Variable costs** are tied directly to the production of finished goods and services. As more goods are produced, variable costs rise. Examples of variable costs are raw materials used in the production process, extra labor needed in peak production periods, and additional capital if expansion is needed.

Exchange

Economic exchange is the basic activity of economics. The circular cycle of exchange from consumer to suppliers and back are the transactions that move an economy. The field of exchange is the marketplace, and money is the medium through which these transactions move. Building an **infrastructure** for market transactions is necessary to allow an orderly and dependable mechanism for economic exchange.

Traditional Economy

In a traditional economy, determinations of the types and amounts of goods produced, methods of production, and distribution of goods are based on long-established customs and habits. Such economies are sometimes referred to as subsistence economies because little surplus is produced, which negates the need for markets.

Market Economy

A market economy is based on supply and demand. **Demand** has to do with what customers want and need, as well as what quantity those consumers are able to purchase based on other economic factors. **Supply** refers to how much can be produced to meet demand, or how much suppliers are willing and able to sell. Where the needs of consumers meet the needs of suppliers is referred to as a market equilibrium price. This price varies depending on many factors, including the overall health of a society's economy and the overall beliefs and considerations of individuals in society. The following is a list of terms defined in the context of a market economy:

- **Elasticity**—this is based on how the quantity of a particular product responds to the price demanded for that product. If quantity responds quickly to changes in price, the supply/demand for that product is said to be elastic. If it does not respond quickly, then the supply/demand is inelastic.
- **Market efficiency**—this occurs when a market is capable of producing output high enough to meet consumer demand.
- **Comparative advantage**—in the field of international trade, this refers to a country focusing on a specific product that it can produce more efficiently and more cheaply, or at a lower opportunity cost, than another country, thus giving it a comparative advantage in production.

Review Video: Basics of Market Economy
Visit mometrix.com/academy and enter code: 791556

Planned Economy vs. Market Economy

In a **market economy**, supply and demand are determined by consumers. In a **planned economy**, a public entity or planning authority makes the decisions about what resources will be produced, how they will be produced, and who will be able to benefit from them. The means of production, such as factories, are also owned by a public entity rather than by private interests. In **market socialism**, the economic structure falls somewhere between the market economy and the planned economy. Planning authorities determine the allocation of resources at higher economic levels, while consumer goods are driven by a market economy.

Microeconomics

While economics generally studies how resources are allocated, **microeconomics** focuses on economic factors such as the way consumers behave, how income is distributed, and output and input markets. Studies are limited to the industry or firm level rather than an entire country or society. Among the elements studied in microeconomics are factors of production, costs of production, and factor income. These factors determine production decisions of individual firms, based on resources and costs.

Classification of Various Markets by Economists

The conditions prevailing in a given market are used to **classify** markets. Conditions considered include:

- Existence of competition
- Number and size of suppliers
- Influence of suppliers over price
- Variety of available products
- Ease of entering the market

Once these questions are answered, an economist can classify a certain market according to its structure and the nature of competition within the market.

Market Failure

When any of the elements for a successfully competitive market are missing, this can lead to a **market failure**. Certain elements are necessary to create what economists call "**perfect competition**." If one of these factors is weak or lacking, the market is classified as having "**imperfect competition**." Worse than imperfect competition, though, is a market failure. There are five major types of market failure:

- Inadequate competition
- Inadequate information
- Immobile resources
- Negative externalities, or side effects
- Failure to provide public goods

Externalities are side effects of a market that affect third parties. These effects can be either negative or positive.

Factors of Production and Costs of Production

Every good and service requires certain resources, or **inputs**. These inputs are referred to as **factors of production**. Every good and service requires four factors of production:

- Labor
- Capital
- Land
- Entrepreneurship

These factors can be fixed or variable and can produce fixed or variable costs. Examples of **fixed costs** include land and equipment. **Variable costs** include labor. The total of fixed and variable costs makes up the cost of production.

Factor Income

Factors of production each have an associated **factor income**. Factors that earn income include:

- **Labor**—earns wages
- **Capital**—earns interest
- **Land**—earns rent
- **Entrepreneurship**—earns profit

Each factor's income is determined by its **contribution**. In a market economy, this income is not guaranteed to be equal. How scarce the factor is and the weight of its contribution to the overall production process determines the final factor income.

Kinds of Market Structures in an Output Market.

The four kinds of market structures in an output market are:

- **Perfect competition**—all existing firms sell an identical product. The firms are not able to control the final price. In addition, there is nothing that makes it difficult to become involved in or leave the industry. Anything that would prevent entering or leaving an industry is called a barrier to entry. An example of this market structure is agriculture.
- **Monopoly**—a single seller controls the product and its price. Barriers to entry, such as prohibitively high fixed cost structures, prevent other sellers from entering the market.
- **Monopolistic competition**—a number of firms sell similar products, but they are not identical, such as different brands of clothes or food. Barriers to entry are low.
- **Oligopoly**—only a few firms control the production and distribution of products, such as automobiles. Barriers to entry are high, preventing large numbers of firms from entering the market.

Types of Monopolies

Four types of monopolies are:

- **Natural monopoly**—a single supplier has a distinct advantage over the others.
- **Geographic monopoly**—only one business offers the product in a certain area.
- **Technological monopoly**—a single company controls the technology necessary to supply the product.
- **Government monopoly**—a government agency is the only provider of a specific good or service.

Actions Taken by the US Government to Control Monopolies

The US government has passed several acts to regulate businesses, including:

- **Sherman Antitrust Act (1890)**—this prohibited trusts, monopolies, and any other situations that eliminated competition.
- **Clayton Antitrust Act (1914)**—this prohibited price discrimination.
- **Robinson-Patman Act (1936)**—this strengthened provisions of the Clayton Antitrust Act, requiring businesses to offer the same pricing on products to any customer.

The government has also taken other actions to ensure competition, including requirements for public disclosure. The **Securities and Exchange Commission (SEC)** requires companies that provide public stock to provide financial reports on a regular basis. Because of the nature of their business, banks are further regulated and required to provide various information to the government.

Marketing and Utility

Marketing consists of all of the activity necessary to convince consumers to acquire goods. One major way to move products into the hands of consumers is to convince them that any single product will satisfy a need. The ability of a product or service to satisfy the need of a consumer is called **utility**. There are four types of utility:

- **Form utility**—a product's desirability lies in its physical characteristics.
- **Place utility**—a product's desirability is connected to its location and convenience.
- **Time utility**—a product's desirability is determined by its availability at a certain time.
- **Ownership utility**—a product's desirability is increased because ownership of the product passes to the consumer.

Marketing behavior will stress any or all of these types of utility when marketing to the consumer.

Producers Determining What Customers Desire for Their Products

Successful marketing depends not only on convincing customers they need the product but also on focusing the marketing towards those who already have a need or desire for the product. Before releasing a product into the general marketplace, many producers will **test** markets to determine which will be the most receptive to the product. There are three steps usually taken to evaluate a product's market:

- **Market research**—this involves researching a market to determine if it will be receptive to the product.
- **Market surveys**—a part of market research, market surveys ask consumers specific questions to help determine the marketability of a product to a specific group.
- **Test marketing**—this includes releasing the product into a small geographical area to see how it sells. Often test marketing is followed by wider marketing if the product does well.

Major Elements of a Marketing Plan

The four major elements of a marketing plan are:

- **Product**—this includes any elements pertaining directly to the product, such as packaging, presentation, or services to include along with it.
- **Price**—this calculates the cost of production, distribution, advertising, etc., as well as the desired profit to determine the final price.
- **Place**—this determines which outlets will be used to sell the product, whether traditional outlets such as brick and mortar stores or through direct mail or internet marketing.
- **Promotion**—this involves ways to let consumers know the product is available, through advertising and other means.

Once these elements have all been determined, the producer can proceed with production and distribution of his product.

DISTRIBUTION CHANNELS

Distribution channels determine the route a product takes on its journey from producer to consumer, and can also influence the final price and availability of the product. There are two major forms of distributions: wholesale and retail. A **wholesale distributor** buys in large quantities and then resells smaller amounts to other businesses. **Retailers** sell directly to the consumers rather than to businesses. In the modern marketplace, additional distribution channels have grown up with the rise of markets such as club warehouse stores as well as purchasing through catalogs or over the internet. Most of these newer distribution channels bring products more directly to the consumer, eliminating the need for middlemen.

DISTRIBUTION OF INCOME IN A SOCIETY

Distribution of income in any society ranges from poorest to richest. In most societies, income is not distributed evenly. To determine **income distribution**, family incomes are ranked from lowest to highest. These rankings are divided into five sections called **quintiles**, which are compared to each other. The uneven distribution of income is often linked to higher levels of education and ability in the upper classes but can also be due to other factors such as discrimination and existing monopolies. The **income gap** in America continues to grow, largely due to growth in the service industry, changes in the American family unit, and reduced influence of labor unions. **Poverty** is defined by comparing incomes to poverty guidelines. Poverty guidelines determine the level of income necessary for a family to function. Those below the poverty line are often eligible for assistance from government agencies.

MACROECONOMICS

Macroeconomics examines economies on a much larger level than microeconomics. While **microeconomics** studies economics on a firm or industry level, **macroeconomics** looks at economic trends and structures on a national level. Variables studied in macroeconomics include:

- Output
- Consumption
- Investment
- Government spending
- Net exports

The overall economic condition of a nation is defined as the **Gross Domestic Product**, or GDP. GDP measures a nation's economic output over a limited time period, such as a year.

Review Video: Microeconomics and Macroeconomics
Visit mometrix.com/academy and enter code: 538837

Review Video: Gross Domestic Product
Visit mometrix.com/academy and enter code: 409020

TAXES

Any assessment or charge to an individual economic unit by a government or quasi-government may be termed a **tax**. Some taxes are **direct**, such as a sales tax on goods and services sold. Other taxes may be **indirect**, property taxes being a prime example. Earlier economic systems received "taxes" as goods and services rendered to a ruling authority. In contemporary economics, we usually think of taxes in terms of legal currency. Taxes have caused revolutions ("No taxation without representation"), have overturned governments, and have become a social and political issue of controversy and debate. Who should pay taxes, how much should be paid, and the use of tax revenue are all critical issues in the fabric of society. The branch of formal economics most concerned with taxes is public finance.

Types of Consumer Behavior

The two major types of consumer behavior as defined in macroeconomics are:

- **Marginal propensity to consume (MPC)** defines the tendency of consumers to increase spending in conjunction with increases in income. In general, individuals with greater income will buy more. As individuals increase their income through job changes or growth of experience, they will also increase spending.
- **Utility** is a term that describes the satisfaction experienced by a consumer in relation to acquiring and using a good or service. Providers of goods and services will stress utility to convince consumers they want the products being presented.

Ways to Measure the Gross Domestic Product of a Country

Gross domestic product (GDP) is the total value of all the goods and services produced within a country during a certain time period. It is often used as a measurement of a country's economic health.

The two major ways to measure the Gross Domestic Product of a country are:

- The **expenditures approach** calculates the GDP based on how much money is spent in each individual sector.
- The **income approach** calculates the GDP based on how much money is earned in each sector.

Both methods yield the same results, and both of these calculation methods are based on four **economic sectors** that make up a country's macro-economy:

- Consumers
- Business
- Government
- Foreign sector

Types of Earnings Generated by an Economy Considered to Calculate GDP

Several factors must be considered in order to accurately calculate the GDP using the incomes approach. **Income factors** are:

- Wages paid to laborers, or compensation of employees (CE)
- Rental income derived from land
- Interest income derived from invested capital
- Entrepreneurial income

Entrepreneurial income consists of two forms. **Proprietor's income** is income that comes back to the entrepreneur himself. **Corporate profit** is income that goes back into the corporation as a whole. Corporate profit is divided by the corporation into corporate profits taxes, dividends, and retained earnings. Two other figures must be subtracted in the incomes approach. These are **indirect business taxes**, including property and sales taxes, and **depreciation**.

Effects of Population of a Country on the Gross Domestic Product

Changes in population can affect the calculation of a nation's **GDP**, particularly since GDP and GNP (Gross National Product) are generally measured per capita. If a country's economic production is low but the population is high, the income per individual will be lower than if the income is high and the population is lower. Also, if the population grows quickly and the income grows slowly, individual income will remain low or even drop drastically.

Population growth can also affect overall **economic growth**. Economic growth requires both that consumers purchase goods and workers produce them. A population that does not grow quickly enough will not supply enough workers to support rapid economic growth.

Problems with Equating GDP Per Capita and Economic Well-Being

Several economic factors may interfere with equating GDP per capita with individual well-being. A significant allocation of assets is used to combat the negative effects of economic growth such as the destruction of natural habitats and air and water pollution. Economic growth increases such **intangibles** as the increase in commuting, which affects quality of life. Perhaps most importantly, GDP does not account for a significant amount of **domestic production,** such as child-raising and homemaking. The money equivalents for these tasks are omitted from the GDP calculation. There are numerous markets that are left out of GDP, including black markets, criminal activity, and alternative economies. There is also no provision in GDP for volunteer activity, "do it yourself" tasks such as home improvements and landscape management. All of these economic activities are omitted from the formal measurement of per capita GDP and fail to give an accurate picture of individual well-being.

Ideal Balance to be Obtained in an Economy

Ideally, an economy functions efficiently, with the **aggregate supply**, or the amount of national output, equal to the **aggregate demand**, or the amount of the output that is purchased. In these cases, the economy is stable and prosperous. However, economies more typically go through **phases**. These phases are:

- **Boom**—GDP is high and the economy prospers
- **Recession**—GDP falls and unemployment rises
- **Trough**—the recession reaches its lowest point
- **Recovery**—unemployment lessens, prices rise, and the economy begins to stabilize again

These phases tend to repeat in cycles that are not necessarily predictable or regular.

Measures of National Income and Output

National income may be defined as the aggregate figure of all consumption, individual, business, and governmental income, plus total investments and the balance of trade accounts for a country. This aggregate number, derived from adding these categories together, is called the **expenditure method** of national income determination. Another calculation to determine the national income is to account for all the goods and services produced in a country during a fixed period. This is called the **production accounting** of national income. Yet another way of computing national income is to total all income received by individuals, businesses, and governments to arrive at total national income. This is the **income approach** to national income accounting. To summarize, there are three ways of calculating national income: total expenditures, total value of production, and the aggregate consumption figures for a country.

Consumer Price Indices

A price index, such as the **Consumer Price Index**, can be used as a measuring tool to compare prices at different times. A fictional "market basket" of commonly consumed staples is measured and charted over a period of time (usually one year). If the price of the representative market basket has gone up, **inflation** has occurred. For example, if a typical basket costs $500 this year as compared to $400 last year for the same basket, inflation has risen over a year. Inflation reduces the buying power of money, and if uncontrolled, can threaten the entire economy.

Unemployment and Inflation

When demand outstrips supply, prices are driven artificially high, or are **inflated**. This occurs when too much spending causes an imbalance in the economy. In general, inflation occurs because an economy is growing too quickly. When there is too little spending, and supply has moved far beyond demand, a **surplus** of product results. Companies cut back on production and reduce the number of employees, and **unemployment** rises as people lose their jobs. This imbalance occurs when an economy becomes sluggish. In general, both these economic instability situations are caused by an imbalance between supply and demand. Government intervention may be necessary to stabilize an economy when either inflation or unemployment becomes too serious.

Different Forms of Unemployment

- **Frictional**—when workers change jobs and are unemployed while waiting for new jobs
- **Structural**—when economic shifts reduce the need for workers
- **Cyclical**—when natural business cycles bring about loss of jobs
- **Seasonal**—when seasonal cycles reduce the need for certain jobs
- **Technological**—when advances in technology result in the elimination of certain jobs

Any of these factors can increase unemployment in certain sectors.

Inflation is classified by the overall rate at which it occurs:

- **Creeping inflation**—this is an inflation rate of about 1%-3% annually.
- **Walking inflation**—this is an inflation rate of 3%-10% annually.
- **Galloping inflation**— a severe inflation rate above 10 percent (to upwards of 100 percent and beyond) annually. Highly detrimental to the economy, this deeply impacts the lower and middle class populus.
- **Hyperinflation**— an inflation rate over 50% monthly or 500+ percent annually. Hyperinflation usually leads to complete monetary collapse in a society. Individuals are unable to have enough income to purchase their needed goods.

Government Intervention Policies That Mitigate Inflation and Unemployment

When an economy becomes too imbalanced, either due to excessive spending or not enough spending, **government intervention** often becomes necessary to put the economy back on track. Government fiscal policy can take several forms, including:

- Contractionary policy
- Expansionary policy
- Monetary policy

Contractionary policies help counteract inflation. These include increasing taxes and decreasing government spending to slow spending in the overall economy. **Expansionary policies** increase government spending and lower taxes in order to reduce unemployment and increase the level of spending in the economy overall. **Monetary policy** can take several forms and affects the amount of funds available to banks for making loans.

Study and Quantification of Populations and Population Growth

Populations are studied by **size**, rates of **growth** due to immigration, the overall **fertility rate**, and **life expectancy**. For example, though the population of the United States is considerably larger than it was two hundred years ago, the rate of population growth has decreased greatly, from about three percent per year to less than one percent per year.

In the US, the fertility rate is fairly low, with most choosing not to have large families, and life expectancy is high, creating a projected imbalance between older and younger people in the near future. In addition, immigration and the mixing of racially diverse cultures are projected to increase the percentages of Asians, Hispanics, and African Americans.

Functions and Types of Money

Money is used in three major ways:

- As an accounting unit
- As a store of value
- As an exchange medium

In general, money must be acceptable throughout a society in exchange for debts or to purchase goods and services. Money should be relatively scarce, its value should remain stable, and it should be easily carried, durable, and easy to divide up. There are three basic types of money: commodity, representative, and fiat. **Commodity money** includes gems or precious metals. **Representative money** can be exchanged for items such as gold or silver that have inherent value. **Fiat money**, or legal tender, has no inherent value but has been declared to function as money by the government. It is often backed by gold or silver but not necessarily on a one-to-one ratio.

Investment and Credit

Investment is committing financial resources to a particular account or asset in order to earn a return at a later time. Each type of **investment** carries a different level of risk and a different potential return, though it can be difficult to determine exactly how profitable a particular endeavor will be in the long run. **Credit** is the process by which a financial institution lends funds to an individual for the purchase of a particular product or service. This means that the financial institution will cover the cost of the product or service in exchange for the individual agreeing to pay back that money, and any interest associated with the loan or credit, at a later time.

Types of Money Available in the US and Economists' Measure of It

Money in the US is not just currency. When economists calculate the amount of money available, they must take into account other factors, such as deposits that have been placed in checking accounts, debit cards, and "near moneys," such as savings accounts, that can be quickly converted into cash. Currency, checkable deposits and traveler's checks, referred to as **M1**, are added up, and then **M2** is calculated by adding savings deposits, CDs, and various other monetary deposits. The final result is the total quantity of available money.

Aspects of Monetary Policy and the Role of the Federal Reserve System

The Federal Reserve System, also known as the **Fed**, implements all monetary policy in the US. Monetary policy regulates the amount of money available in the American banking system. The Fed can decrease or increase the amount of available money for loans, thus helping regulate the national economy. Monetary policies implemented by the Fed are part of expansionary or contractionary monetary policies that help counteract inflation or unemployment. The **discount rate** is an interest rate charged by the Fed when banks borrow money from them. A lower discount rate leads banks to borrow more money, leading to increased spending. A higher discount rate has the opposite effect.

How Banks Function

Banks earn their income by **loaning** out money and charging **interest** on those loans. If less money is available, fewer loans can be made, which affects the amount of spending in the overall economy. While banks function by making loans, they are not allowed to loan out all the money they hold in deposit. The amount of money they must maintain in reserve is known as the **reserve ratio**. If the reserve ratio is raised, less money is available for loans and spending decreases. A lower reserve ratio increases available funds and increases spending. This ratio is determined by the Federal Reserve System.

Central Banks

Central banks of countries are the institutions that control currency (and the money supply) through monetary and fiscal policy. These central banks or other monetary authorities (set up as an agency by the government) control and implement monetary policy and activity. Such authorities differ in their power from country to country. For example, in the United States, the Federal Reserve is a wholly independent agency free of political controls. Although Congress legislated the Federal Reserve into existence, it remains completely independent in its activity.

Open Market Operations

The Federal Reserve System can also expand or contract the overall money supply through **open market operations**. In this case, the Fed can buy or sell **bonds** it has purchased from banks or individuals. When the Fed buys bonds, more money is put into circulation, creating an expansionary situation to stimulate the economy. When the Fed sells bonds, money is withdrawn from the system, creating a **contractionary** situation to slow an economy suffering from inflation. Because of international financial markets, however, American banks often borrow and lend money in markets outside the US. By shifting their attention to international markets, domestic banks and other businesses can circumvent whatever contractionary policies the Fed may have put into place.

Major Characteristics of International Trade

International trade can take advantage of broader markets, bringing a wider variety of products within easy reach. By contrast, it can also allow individual countries to specialize in particular products that they can produce easily, such as those for which they have easy access to raw materials. Other products, more difficult to make domestically, can be acquired through trade with other nations. **International trade** requires efficient use of **native resources** as well as sufficient **disposable income** to purchase native and imported products. Many countries in the world engage extensively in international trade, but others still face major economic challenges.

Major Characteristics of a Developing Nation

The five major characteristics of a developing nation are:

- Low GDP
- Rapid growth of population
- Economy that depends on subsistence agriculture

- Poor conditions, including high infant mortality rates, high disease rates, poor sanitation, and insufficient housing
- Low literacy rate

Developing nations often function under oppressive governments that do not provide private property rights and withhold education and other rights from women. They also often feature an extreme disparity between upper and lower classes, with little opportunity for the lower classes to improve their position.

Stages of Economic Development

Economic development occurs in three stages that are defined by the activities that drive the economy:

- Agricultural stage
- Manufacturing stage
- Service sector stage

In developing countries, it is often difficult to acquire the necessary funding to provide equipment and training to move into the advanced stages of economic development. Some can receive help from developed countries via foreign aid and investment or international organizations such as the **International Monetary Fund** or the **World Bank**. Having developed countries provide monetary, technical, or military assistance can help developing countries move forward to the next stage in their development.

Controls

An imposition of wage and price controls is a more drastic way to slow or halt inflation. These measures have many drawbacks, including the possibility of depressing the economy too far. Controls also promote hoarding and artificial shortages and sometimes encourage the creation of alternative marketplaces that impair economic growth.

Labor Demand

The totality of all firms' demand for labor is called the **total market demand for labor**. The market supply of labor depends on the population, level of skill required, prevalent economic condition, and effective wage rate. When the demand and supply curves for labor intersect, the **competitive equilibrium wage rate** is determined. Firms will continue to hire labor until the marginal revenue product of labor, or its demand for labor, reaches the wage rate. **Labor unions** can distort the supply and demand for labor, and thus the wage determination, by increasing productivity, reducing the labor force with excessive union dues, and bargaining with businesses and threatening strikes.

Obstacles Developing Nations Face Regarding Economic Growth

Developing nations typically struggle to overcome obstacles that prevent or slow economic development. Major **obstacles** can include:

- Rapid, uncontrolled population growth
- Trade restrictions
- Misused resources, often perpetrated by the government
- Traditional beliefs that can slow or reject change

Corrupt, oppressive governments often hamper the economic growth of developing nations, creating huge **economic disparities** and making it impossible for individuals to advance, in turn preventing overall growth. Governments sometimes export currency, called **capital flight**, which is detrimental to a country's economic development. In general, countries are more likely to experience economic growth if their governments encourage entrepreneurship and provide private property rights.

Problems When Industrialization Occurs Too Quickly

Rapid growth throughout the world leaves some nations behind and sometimes spurs their governments to move forward too quickly into **industrialization** and **artificially rapid economic growth**. While slow or nonexistent economic growth causes problems in a country, overly rapid industrialization carries its own issues. Four major problems encountered due to rapid industrialization are:

- Use of technology not suited to the products or services being supplied
- Poor investment of capital
- Lack of time for the population to adapt to new paradigms
- Lack of time to experience all stages of development and adjust to each stage

Economic failures in Indonesia were largely due to rapid growth that was poorly handled.

Importance of E-Commerce in Today's Marketplace

The growth of the internet has brought many changes to our society, not the least of which is the modern way of business. Where supply channels used to move in certain necessary ways, many of these channels are now bypassed as **e-commerce** makes it possible for nearly any individual to set up a direct market to consumers, as well as direct interaction with suppliers. Competition is fierce. In many instances, e-commerce can provide nearly instantaneous gratification, with a wide variety of products. Whoever provides the best product most quickly often rises to the top of a marketplace. How this added element to the marketplace will affect the economy in the future remains to be seen. Many industries are still struggling with the best ways to adapt to the rapid, continuous changes.

Knowledge Economy and Possible Effect on Future Economic Growth

The knowledge economy is a growing sector in the economy of developed countries, and includes the trade and development of:

- Data
- Intellectual property
- Technology, especially in the area of communications

Knowledge as a resource is steadily becoming more and more important. What is now being called the **Information Age** may prove to bring about changes in life and culture as significant as those brought on by the Agricultural and Industrial Revolutions.

Cybernomics

Related to the knowledge economy is what has been dubbed "**cybernomics**," or economics driven by e-commerce and other computer-based markets and products. Marketing has changed drastically with the growth of cyber communication, allowing suppliers to connect one-on-one with their customers. Other issues coming to the fore regarding cybernomics include:

- Secure online trade
- Intellectual property rights
- Rights to privacy
- Bringing developing nations into the fold

As these issues are debated and new laws and policies developed, the face of many industries continues to undergo drastic change. Many of the old ways of doing business no longer work, leaving industries scrambling to function profitably within the new system.

Chapter Quiz

Ready to see how well you retained what you just read? Scan the QR code to go directly to the chapter quiz interface for this study guide. If you're using a computer, simply visit the online resources page at **mometrix.com/resources719/praxsocst** and click the Chapter Quizzes link.

99/140

Praxis Practice Test

Want to take this practice test in an online interactive format? Check out the online resources page, which includes interactive practice questions and much more: **mometrix.com/resources719/praxsocst**

1. Which of the following empires still existed following the armistice ending World War I?

a. The Austro-Hungarian Empire
b. The Ottoman Empire
c. The German Empire
d. The British Empire

2. Which of the following is associated with market failure?

I. When a firm in a non-competitive industry hires labor at a lower wage
II. When the firms in a non-competitive industry create less than the efficient amount of a good or service
III. When production of a good creates negative externalities born by third parties
IV. Public goods

a. I and II only
b. I and III only
c. I, II, and III only
d. I, II, III, and IV

3. Which of the following statements is NOT true about slavery in America?

a. The Spanish brought African slaves to Florida by the 1560s.
b. Chattel (ownership) slavery was legal in America from 1654 to 1865.
c. Indentured servants preceded slavery in America as sources of labor.
d. Southern colonies imported more slaves in the 1600s to farm cotton.

4. Congressional elections are held every ____________ years.

a. four
b. two
c. six
d. three

5. Which statement regarding US international trade policy in the 1990s is NOT correct?

a. In 1994, the General Agreement on Tariffs and Trade (GATT) was approved by Congress.
b. The 57 countries that signed the GATT agreed to remove or reduce many of their tariffs.
c. The GATT created the World Trade Organization (WTO) to settle international trade differences.
d. The NAFTA (North American Free Trade Agreement), ratified in 1994, had originally been set up by George H.W. Bush's administration.

6. Before the Civil War, to which of the following did Southern states object?

a. An increase in Southern tobacco production
b. An increase in tariffs on Northern manufactured goods
c. An increase in western mining for gold
d. An increase in the voting rights of slaves

7. The Andes Mountain Range is located on which continent?

a. North America
b. South America
c. Australia
d. Asia

8. The Erie Canal is 363 miles long and connects which body of water to Lake Erie?

a. The Mississippi River
b. The Hudson River
c. The Susquehanna River
d. The Lehigh River

9. What portion of the federal budget is dedicated to transportation, education, national resources, the environment, and international affairs?

a. Mandatory spending
b. Discretionary spending
c. Undistributed offsetting receipts
d. Official budget outlays

10. Which of the following laws was instrumental in spurring westward migration to the Great Plains between 1860 and 1880?

a. The Homestead Act
b. The Timber Culture Act
c. The Desert Land Act
d. All of these laws were instrumental in spurring westward migration to the Great Plains during that period.

Refer to the following for question 11:

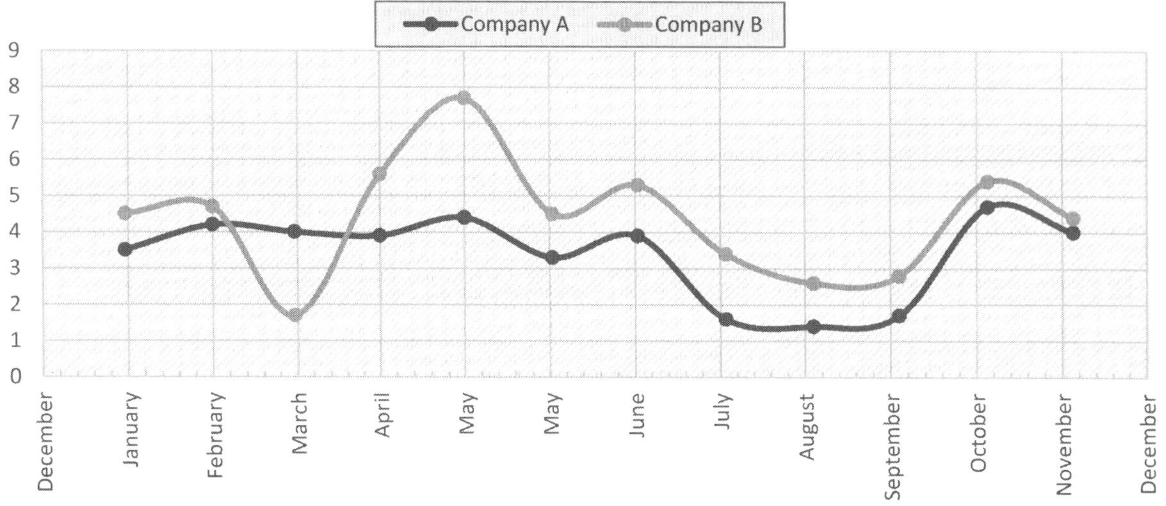

11. Based on the graph, which of the following is TRUE?

a. Company B performed better than Company A in each month.
b. March was a high-performance time for both companies.
c. Sales performance dropped faster for Company A than for Company B from June to July.
d. Company B performed better than Company A during January to May and from July to November.

12. The price of oil drops dramatically, saving soda pop manufacturers great amounts of money spent on making soda pop and delivering their product to market. Prices for soda pop, however, stay the same. This is an example of what?

a. Sticky prices
b. Indiscriminate costs
c. Stable demand
d. Aggregate expenditure

13. In the Constitution of the United States, which of the following powers is reserved for the states?

a. Taxation
b. Declaring war
c. Regulation of intrastate trade
d. Granting patents and copyrights

14. A filibuster is used to delay a bill. Where can a filibuster take place?

a. The House of Representatives
b. The Senate
c. Committees
d. The Supreme Court

15. Which Supreme Court case enforced the civil rights of citizens to not incriminate themselves?

a. Marbury v. Madison
b. Miranda v. Arizona
c. Youngstown Sheet and Tube Company v. Sawyer
d. United States v. Carolene Products Company

16. Which statement about factors related to the growth of the US economy between 1945 and 1970 is NOT correct?

a. The Baby Boom's greatly increased birth rates contributed to economic growth during this time.
b. The reduction in military spending after World War II contributed to the stronger US economy.
c. Government programs and growing affluence nearly quadrupled college enrollments in 20 years.
d. Increased mobility and bigger families caused fast suburban expansion, especially in the Sunbelt.

17. Which group(s) of people were originally responsible for selecting the members of the US Senate?

a. State legislatures
b. State governors
c. State electors
d. State residents, subject to voting eligibility

18. In 1983, Dianne Feinstein was mayor of San Francisco. She called for a women-mayors' caucus to be part of the US Conference of Mayors. The organization exists to encourage women to run for mayor and to be more involved in the larger organization. This goal is an example of:

a. cronyism
b. networking
c. lobbying
d. patronage

19. Which of the following statements does NOT describe Rome's relationship with its conquered peoples?

a. All subjects were granted the full range of rights entitled to Roman citizens.
b. The Romans allowed some degree of cultural autonomy.
c. Subjects were expected to follow Roman laws.
d. Subjects were obligated to pay taxes.

20. The concept of checks and balances is evident in which of the following?

a. Federal judiciary appeals
b. Presidential veto
c. States' rights
d. The House and the Senate

21. During which stage of spatial diffusion does the process slow to a stop?

a. Primary
b. Diffusion
c. Condensing
d. Saturation

22. Which of these is NOT true relative to the rise of Fascism in Europe?

a. Fascism was opposed to nationalism and to patriotism.
b. Fascism was opposed to Marxism and the bourgeoisie.
c. Fascism purported to be an alternative to Bolshevism.
d. Fascism had some things in common with Bolshevism.

23. Which of the following statements does NOT describe the average European diet before the expansion of trade routes?

a. Europeans ate for survival, not enjoyment.
b. They had an abundance of preservatives such as salt that could make food last longer.
c. Grain-based foods such as porridge and bread were staple meals.
d. Spices were unavailable.

24. In the long run, firms will exit a monopolistically competitive market when:

a. Profit is maximized
b. Price = marginal cost
c. Price exceeds marginal cost
d. Price is less than the minimum of the average total costs curve

25. Which of the following statements regarding events in the Middle East that took place during the Reagan administration is NOT correct?

a. Israel invaded Lebanon to get rid of the Palestine Liberation Organization's camps there.
b. When a terrorist bombing killed 240 US Marines, Reagan escalated military action.
c. Lebanon was already in the midst of a civil war when Israeli troops invaded the country.
d. President Reagan deployed US Marines to Lebanon in 1982 on a peacekeeping mission.

26. Which of the following is true regarding the Tropic of Capricorn?

a. It separates the northern and southern hemispheres.
b. It separates the eastern and western hemispheres.
c. It is the southernmost latitude at which the sun can appear directly overhead at noon.
d. It is the northernmost latitude at which the sun can appear directly overhead at noon.

27. Which of the following is *not* one of the Baltic states?

a. Moldova
b. Latvia
c. Lithuania
d. Estonia

28. Which statement is NOT true regarding ancient Greek democracy?

a. Democracy began to develop approximately 500 BC.
b. One of the first, best-known democracies was in Athens.
c. It was a direct democracy, not using any representatives.
d. It was a democracy completely open to all of the public.

29. Which of the following was the reason the economy of colonial New England focused mainly on manufacture and trade?

a. The soil and climate conditions in New England were not conducive to year-round farming.
b. The New England colonists were primarily merchants from England and Scotland.
c. Slavery did not exist in the northern colonies.
d. The New England colonists wanted to achieve economic dominance over the Middle Atlantic colonies.

30. The two new states admitted under the Missouri Compromise of 1820 were Missouri and what other state?

a. Ohio
b. Alabama
c. Kansas
d. Maine

31. Which list is in the correct chronological order?

a. Great Papal Schism, Norman Conquest, French Revolution
b. Great Papal Schism, French Revolution, Norman Conquest
c. Norman Conquest, Great Papal Schism, French Revolution
d. French Revolution, Norman Conquest, Great Papal Schism

32. Guaranteed rights enumerated in the Declaration of Independence, possessed by all people, are referred to as:

a. Universal rights
b. Unalienable rights
c. Voting rights
d. Peoples' rights

33. After the Civil War, President Andrew Johnson disagreed with Congress over Reconstruction policies. Which action by President Johnson best describes the grounds for which he was impeached?

a. He dismissed a Cabinet member without congressional permission.
b. He refused to enforce the Fourteenth Amendment.
c. He sought to disenfranchise former Confederate officers.
d. He violated Constitution law in forming a third political party.

34. Which of the following is NOT a method of representing relief on a physical map?

a. Symbols
b. Color
c. Shading
d. Contour Lines

35. Which of the following is considered to be the largest cause of death among Native Americans following the arrival of European colonists in North America?

a. Wounds from wars with the European settlers
b. Wounds from wars with the other Native American tribes
c. European diseases
d. Exposure during the wintry, forced marches on which the European settlers forced them

36. As a form of government, what does *oligarchy* mean?

a. Rule by one
b. Rule by a few
c. Rule by law
d. Rule by many

37. In the 16th century, Akbar ruled the Mughal Empire, which covered much of present-day India. Which statement best describes one means by which Akbar maintained control of the Empire?

a. He paid administrative officials with land instead of money.
b. He accommodated the religious practices of Hindus as well as Muslims.
c. He refused to allow certain defeated rulers to keep their land.
d. He refused to allow the construction of Hindu temples.

38. In order to be accepted, amended, or rejected completely, a newly introduced bill is first given to what type of committee?

a. Full committee
b. Conference committee
c. Subcommittee
d. Senate committee

39. For thousands of years, Africans have cultivated the grasslands south of the Sahara Desert, an area known as the

a. Qattara Depression.
b. Great Rift Valley.
c. Congo Basin.
d. Sahel.

40. The civil rights act that outlawed segregation in schools and public places also did which of the following?

a. Gave minorities the right to vote
b. Established women's right to vote
c. Outlawed unequal voter registration
d. Provided protection for children

41. The telephone was a solution to which of the following problems with the telegraph?

a. Telegraph lines were thick and difficult to maintain.
b. Telegraph messages could only be received by people who had specialized equipment.
c. Telegraphs could only relay one message at a time.
d. Telegraphs frequently broke down if subject to extended use.

42. Civic responsibility differs from personal responsibility in that the subject matter of civic responsibility is mainly which of the following?

a. Fair reporting of government actions
b. Fair dealings between governments
c. A person's responsibilities as a citizen
d. A person's responsibilities as a government worker

43. Who established the precedent for the two-term limit for the US presidency?

a. Abraham Lincoln
b. Alexander Hamilton
c. George Washington
d. Thomas Jefferson

44. Which of the following statements is NOT an accurate statement about the Puritans in England?

a. The Puritans unconditionally gave all their support to the English Reformation.
b. The Puritans saw the Church of England as too much like the Catholic Church.
c. The Puritans became a chief political power because of the English Civil War.
d. The Puritans' clergy mainly departed from the Church of England after 1662.

45. Which of the following is NOT true about the Crusades?

a. Their purpose was for European rulers to retake the Middle East from Muslims.
b. The Crusades succeeded at European kings' goal of reclaiming the "holy land."
c. The Crusades accelerated the already incipient decline of the Byzantine Empire.
d. Egypt saw a return as a major Middle Eastern power as a result of the Crusades.

46. Which of the following represents a discretionary expense?

a. Textbook
b. Rent
c. DVD
d. Groceries

47. Which of the following is NOT true about democracy and the formation of the United States?

a. The founding fathers stated in the Constitution that the United States would be a democracy.
b. The Declaration of Independence did not dictate democracy but stated its principles.
c. The United States Constitution stipulated that government be elected by the people.
d. The United States Constitution had terms to protect some, but not all, of the people.

48. The Populist Party most contributed to the prominence of which issue in the United States in the late 19th and early 20th centuries?

a. The rising cost of farm crops
b. The justification for the Electoral College
c. The basis for US currency
d. The rights of organized labor

49. Most federal judges have served as local judges, lawyers, and law professors. These are ________ qualifications.

a. Formal
b. Required
c. Informal
d. Recommended

50. With the end of Reconstruction in 1877, which of the following was true regarding African Americans in the South?

a. They soon took control of state legislatures
b. They formed a new political party to protect their own interests
c. They were able to rise quickly into the economic middle class
d. They were kept from voting by poll taxes and literacy tests

51. Which of the following is NOT correct regarding assumptions of mercantilism?

a. The money and the wealth of a nation are identical properties.
b. In order to prosper, a nation should try to increase its imports.
c. In order to prosper, a nation should try to increase its exports.
d. Economic protectionism by national governments is advisable.

52. To whom was the Declaration of Independence addressed and why?

a. To the British Parliament because the colonists were opposed to being ruled by a king who had only inherited his throne and only considered the popularly elected Parliament to hold any authority over them
b. To the King of England because the colonists were upset that Parliament was passing laws for them even though they did not have the right to elect members of Parliament to represent their interests
c. To the governors of the rebelling colonies so that they would know that they had 30 days to either announce their support of the Revolution or to return to England
d. To the colonial people as a whole because the Declaration of Independence was intended to outline the wrongs that had been inflicted on them by the British military and inspire them to rise up in protest

53. In economic terms, which of the following is considered investment?

a. Buying a new home computer
b. Construction of a new manufacturing plant
c. Purchase of a college education
d. Selling finished goods to a customer

54. Most of the region known in ancient times as Mesopotamia is located in which present-day nation?

a. Iran
b. Saudi Arabia
c. Turkmenistan
d. Iraq

55. Which of the following is true of social changes and the Industrial Revolution in Europe in the 18th and early 19th centuries?

a. They gave rise to a new middle-class
b. They improved working conditions
c. They were the result of urbanization
d. They were caused by the labor unions

56. Which of the following best defines American GDP?

a. The value, in American dollars, of all goods and services produced within American borders during one calendar year
b. The value, in American dollars, of all goods and services produced by American companies during one calendar year
c. The total value, in American dollars, of all American household incomes during one calendar year
d. The value, in American dollars, of a "market basket" of goods and services in one year divided by the value of the same market basket in a previous year multiplied by 100

57. Some American colonists reacted angrily to Great Britain's Navigation Acts in the seventeenth and eighteenth centuries primarily because of which of the following?

a. The Acts restricted manufacturing in the colonies.
b. The Acts forced the colonists to buy sugar from the French West Indies.
c. The Acts gave the British a monopoly on tobacco.
d. The Acts placed high taxes on the cost of shipping goods to Britain.

58. Unlike slaves, who were considered to be the property of their masters, which of the following was true regarding most indentured servants in colonial times?

a. They received wages for their labor
b. They were generally treated kindly by their employers
c. They were highly educated
d. They voluntarily entered into servitude

59. On which type of map would Nigeria be bigger than Australia?

a. Contour map of elevation
b. Flow-line map of the spice trade
c. Mercator projection
d. Cartogram of population

60. Which of the following are the leading producers of petroleum in Latin America?

a. Argentina and Bolivia
b. Mexico and Guatemala
c. Brazil and Venezuela
d. Colombia and Uruguay

61. Which of the following is the best example of a factor resulting from Europe's Commercial Revolution that contributed to the 1700s' Industrial Revolution?

a. The rediscovery of concrete
b. New advances in making iron
c. The steam engine's invention
d. Increases in population growth

62. How did the ruling in *Marbury v. Madison* alter the Supreme Court's power in the federal government?

a. It lessened it. The Supreme Court was concerned about the possibility of judges overturning laws enacted by voters through referendums and took away that power.
b. It increased it. The decision in *Marbury v. Madison* gave the Supreme Court its now traditional right to overturn legislation.
c. It increased it. The decision in *Marbury v. Madison* strengthened the Supreme Court's Constitutional right to overturn legislation.
d. There was no change. *Marbury v. Madison* was a case involving a president who was unwilling to obey laws enacted by his predecessor; there was nothing about the case or decision that would have more than a cursory connection to federal powers of government

63. Which of the following accurately describes the process by which government officials may be impeached and removed from office?

a. Charges are brought by the House of Representatives and tried in the Senate.
b. Charges are brought by the Senate and tried in the House of Representatives.
c. Charges are brought by the Attorney-General and tried in Congress.
d. Charges are brought by both houses of Congress and tried in the Supreme Court.

64. The results of increased production of crops and a managed approach to agriculture is called:

a. The industrial revolution
b. The information revolution
c. The agricultural revolution
d. The scientific revolution

65. Which statement best describes the role of the Catholic Church in medieval Western Europe?

a. Powerful and wealthy, the Church was important to both poor and rich people.
b. The Church concerned itself mainly with the poorer members of medieval society.
c. Weakened by infighting about Church doctrine, the Church struggled to wield power.
d. The Catholic Church served as a neutral force between competing political leaders.

66. Decolonization was difficult or impossible in countries with large, long-term settler populations where the settler population was too important and/or the indigenous population had become a minority. Of the following countries, which one had a settler population that moved out and relocated upon the country's decolonization?

a. The Chinese population of Singapore
b. The large Jewish population of Algeria
c. The British population of Cayman Islands
d. The Russian population of Kazakhstan

67. To be President of the United States, one must meet these three requirements:

a. The President must be college educated, at least 30 years old, and a natural citizen.
b. The President must be a natural citizen, have lived in the US for 14 years, and have a college education.
c. The President must be a natural citizen, be at least 35 years old, and have lived in the US for 14 years.
d. The President must be at least 30 years old, be a natural citizen, and have lived in the US for 14 years.

68. According to Karl Marx, which two groups are in continual conflict?

a. Farmers and landowners
b. Workers and owners
c. Kings and nobles
d. Politicians and voters

69. How did Russia's participation in World War I influence the Russian Revolution?

a. Civilian suffering and military setbacks served as a catalyst for revolutionary forces.
b. Nicholas III capitalized on battlefield successes to temporarily silence critics.
c. The government eased laws banning collective action by factory workers to appease social discontent about the war.
d. Anti-government protesters temporarily ceased protesting to show patriotism in a difficult war.

70. Which is NOT correct regarding black activism during the 1960s?

a. There was a riot in the Los Angeles ghetto of Watts in 1965.
b. There was a riot involving black activists in Newark, New Jersey, after the Watts riot.
c. The Mississippi Freedom Democrats unseated that state's delegation at the convention.
d. There was a riot involving black activists in Detroit, Michigan, after the riot in Watts.

71. On a map of Africa, there is a small box around Nairobi. This city is depicted in greater detail in a box at the bottom of the map. What is the name for this box at the bottom of the map?

a. Inset
b. Legend
c. Compass rose
d. Key

72. The physical geography of a region most directly affects which of the following?

a. The religious beliefs of the native population
b. The family structure of the native population
c. The dietary preferences of the native population
d. The language spoken by the native population

73. Which of the following rivers did NOT play an important role in the development of the earliest civilizations?

a. The Tiber River
b. The Yangtze River
c. The Euphrates River
d. The Nile River

74. During World War I, which group joined with the Central Powers after it formed?

a. Austria-Hungary
b. Germany
c. Ottoman Empire
d. Italy

75. Which of the following is true concerning the formation of new state governments in the United States of America following freedom from British rule?

a. By the end of 1777, new constitutions had been created for twelve of the American states.
b. The states of Connecticut and Massachusetts retained their colonial charters, minus the British parts.
c. The state of Massachusetts required a special convention for its constitution, setting a good example.
d. The state of Massachusetts did not formally begin to use its new constitution until 1778.

76. Which of the following would NOT happen if the FOMC uses Treasury Bills to pursue a contractionary monetary policy?

a. The money supply decreases
b. The international value of the American dollar increases
c. The price of US goods to foreigners increases
d. Lower interest rates

77. The House Committee on Oversight and Government Reform oversees and reforms government operations. Which Senate committee works with that committee?

a. Senate Committee on Banking, Housing, and Urban Affairs
b. Senate Committee on Homeland Security and Government Affairs
c. Senate Committee on Rules and Administration
d. Senate Appropriations Committee

78. Which of the following is NOT correct concerning the growth of American labor unions?

a. The new factory system separated workers from owners, which tended to depersonalize workplaces.
b. The goal of attaining an 8-hour work day stimulated growth in labor organizing in the early 1800s.
c. The first organized workers' strike was in Paterson, New Jersey in 1828, and was by child laborers.
d. Recurring downturns in the economy tended to limit workers' demands for rights until the 1850s.

79. Who may write a bill?

a. Anyone
b. A member of the House
c. A Senator
d. Any member of Congress

80. Article III judges who can retire but still try cases on a full-time or part-time basis are called ____________.

a. Recalled judges
b. Senior judges
c. Chief judges
d. Elder judges

81. Which of the following conquistadores unwittingly gave smallpox to the indigenous peoples and destroyed the Aztec empire in Mexico?

a. Vasco Núñez de Balboa
b. Juan Ponce de León
c. Hernán Cortés
d. Álvar Núñez Cabeza de Vaca

82. The economic theories of John Maynard Keynes are most closely associated with which of the following?

a. The view that deficit spending leads to inflation
b. Advocating government action against monopolies
c. The view that supply creates its own demand
d. Advocating government action to stimulate economic growth

83. When the euro was introduced in January 2002, a single euro was valued at 88 cents in United States currency. In the summer of 2008, at one point it required $1.60 US to buy 1 euro. In late October 2008, the euro fell to its lowest level against the dollar in two years. Which of the following statements is a correct conclusion?

a. The global economy in 2008 was headed for another Great Depression.
b. The dollar regained strength after much devaluing against the euro.
c. The euro is the world's strongest currency.
d. Investors need to keep buying stocks.

84. Which of the following is most likely to benefit from inflation?

a. A bond investor who owns fixed-rate bonds
b. A retired widow with no income other than fixed Social Security payments
c. A person who has taken out a fixed-rate loan
d. A local bank who has loaned money out at fixed rate

85. Which statement best describes how Martin Luther's religious Reformation influenced Western civilization?

a. It contributed to the decline of women's and girls' education.
b. It weakened civil authorities in European towns.
c. It contributed to the rise of individualism.
d. It delayed reform within the Catholic Church itself.

86. How are members of the Federal Judiciary chosen?

a. They are elected by voters.
b. They are appointed by the president and confirmed by the House of Representatives.
c. They are chosen by a committee.
d. They are appointed by the president and confirmed by the Senate.

87. In about 1428, the Mesoamerican city-states Tenochtitlan, Texcoco, and Tlacopan formed a Triple Alliance. How did this influence Aztec history?

a. Texcoco and Tlacopan secretly conspired against Tenochtitlan, using the Alliance as a front.
b. Disagreements about strategy between the city-states weakened Aztec resistance to Spanish invaders.
c. The alliance agreed that each city-state would offer a specific number of human sacrifices each year.
d. The allied city-states joined forces to conquer other city-states, incorporating them into an Aztec Empire.

88. What major US event took place around the same time that the Judiciary Act set up the federal judiciary system?

a. The Neutrality Act was passed.
b. The United States entered WWII.
c. The Korean War ended.
d. George Washington was inaugurated president.

89. Among the following, which is correct regarding some essential geography concepts?

a. An example of absolute location is urban vs. rural land prices.
b. Relative location equals the latitude and longitude of a place.
c. Product and land prices are affected by geographical distance.
d. Achievability relates to surface conditions and never changes.

90. The strategy of containment was a major element of American foreign policy during:

a. The Spanish-American War
b. World War I
c. World War II
d. The Cold War

91. European colonization of present-day Pennsylvania in the late 17th century is most closely associated with:

a. The desire for freedom of the press
b. Escape from high taxes
c. The desire for religious freedom
d. Escape from trade restrictions

92. Which of the following resources in the West Bank is the most significant motivation for Israel's continuing occupation of that territory?

a. The Mediterranean Sea
b. Oil reserves
c. Olive groves
d. Aquifers

93. How can Congress override the presidential veto of a bill?

a. By a majority vote in the House and a two-thirds majority in the Senate
b. By a two-thirds vote in the House and a majority in the Senate
c. By a majority vote in both the House and the Senate
d. By a two-thirds vote in both the House and the Senate

94. How did the Homestead Act impact westward migration to the Great Plains between 1860 and 1880?

a. It allowed business owners tax breaks for opening new businesses in the Great Plains.
b. It provided settlers with free land in exchange for a commitment to cultivate the land.
c. It gave buyers monetary incentives for irrigating the land to improve the land quality.
d. It provided farmers with monetary aid in planting trees on newly purchased land.

95. What was the earliest written language in Mesopotamia?

a. Sumerian
b. Elamite
c. Akkadian
d. Aramaic

96. Which of the following statements is *not* true of the rash of witch hunts that took place in the 14th through 16th centuries in Europe?

a. The witch hunts used the Inquisition's techniques for rooting out heretics.
b. Many hunts followed careful legal codes.
c. Much of the evidence used was based on hearsay.
d. Belief in magic and superstition was commonplace even among educated Europeans.

97. Which invention had a major role in communication during the Civil War?

a. Morse Code
b. Telephone
c. Radio
d. Computer

98. What judicial system did America borrow from England?

a. Due process
b. Federal law
c. Commerce law
d. Common law

99. Parks and recreation services, police and fire departments, housing services, emergency medical services, municipal courts, transportation services, and public works usually fall under the jurisdiction of which body of government?

a. State government
b. Federal government
c. Federal agencies
d. Local government

100. Inflation has what effects?

a. Harms all members of an economy
b. Helps all members of an economy
c. Harms no members of an economy
d. Harms some members of an economy, helps others

101. Which of the following is a correct statement regarding consequences of the French Revolution?

a. De Tocqueville wrote that it showed the rising middle class's growing self-awareness.
b. Conservative Edmund Burke felt it was a minority conspiracy with no valid claims.
c. Marxists viewed it as a huge class struggle with lower and middle classes revolting.
d. All of these statements are correct regarding consequences of the French Revolution.

102. The vice president succeeds the president in case of death, illness or impeachment. What is the order of succession for the next three successors, according to the Presidential Succession Act of 1947?

a. President pro tempore of the Senate, secretary of state, and secretary of defense
b. Speaker of the House, president pro tempore of the Senate, and secretary of state
c. President pro tempore of the Senate, Speaker of the House, and secretary of state
d. Secretary of state, secretary of defense, and Speaker of the House

103. How does the prevalence of ziggurats in ancient Mesopotamia illustrate a central factor of Mesopotamian culture?

a. Intended as lookouts, the number of ziggurats illustrates a Mesopotamian concern for security from invaders.
b. Used for stargazing, the number of ziggurats shows how Mesopotamian culture depended on astrology.
c. Dedicated to Mesopotamian rulers, the ziggurats illustrate the complete control Mesopotamian kings held over their subjects.
d. Structures dedicated to gods, the ziggurats illustrate the importance of religion in Mesopotamian culture.

104. What significance did *Brown* v. *Board of Education of Topeka* have on the system if education in the United States?

a. Students were educated separately but equally.
b. Students were taught creationism.
c. Students were taught evolution.
d. The "separate but equal" ruling was reversed.

105. The French and Indian War ended in 1763. Which subsequent British policy regarding the American colonies was most important to the American Revolution?

a. Increasingly limited oversight of the colonies in order to focus on Canadian territories
b. A determination that the colonies should help pay for the War
c. The Proclamation of 1763 limiting the location of new American colonies
d. Increasing the colonies' dependence on the British military

106. How did isolationism most influence American society in the decade following World War I?

a. It shaped a temporarily strong economy as the US avoided the troubled economies of postwar Europe.
b. It led to a system of admitting immigrants according to quotas based on their national origins.
c. It guided the US government's decision to strengthen its navy as a safeguard against foreign attacks.
d. It influenced the collapse of trade deals, allowing US companies access to oil in Colombia and in Middle Eastern countries.

107. What is a committee that raises money for political candidates and is formed by business, labor, or other special interest groups?

a. Party
b. Lobby
c. PLEO
d. PAC

108. Which statement best describes the role played by the French economy in causing the 1789 French Revolution?

a. France's very large national debt led to heavy tax burdens on the French peasantry.
b. Nearly seventy percent of annual national expenditures financed luxuries for the French nobility.
c. Reforms in the guild system allowed many peasants to rise to the middle class.
d. The king's attempt to curtail free trade led skilled journeymen to rebel against the monarchy.

109. The popularity of hockey in Canada and the northern United States is an example of

a. Expansion diffusion
b. Indirect diffusion
c. Forced diffusion
d. Direct diffusion

110. Which of the following is NOT true regarding the Virginia Companies?

a. One of these companies, the Virginia Company of Plymouth, made its base in North America.
b. One of these companies, the Virginia Company of London, made its base in Massachusetts.
c. One company had a charter to colonize America between the Hudson and Cape Fear rivers.
d. One company had a charter to colonize America from the Potomac River to north Maine.

111. The president may serve a maximum of _____ according to the ___ Amendment.

a. Three four-year terms; 23rd
b. Two four-year terms; 22nd
c. One four-year term; 22nd
d. Two four-year terms; 23rd

112. During the 15th century, Johann Gutenberg invented a printing press with moveable type. How did his invention influence science?

a. It did not influence science; the printing of Gutenberg Bibles directed public attention away from science and toward reforming the Catholic Church.
b. It led to scientific advances throughout Europe by spreading scientific knowledge.
c. It influenced scientific advancement in Germany only, where Gutenberg's press was based.
d. It did not influence science; though texts with scientific knowledge were printed, distribution of these texts was limited.

113. How is a tie in the Electoral College broken to choose the President?

a. Each state's delegation in the House of Representatives gets a vote, and the majority wins
b. Each state's delegation in the Senate gets a vote, and the majority wins
c. The former Vice President becomes President
d. The Speaker of the House casts the deciding vote

114. What do the executive, legislative, and judicial branches of government compose?

a. The federal government
b. The democratic process
c. Bicameralism
d. Rule of law

Refer to the following for questions 115–116:

For a geography unit, students are learning about the state of Wisconsin. To help better understand the climate of the state, students are asked to record how the elevation of certain regions correlates to temperature. They are also expected to locate and label the major cities of the state, such as Madison and Milwaukee.

115. What would be the best map to use to find the highest elevation in Wisconsin?

a. Political map
b. Topographic map
c. Resource map
d. Road map

116. Which of the following gives the clearest relative location of Milwaukee?

a. In Wisconsin
b. On Lake Michigan
c. 44° N, 88° W
d. 100 miles north of Chicago

117. Which of the following statements is NOT correct regarding these religions under the Roman Empire?

a. The Romans generally protected the Jews until the rebellion in Judea (66 AD).
b. Julius Caesar circumvented Roman law to help Jews have freedom of worship.
c. The Druids were a religious group that the Romans ignored but also tolerated.
d. Romans viewed Christianity as a Jewish sect for its first two centuries.

118. Which of the following was NOT an immediate effect of rapid urban growth in the 1800s?

a. Poor sanitation conditions in the cities
b. Epidemics of diseases in the cities
c. Inadequate police and fire protection
d. Widespread urban political corruption

119. Which of these pre-Columbian civilizations was Mesoamerican rather than Andean?

a. Inca
b. Aztec
c. Moche
d. Cañaris

120. Which Italian Renaissance figure was best known as a political philosopher?

a. Dante Alighieri
b. Leonardo Da Vinci
c. Francesco Petrarca
d. Niccolò Machiavelli

121. Which of these factors was NOT a direct contributor to the beginning of the American Revolution?

a. The attitudes of American colonists toward Great Britain following the French and Indian War
b. The attitudes of leaders in Great Britain toward the American colonies and imperialism
c. James Otis's court argument against Great Britain's Writs of Assistance as breaking natural law
d. Lord Grenville's Proclamation of 1763, the Sugar Act, the Currency Act, and especially the Stamp Act

122. Of the following international diplomatic conferences, which one made US-Soviet differences apparent?

a. The Potsdam conference
b. The conference at Yalta
c. Dumbarton Oaks conference
d. The Tehran conference

123. Land is typically more expensive in urban areas than in rural areas. Which geography concept does this reflect?

a. Location
b. Distance
c. Pattern
d. Interaction

124. How did the Crusader army that went on the First Crusade differ from the Crusader armies that Pope Urban II envisioned?

a. There was no difference. The people of Europe were accustomed to obeying clerical direction and eagerly joined the cause. They created an army that was primarily made up of faithful Christians from all social classes led by a select group of knights who were responsible for leading and training their armies.
b. There was no difference. The people of Europe obeyed clerical direction and stayed home to pray for the success of an army composed entirely of knights and other professional military personnel.
c. Pope Urban II had envisioned an army of skilled knights and professional soldiers; instead, men and women from all classes joined together to retake the Holy Land.
d. Pope Urban II had envisioned an army composed of faithful Christians from all social classes led by a group of select knights; instead, the army was primarily made up of knights and other professional military personnel.

125. Which of the following BEST describes the significance of the US Supreme Court's decision in the Dred Scott case?

a. The ruling effectively declared slavery to be a violation of the Constitution.
b. The ruling guaranteed full citizenship rights to freed slaves.
c. The ruling turned many Southerners against the Supreme Court.
d. The ruling furthered the gap between North and South and hastened the Civil War.

126. On a globe, the distance between Buenos Aires and Tokyo is 35 cm. If the globe has a scale of 1 cm for every 516 km, what is the real distance?

a. 18,060 km
b. 35 km
c. 21,080 km
d. 14,740 km

127. Which of the following is the most significant justification for United States expansion as advocated by the Manifest Destiny?

a. It was the duty of the United States to spread democracy.
b. The United States would spread material wealth.
c. It was the duty of the United States to prevent the spread of slavery.
d. The United States would spread religious freedom.

128. Approximately what percentage of the Earth's surface is land?

a. 50
b. 10
c. 30
d. 85

129. Which of the following is NOT a true statement regarding the Louisiana Purchase?

a. Jefferson sent a delegation to Paris to endeavor to purchase only the city of New Orleans from Napoleon.
b. Napoleon, anticipating US intrusions into Louisiana, offered to sell the US the entire Louisiana territory.
c. The American delegation accepted Napoleon's offer, though they were only authorized to buy New Orleans.
d. The Louisiana Purchase, once it was completed, increased the territory of the US by 50% overnight.

130. The Trail of Tears was:

a. The forced removal of British soldiers after the American Revolution
b. The forced evacuation of Cherokee peoples into Oklahoma
c. The forced evacuation of freed slaves from the South after the Civil War
d. The tears of Betsy Ross while she sewed the first American flag

131. Tracy needs to determine the shortest route between Lima and Lisbon. Which of the following maps should she use?

a. Azimuthal projection with the North Pole at the center
b. Azimuthal projection with Lisbon at the center
c. Robinson projection of the Eastern Hemisphere
d. Robinson projection of the Western Hemisphere

132. The Seven Years' War, called the French and Indian War by the Colonists:

a. Was the precursor to the American Revolution
b. Was a conflict related to European colonization
c. Primarily took place in Canada
d. Ended European conquests

133. During which of these periods were pyramids NOT built in Egypt?

a. The Old Kingdom
b. The Middle Kingdom
c. The New Kingdom
d. The Third Dynasty

134. Power divided between local and central branches of government is a definition of what term?

a. Bicameralism
b. Checks and balances
c. Legislative oversight
d. Federalism

135. "This era represents the golden age of the Roman Empire. For about 200 years, the Empire experienced relatively few attacks, stability among its conquered lands, and significant developments in architecture and the engineering of roads and bridges. This time period saw the greatest expansion of the empire and the Romanization of the western world."

The above passage refers to which era of Roman history?

a. The reign of Julio-Claudian line of emperors
b. The reign of the Five Good Emperors
c. Pax Romana
d. The reign of the Flavian Emperors

136. Which statement best describes the significance of the Battle of Chapultepec during the US-Mexican War?

a. General Zachary Taylor's performance gained him recognition as an American hero.
b. It was the first Mexican victory after a long string of Mexican defeats.
c. General Santa Ana narrowly escaped capture during the battle.
d. It was the last major US assault prior to capturing Mexico City.

137. Which of the following statements does NOT characterize the Age of Absolutism?

a. Nobles gained more power as monarchs had them live in their palaces.
b. The influence of the Church upon government diminished at this time.
c. The partitioning characteristic of feudal systems no longer took place.
d. All of these were characteristics found during the Age of Absolutism.

138. An action's opportunity cost is best explained in terms of which of the following?

a. The minimum amount a business must borrow for the action
b. The opportunities given up in order to pursue that action
c. The percentage of one's overall budget that the action requires
d. The cost of a long-term action adjusted for inflation

139. Virginian ____________ advocated a stronger central government and was influential at the Constitutional Convention.

a. Benjamin Franklin
b. James Madison
c. George Mason
d. Robert Yates

140. What was generally the sentiment towards Chinese laborers in the United States in the 1880s?

a. Chinese laborers were viewed as cheap laborers and were generally discriminated against.
b. Chinese laborers were highly valued members of US society.
c. Chinese laborers were forced out of the country.
d. Chinese laborers were welcomed through several immigration laws.

Answer Key and Explanations

1. D: Only the British Empire existed following the armistice ending WWI. The Austro-Hungarian Empire, the Ottoman Empire, and the German Empire were all among the Central powers that lost the war. As empires capitulated, armistices and peace treaties were signed and the map of Europe was redrawn as territories formerly occupied by Central powers were partitioned. For example, the former Austro-Hungarian Empire was partitioned into Austria, Hungary, Czechoslovakia, Yugoslavia, Transylvania, and Romania. The Treaty of Lausanne (1923) gave Turkey both independence and recognition as successor to the former Ottoman Empire after Turkey refused the earlier Treaty of Sèvres (1920), and Mustafa Kemal Ataturk led the Turkish Independence War. Greece, Bulgaria, and other former Ottoman possessions became independent. The Lausanne Treaty defined the boundaries of these countries as well as the boundaries of Iraq, Syria, Cyprus, Sudan, and Egypt.

2. D: A market failure is any situation in which the production of a good or service is not efficient. In the cases listed, non-competitive markets allow for the underpayment of labor and the underproduction of a good or service; externalities are negative consequences assumed by parties not involved in a transaction; and public goods are an example of a good the market will not produce at all, or at efficient levels.

3. D: It is not true that cotton farming was the reason Southern colonies imported more slaves in the 1600s. Tobacco farming was the reason. Tobacco became a very successful cash crop at that time in the American colonies. Growing tobacco was extremely labor-intensive, so planters needed more laborers as tobacco became more popular and valuable. Cotton was grown in America by the end of the 16th century and increased around the end of the 18th century due to Eli Whitney's invention of the cotton gin in 1793. It is true that slaves were brought from Africa to Florida by the Spanish as early as the 1560s (A), although this practice became more widespread practice in the 1600s. Chattel slavery (meaning outright ownership of a person for that person's lifetime) was legal in America from 1654 until 1865 (B) when Lincoln's Emancipation Proclamation abolished it. Furthermore, indentured servants provided sources of labor in America before slaves (C). Early indentured servitude was not race based, as the modern concept of race did not begin until the 1700s. Indentured servants were people who were bonded into servitude for a period of several years, often as a result of poverty, after which they could gain their freedom. An eventual shortage of indentured servants led to the importation of slaves and the enslavement of some indentured servants of African descent. By the end of the 17th century, court rulings had confined American slavery to people of African descent.

4. B: Members of the House are elected for two-year terms. Senators serve six-year terms, but the elections are staggered so roughly one-third of the Senate is elected every two years.

5. B: The GATT countries did agree to abolish or decrease many of their tariffs, but this agreement did not include only 57 countries. The number of signatories was much larger, totaling 117 countries. The GATT was approved by Congress in 1994. In addition to having 117 countries agree to increase free trade, the GATT also set up the World Trade Organization (WTO) for the purpose of settling any differences among nations related to trade. Another instance of free trade policy established in the 1990s was the Senate's ratification of NAFTA. The negotiation of this agreement was originally made by the first Bush administration, with President Bush and the leaders of Canada and Mexico signing it in 1992, but it still needed to be ratified. When he was elected

President following the senior Bush's term, Bill Clinton also supported NAFTA, and the Senate ratified it in 1994.

6. B: Southern states provided raw materials that were manufactured into commodities in Northern states. Southerners resented paying taxes to Northern states for these products (textiles, furniture, etc.).

7. B: The Andes mountain range is the world's longest continental mountain range. It lies as a continuous chain of mountains along the western coast of South America.

8. B: The Erie Canal opened in 1825 and created a water route between the Hudson River and Lake Erie. Water routes have historically been cheaper and easier than overland ones and the Erie Canal was originally proposed in the 1700s as a means of providing a shipping route to assist in settling the areas west of the Appalachian Mountains. The Mississippi River is to the west of the Great Lakes; its source is in Minnesota and it discharges into the Gulf of Mexico approximately 100 miles downstream of New Orleans, Louisiana. The Susquehanna River runs through New York, Pennsylvania, and Maryland and is the home of Three Mile Island, the site of the United States' largest nuclear disaster. The Lehigh River is located in eastern Pennsylvania.

9. B: Discretionary spending is dedicated to transportation, education, national resources, the environment, and international affairs. State and local governments use this money to help finance programs. Mandatory spending covers entitlements such as Medicare, Social Security, Federal Retirement, and Medicaid.

10. D: All the laws (D) named were instrumental in spurring westward migration to the Great Plains. The Homestead Act (A), passed in 1862, gave settlers 160 acres of land at no monetary cost in exchange for a commitment to cultivating the land for five years. The Timber Culture Act (B), passed in 1873, gave the settlers 160 acres more of land in exchange for planting trees on one quarter of the acreage. The Desert Land Act (C), passed in 1877, allowed buyers who would irrigate the land to buy 640 acres for only 25 cents an acre. Thus, (D), all of these laws were instrumental in spurring westward migration to the Great Plains during that period, is correct.

11. C: Company A outperformed Company B in March, March was not a peak performance for either company, and Company B did not perform better than Company A during all of January to May. The only true statement is that sales performance dropped faster for Company A than Company B from June to July.

12. A: The phenomenon of "sticky prices" refers to prices that stay the same even though it seems they should change (either increasing or decreasing).

13. C: Intrastate trade is solely within a state, so the state has jurisdiction over it. Taxation is a right granted to both federal and state authorities. Declaring war is a national decision. Patents and copyrights apply to goods made and/or sold throughout the country; therefore, they are a federal responsibility.

14. B: The House has strict rules that limit debate. A filibuster can only occur in the Senate where senators can speak on topics other than the bill at hand and introduce amendments. A filibuster can be ended by a supermajority vote of 60 senators.

15. B: The Supreme Court ruled that statements made in interrogation are not admissible unless the defendant is informed of the right to an attorney and waives that right. The case of Miranda v.

Arizona was consolidated with Westover v. United States, Vignera v. New York, and California v. Stewart.

16. B: There was not a reduction in military spending after the war. Although the manufacturing demand for war supplies and the size of the military decreased, the government had increased military spending from $10 billion in 1947 to more than $50 billion by 1953—a more than fivefold increase. This increase strengthened the American economy. Other factors contributing to the strengthened economy included the significantly higher birth rates during the Baby Boom from 1946 to 1957, which stimulated the growth of the building and automotive industries by increased demand. Government programs, such as the GI Bill (the Servicemen's Readjustment Act of 1944), other veterans' benefits, and the National Defense Education Act all encouraged college enrollments, which increased by nearly four times. Additionally, larger families, increased mobility and low-interest loans offered to veterans led to suburban development and growth as well as increased home construction. Improvements in public health were also results of the new affluence; the rate of infant deaths decreased significantly, and as a result, from 1946–1957, the American life span rose from 67 to 71 years. Moreover, Dr. Jonas Salk developed the polio vaccine in 1955, which virtually wiped out poliomyelitis, preventing many deaths and disabilities in children.

17. A: The US Constitution, Article I, Section 3 states that: "The Senate of the United States shall be composed of two Senators from each state, chosen by the legislature thereof, for six years; and each Senator shall have one vote." This was the practice until the Seventeenth Amendment was ratified on April 8, 1913. The Seventeenth Amendment states that US Senators are to be elected by the people of the states which they serve and that the state executive branches may appoint replacement Senators if a Senate seat becomes vacant mid-term, until the state legislature can arrange for a popular election.

18. B: Women in the organization have the opportunity to meet others and bring their involvement into the larger organization. Choice A is wrong because cronyism is using power to place your friends and associates in power. Choice C is also incorrect because lobbyists are not mayors. Instead, they are people who try to influence legislators. Patronage is a system of supporting worthy persons or causes. So, this makes choice D incorrect.

19. A: Most of the conquered peoples were not granted Roman citizenship. Each conquered state was allowed some degree of cultural autonomy. Subjects were expected to follow the laws of Rome, pay taxes, and hand over land and supplies to the Roman government.

20. B: The President may veto legislation passed by Congress. The executive branch has this "check" on the legislative branch.

21. D: In the saturation stage of spatial diffusion, the process slows down and eventually stops altogether. The Swedish geographer Torsten Hägerstrand outlined four stages in spatial diffusion, which is the spread of innovation throughout a geographical region. In the primary stage, the innovation first appears and is adopted in the immediate vicinity. In the diffusion stage, the innovation is used in increasingly far-flung areas. In the condensing stage, any areas that had not already received the innovation do so. In the saturation stage, the innovation is either replaced or abandoned because it is no longer believed to have utility.

22. A: Fascism was not opposed to nationalism and patriotism. Fascism was a radical political movement that was nationalistic in character. In fact, Fascism opposed Marxism (B) because Fascists saw Marxism as anti-nationalist and anti-patriotic. Fascism was both collectivist and saw itself as patriotic. Fascists were also against the bourgeoisie (B) for their individualism, which was the opposite of collectivism. Fascism did purport to be an alternative to Bolshevism (C). Nonetheless, despite this, the Fascist movement did have several things in common with Bolshevism (D). For example, both political movements believed in a single-party state, in appealing to the proletariat, and in the ruling over the masses by an elite group.

23. B: Salt and other preservatives were known in Europe long before major trade expansions, but they were costly and not abundant for most people; therefore, the claim of an 'abundance of preservatives' is inaccurate.

24. D: A market that is monopolistically competitive is relatively easy to enter and exit and has high levels of competition. Therefore, firms will enter and exit the market if it is not in long-run equilibrium. When price/quantity is below the minimum of the average total cost curve firms will exit the market.

25. B: Reagan did not escalate military action in response to a terrorist bombing that killed 240 US Marines. Reagan sent the Marines to Lebanon in 1982 as part of a peacekeeping effort after Israel invaded Lebanon on a mission to eradicate its PLO camps. At the time, Lebanon was already engaged in a civil war. When the terrorist attack killed 240 Marines, Reagan withdrew the rest of the troops rather than escalate the action.

26. C: Lying at a little more than 23° south of the equator, the Tropic of Capricorn is the border between the Southern Temperate Zone to the south and the Tropical Zone to the north. The southern hemisphere is tilted toward the sun to its maximum extent each year at the winter solstice in December. The northernmost latitude at which the sun can appear directly overhead is at the Tropic of Cancer during the summer solstice. The northern and southern hemispheres are separated by the equator at 0° latitude. The eastern and western hemispheres are separated by the prime meridian at 0° longitude.

27. A: Moldova is not one of the Baltic states. Latvia, Lithuania, and Estonia all border the Baltic Sea, which has enabled them to become major traders. Unfortunately, the smallness and advantageous locations of these nations has made them attractive to invaders. The Soviet Union took over these lands in 1939, and it was not until 1991 that they regained independence. All three of these nations are now struggling to establish themselves as viable economic actors.

28. D: Ancient Greek democracy was not completely open to all of the public. However, participating persons were not chosen or excluded based on their respective socioeconomic levels. The city-state of Athens had one of the first and most well-known democracies in ancient Greece. It began around 500 BC. The experiment of Athenian democracy was unique in that it was a direct democracy, meaning people voted directly for or against proposed legislation without any representation such as the House of Representatives and the Senate, as we have in modern democracies.

29. A: Agriculture was not a viable economic model for New Englanders. Although the colonists were mainly from England and Scotland, few were merchants before arriving in the colonies. Slavery existed in the north, although it was less important to the economy than it was in the agricultural south. New England colonists were not actively competing with their neighbors to the immediate south.

30. D: Under the Missouri Compromise, Maine would be admitted as a free state while Missouri would enter as a slave state. Slavery would be prohibited in the former Louisiana Territory north of the 36°30' parallel except in the new state of Missouri. Ohio had entered the Union in 1803 under the Northwest Ordinance. Alabama had been admitted as a slave state shortly before the Missouri Compromise. After years of bloody conflict, Kansas entered the Union as a free state in 1861.

31. C: The Norman Conquest was the English historical period beginning in 1066. It began with the defeat of Anglo-Saxon King Harold II. With this defeat, the customs, laws, and language of the Normans was introduced in England. The Great Papal Schism was the division in the Roman Catholic Church from 1378–1417 when two rival popes emerged.

The French Revolution was the prolonged political and social struggle between 1789 and 1799 in France. It encompassed the regicide of the king, Louis XVI, and the queen, Marie-Antoinette, included the Reign of Terror, the establishment of the First Republic, and led to the rise of Napoleon Bonaparte as Emperor of France, leading Europe to war.

32. B: "...endowed by their Creator with certain unalienable Rights," is excerpted from the Declaration of Independence. These rights are unable to be taken away from individuals, referring to the colonists' rights that Great Britain could not oppress.

33. A: After a series of disagreements over Reconstruction Policy, Congress passed the Tenure of Office Act, according to which the President needed congressional consent to dismiss from office anyone who had been confirmed by the Senate. President Johnson violated the Act by dismissing Secretary of War Edwin Stanton, whom radical Republicans wanted to keep in office. Congress accordingly impeached President Johnson. Regarding option B, Southern states did enact "Black Laws" to prevent African Americans from voting, but President Johnson was not impeached because he allowed such laws (and thus failed to enforce the Fourteenth Amendment). Johnson did seek to disenfranchise former Confederate officers, and he did attempt to form a third political party; but neither of these actions were grounds for his impeachment (with respect to the former action, radical Republicans were in agreement). This eliminates choices C and D respectively.

34. A: Symbols are not used to represent relief on a physical map. A physical map is dedicated to illustrating the landmasses and bodies of water in a specific region, so symbols do not provide enough detail. Color, shading, and contour lines, on the other hand, are able to create a much more complicated picture of changes in elevation, precipitation, etc. Changes in elevation are known in geography as relief.

35. C: While wounds from war most certainly killed more than a few, European disease laid waste to vast swaths of Native American people who had no immunity to the foreign diseases which the Europeans carried. The forced marches took place in the mid-19th century under Andrew Jackson's presidency and are thus removed from the time frame in question.

36. B: Oligarchy is defined as the rule by few. An example is aristocracy, which in ancient Greece, was government by an elite group of citizens as opposed to a monarchy. In later times, it meant government by the class of aristocrats, a privileged group, as opposed to democracy. The rule of one is called autocracy. Examples include monarchy, dictatorship, and many others. The rule by law is called a republic. Some examples are constitutional republics, parliamentary republics, and federal republics. The rule by many could apply to democracy, which governs according to the people's votes, or to the collective leadership form of socialism, where no one individual has too much power.

37. B: Akbar allowed the practice of both Hinduism and Islam, despite pressure from Islamic religious leaders to do otherwise. Akbar specifically permitted the construction of Hindu temples, which freed Akbar from Hindu resistance that he might otherwise have faced. This fact eliminates answer D. Breaking from some past practices, Akbar also used cash instead of land to pay empire officials, allowing him to control more land. Because of this, option A can be rejected. Option C can be rejected because Akbar allowed certain defeated princes to keep their lands.

38. C: A bill is usually first reviewed by the appropriate subcommittee. The subcommittee can accept the bill, amend the bill, or reject the bill. If the subcommittee accepts or amends the bill, they send it to the full committee for review. Expert witnesses and testimony are all part of committee review.

39. D: The Sahel, a belt of grasslands just south of the Sahara Desert, has long been a focus of agricultural efforts in Africa. This semiarid region has provided sustenance to people and animals for thousands of years. In the last thousand years, stores of salt and gold were found there, giving rise to empires in Ghana and Mali. Changes in climate have expanded the Sahara, however, and pushed the Sahel farther south. The Qattara Depression is a low-lying desert in Egypt. The Great Rift Valley is a region of faults and rocky hills that extends along the southeastern coast of Africa. The Congo Basin is a repository of sediment from the Ubangi and Congo rivers. It is in the northern half of what is now called the Democratic Republic of the Congo.

40. C: The Civil Rights Act of 1964 affected the Jim Crow laws in the Southern states. Many minorities suffered under unfair voting laws and segregation. President Lyndon Johnson signed the Civil Rights Act of 1964 into law after the 1963 assassination of President Kennedy, who championed the reform.

41. C: The telegraph was a gigantic leap forward in the realm of communications. Before the telegraph, messages could take days, weeks, or months to reach their intended recipient, based upon the distance that they had to travel. The telegraph allowed people to send messages through use of electric signals transmitted over telegraph wires, allowing for instantaneous communications. The main drawbacks to the telegraph included the need to "translate" the message into and out of the appropriate telegraphic code and that the telegraph could only relay one message at a time. In contrast, the telephone allowed for spoken communication between people at different locations, increasing the efficiency and speed as the people on each end of the conversation could communicate multiple messages quickly and in one telephone conversation.

42. C: The main subject matter of civic responsibility is a person's responsibilities as a citizen. By contrast, the main subject matter of personal responsibility is one's responsibilities as a person. For example, keeping a promise to a friend is often a matter of personal responsibility because such a duty arises from the friendship. Serving on a jury when called to do so is an example of civic responsibility because such a duty arises from the person's citizenship. None of the other options given accurately describe the main subject matter of civic responsibility. For example, while a journalist might see accurate reporting of government actions as his or her civic responsibility, such reporting is not the main subject matter of civic responsibility and is also a responsibility that arises from that journalist's employment. Similar reasoning applies to a person's responsibilities as a government worker. This eliminates options A and D. Civic responsibility does not primarily concern inter-government relations; this eliminates option B.

43. C: George Washington served 2 four-year terms as president. This interval of time was not specified in the Constitution, but future presidents followed suit (until FDR).

44. A: The inaccurate statement is the Puritans unconditionally supported the English Reformation. While they agreed with the Reformation in principle, they felt that it had not pursued those principles far enough and should make greater reforms. Similarly, they felt that the Church of England (or Anglican Church), though it had separated from the Catholic Church in the Protestant

Reformation, still allowed many practices they found too much like Catholicism. The Puritans did become a chief political power in England because of the first English Civil War between Royalists and Parliamentarians. The Royalists had a profound suspicion of the radical Puritans. Among the Parliament's elements of resistance, the strongest was that of the Puritans. They joined in the battle initially for ostensibly political reasons as others had, but soon they brought more attention to religious issues. Following the Restoration in 1660 and the Uniformity Act of 1662, thereby restoring the Church of England to its pre-English Civil War status, the great majority of Puritan clergy defected from the Church of England. It is also accurate that the Puritans in England disagreed about separating from the Church of England. Some Puritans desired complete separation; they were known first as Separatists and after the Restoration as Dissenters. Others did not want complete separation but instead desired further reform in the Church of England. While they remained part of the Church of England, they were called Non-Separating Puritans, and after the Restoration, they were called Nonconformists.

45. B: It is not true that the Crusades succeeded at Christians' reclaiming the "holy land" (the Middle East) from Muslims. Despite their number (nine not counting the Northern Crusades) and longevity (1095-1291 not counting later similar campaigns), the Crusades never accomplished this purpose. While they did not take back the Middle East, the Crusades did succeed in exacerbating the decline of the Byzantine Empire, which lost more and more territory to the Ottoman Turks during this period. In addition, the Crusades resulted in Egypt's rise once again to become a major power of the Middle East as it had been in the past.

46. C: Purchasing a DVD is a discretionary expense because it is based on personal desire rather than need. In other words, it is an expense made at the discretion of the consumer. Discretionary expenses are those over which a consumer has the most control. A comprehensive budget must include discretionary expenses as well as fixed and variable expenses. Fixed expenses, such as rent, are the same every month. Variable expenses, including groceries, school supplies, and heating oil, are always present but vary in amount over the course of a year.

47. A: It is not true that the founding fathers specifically stated in the Constitution that the United States would be a democracy. The founding fathers wanted the new United States to be founded on principles of liberty and equality, but they did not specifically describe these principles with the term *democracy*. Thus, the Declaration of Independence, like the Constitution after it, did not stipulate a democracy, although both did state the principles of equality and freedom. The Constitution also provided for the election of the new government, and for protection of the rights of some, but not all, of the people. Notable exceptions at the time were black people and women. Only later were laws passed to protect their rights over the years.

48. C: A central plank in the platform of the Populist Party was free coinage of silver, which allowed citizens to exchange their silver at US mints for US currency. This platform was subsequently adopted by the Democratic Party and was a major domestic issue in the 1892 and 1896 presidential elections. The heart of the issue was the standard on which US currency would be based. Option A can be rejected because the Populist Party was formed in part by farmers unhappy about the decreasing cost of farm crops; the elevation of these costs contributed to the dissolution of the Populist Party. Options B and D can both be rejected because neither were influential planks in the platform of the Populist Party.

49. C: There are no formal qualifications for members of the judicial branch. However, having a background in law is an informal qualification that is considered when appointing Article III judges.

50. D: Although the Thirteenth, Fourteenth, and Fifteenth Amendments guaranteed certain legal protection to African Americans, Southern whites were able to retain power by enacting various restrictions on voting. Lacking formal education and deprived of their right to vote, freed slaves were unable to attain political or economic power in the South.

51. B: In order to prosper, a nation should not try to increase its imports. Mercantilism is an economic theory including the idea that prosperity comes from a positive balance of international trade. For any one nation to prosper, that nation should increase its exports but decrease its imports. Exporting more to other countries while importing less from them will give a country a positive trade balance. This theory assumes that money and wealth are identical assets of a nation. In addition, this theory also assumes that the volume of global trade is an unchangeable quantity. Mercantilism dictates that a nation's government should apply a policy of economic protectionism by stimulating more exports and suppressing imports. Some ways to accomplish this task have included granting subsidies for exports and imposing tariffs on imports. Mercantilism can be regarded as essentially the opposite of the free trade policies that have been encouraged in more recent years.

52. B: The Founding Fathers decided that because the colonies did not have the right to elect members of Parliament, Parliament should not pass laws for them. The Declaration of Independence recognized the British Empire's government as being headed by the King of England, under whom the various local parliaments and legislative bodies served to enact laws for the peoples whom they represented. By addressing their ills to the King, the Founding Fathers sought to prevent the appearance that they acknowledged the British Parliament in London as having any authority over the American colonies.

53. B: Any expenditure that will increase a firm's future productivity is considered investment. Of the items listed, only the construction of a new plant matches the definition.

54. D: Lying between the Tigris and Euphrates rivers, the Mesopotamian region gave rise to many prominent cultures. Today, the land belongs mainly to Iraq while extending to parts of northeastern Syria, southeastern Turkey, and southwestern Iran.

55. A: The Industrial Revolution did create a new working class composed of professionals like doctors and lawyers, industrialists, and businessmen. Formerly, Europe was dominated by royalty and landed gentry over the poor working class. Industrialization allowed many ordinary people to start and run businesses. It did NOT, however, improve working conditions in the 18th and early 19th centuries, but the opposite occurred: Big factories with machines made conditions more dangerous, and child labor caused many deaths, injuries, illnesses, and so on. Women and children were only banned from working in mines in the mid-19th century; housing and work conditions only improved in the late 19th century. Urbanization was the result of industrialization and not vice versa: Mechanization allowed factory construction, and people moved to cities for jobs. Labor unions developed out of the Industrial Revolution, not vice versa, to establish and defend factory workers' rights.

56. A: GDP (Gross Domestic Product) is restricted to value produced within borders, whereas GNP (Gross National Product) is focused on value produced by companies regardless of borders.

57. A: The Navigation Acts in the seventeenth and eighteenth centuries restricted commercial activity in the American colonies and resulted in the constraint of manufacturing. The Acts were a logical extension of British mercantilism, a view according to which the colonies existed primarily to benefit Great Britain. Answer B can be rejected because one Navigation Act forced the colonists to buy more expensive sugar from the British West Indies, rather than the French West Indies. Option C can be eliminated because a positive result of the Navigation Acts was giving the American colonists a monopoly on tobacco by restricting tobacco production in Great Britain itself. Option D can be eliminated because the Acts did not place a tax on shipping goods to Great Britain.

58. D: Indentured servants agreed to work for a set period of time in exchange for transportation to the New World and such basic necessities as food and shelter. They did not receive wages and were generally not highly-educated people. Employers often viewed indentured servants with scorn and treated them as harshly as they treated slaves.

59. D: On a cartogram of population, Nigeria would be bigger than Australia. Even though the area of Australia is several times greater than that of Nigeria, Nigeria has a much larger population. A cartogram is a map on which countries or regions are sized according to a certain variable. So, in a cartogram of population, the country with the most people will be the biggest. The countries would be depicted at their usual size in a contour map of elevation or in a flow-line map. On a Mercator projection, Nigeria would actually be smaller relative to Australia because it is closer to the equator.

60. C: Brazil is the 10th largest producer of oil in the world and the largest in South America. Venezuela is the second largest producer of oil in South America and has the world's largest oil reserves. Bolivia and Guatemala produce oil but are not major producers in Latin America. Uruguay has no significant petroleum production.

61. D: Increases in population growth supplied additional labor forces, helping to enable the Industrial Revolution. These increases were due to the prosperity brought through Europe's Commercial Revolution, which preceded the Industrial Revolution. The rediscovery of concrete, new advances in iron making, and the invention of the steam engine are all examples of developments that occurred during the Industrial Revolution.

62. B: *Marbury v. Madison* started with the election of Thomas Jefferson as third President of the United States. The lame-duck Congress responded by issuing a large number of judicial patents, which the incoming president and Secretary of State refused to deliver to their holders. Marbury, who was to receive a patent as Justice of the Peace, sued to demand delivery. What makes this case important is the decision which declared the judiciary's ability to overturn legislation that conflicted with the Constitution. The case states:

"It is emphatically the province and duty of the judicial department to say what the law is. Those who apply the rule to particular cases must, of necessity, expound and interpret that rule. If two laws conflict with each other, the courts must decide on the operation of each.

"So if a law be in opposition to the Constitution; if both the law and the constitution apply to a particular case, so that the court must either decide that case conformably to the law, disregarding the Constitution; or conformably to the Constitution, disregarding the law; the court must determine which of these conflicting rules governs the case. This is of the very essence of judicial duty.

"If, then, the courts are to regard the Constitution, and the Constitution is superior to any ordinary act of the legislature, the Constitution, and not such ordinary act, must govern the case to which they both apply."

Later, the ruling states: "The judicial power of the United States is extended to all cases arising under the Constitution." It was in this way that the Supreme Court achieved its now traditional ability to strike down laws and to act as the final arbitrator of what is and is not allowed under the US Constitution.

63. A: Article II of the Constitution gives the House of Representatives the sole power of impeachment and the Senate the sole power to convict. The Chief Justice of the United States is empowered to preside over the Senate trial of a President.

64. C: The agricultural revolution. A dependable food supply is essential to all populations. The agricultural revolution, an organized, almost scientific approach to agriculture, increased the food supply necessary for a growing world population.

65. A: The Catholic Church was both powerful and wealthy in medieval Europe. It affected the lives of both the rich and poor; for example, wealthy families often donated to monasteries in exchange for prayers on the donors' behalf. This eliminates option B. Because of these donations, some monasteries became quite wealthy. Rather than being a neutral force, the Catholic Church wielded political power. In medieval times, some claimed that rulers derived their authority to rule from the Catholic Church itself. These facts eliminate options C and D.

66. B: The country and population that moved out and relocated was the large population of Sephardic and Ashkenazi Jews in Algeria when that country became independent from France. The majority of these Algerian Jews evacuated Algeria and repatriated to France after the Second World War. The Chinese population in Singapore (A), the British population in Cayman Islands (C), and the Russian population in Kazakhstan (D) represent situations in which the longtime settler populations and the minority indigenous populations make decolonization impractical (even when the minority and majority are somewhat close in numbers).

67. C: The President must be a natural citizen, be at least 35 years old, and have lived in the US for 14 years. There is no education requirement for becoming President. Truman did not have a college education, but most Presidents have had college degrees.

68. B: Marx's focus in *The Communist Manifesto* (1848) and *Das Kapital* (1867) was on the inevitable conflict between the working class and the capitalists who own the means of production. He identified these two opposing forces as the proletariat and the bourgeoisie.

69. A: Russian involvement in World War I brought social tension in Russia to a head. Contributing factors included military defeats and civilian suffering. Prior to Russia entering the war, Russian factory workers could legally strike, but during the war, it was illegal for them to act collectively. This eliminates answer C. Protests continued during World War I, and the Russian government was overthrown in 1917. This eliminates answer D. Answer B can be rejected because World War I did not go well for the Russian Army; Nicholas III, therefore, had no successes upon which to capitalize.

70. C: The Mississippi Freedom Democratic Party did attend the 1964 Democratic convention; however, they were unable garner Lyndon Johnson's support to unseat the regular delegation from Mississippi. A riot did break out in Watts in 1965, and in the following three years, more riots occurred in Newark, New Jersey and in Detroit, Michigan. These riots were manifestations of the frustrations experienced by blacks regarding racial inequities in American society. Another demonstration of black unrest was the increasing activity of the Black Panthers and the Black Muslims in the 1960s. Both were militant organizations demanding civil rights reforms.

71. A: A smaller box in which some part of the larger map is depicted in greater detail is known as an inset. Insets provide a closer look at parts of the map that the cartographer deems to be more important (for instance, cities, national parks, or historical sites). Often, traffic maps will include several insets depicting the roads in the most congested area of the city. Legends, also known as keys, are the boxes in which the symbols used in the map are explained. A legend, or key, might indicate how railroads and boundaries are depicted, for example. A compass rose indicates how the map is oriented along the north-south axis. It is common for cartographers to tilt a map for ease of display, such that up may not be due north.

72. C: Physical geography focuses on processes and patterns in the natural environment. What people eat in any given geographic region is largely dependent on such environmental factors as climate and the availability of arable land. Religion, family, and language may all be affected by geographical factors, but they are not as immediately affected as dietary preferences.

73. A: Roman civilization developed on the Tiber River, but it is not considered one of the earliest civilizations. Major civilizations developed along the other rivers listed: Chinese civilization developed in the Yangtze and Huang River valleys; Mesopotamian civilization emerged between the Tigris and Euphrates; and Egyptian culture developed in the Nile River valley.

74. C: The Ottoman Empire joined with the Central Powers in 1914 during World War I. The original Triple Alliance was formed by Austria-Hungary, Germany, and Italy in 1882 and renewed in 1902. The Ottoman Empire signed the Turco-German Alliance in August 1914, joining with the Central Powers. In October 1914, with the bombing of Russian ports on the Black Sea, Turkey formally entered World War I. The Allied Powers of the Triple Entente (Great Britain, France, and Russia) declared war on the Ottoman Empire in November 1914.

75. C: Massachusetts did set a valuable example for other states by stipulating that its constitution should be created via a special convention rather than via the legislature. This way, the constitution would take precedence over the legislature, which would be subject to the rules of the constitution. It is not true that twelve states had new constitutions by the end of 1777. By this time, ten of the states had new constitutions. It is not true that Connecticut and Massachusetts retained their colonial charters minus the British parts. Connecticut and Rhode Island were the states that preserved their colonial charters. They simply removed any parts referring to British rule. Massachusetts did not formalize its new constitution in 1778. This state did not actually finish the process of adopting its new constitution until 1780.

76. D: When the FOMC sells bonds, they raise interest rates. This draws money out of the American economy, and attracts foreign investors. This causes the value of the American dollar to rise overseas, which makes American goods more expensive to overseas buyers and causes American exports to drop.

77. B: The Senate Committee on Homeland Security and Government Affairs is a standing committee that oversees and reforms government operations and exercises the congressional power of government oversight.

78. B: Growth in labor organizing was stimulated by organizers wanting to achieve the goal of a shorter workday. However, what they were aiming for in the 1800s was a 10-hour day, not an 8-hour day, which was not realized until 1936. It is true that when the factory system supplanted the cottage industry, owners and workers became separate, and this depersonalized workplaces. Child laborers did conduct the first organized workers' strike in Paterson, NJ, in 1828. Although the first strike did occur this early, there were not a lot of strikes or labor negotiations during this time period due to periodic downturns in the economy, which had the effect of keeping workers dependent and less likely to take action against management. The campaign to attain a 10-hour work day did stimulate a period of growth in labor organizing, but this growth period ended with the depression of 1837.

79. A: Anyone may write a bill, but only a member of Congress can introduce a bill. The President often suggests bills. Bills can change drastically throughout the review process.

80. B: Judges who are eligible to retire but still work are called senior judges. Retired judges who occasionally hear cases are called recalled judges. Both senior and recalled judges handle about 15-20 percent of district and appellate court caseloads.

81. C: Hernán Cortés conquered the Mexican Aztecs in 1519. He had several advantages over the indigenous peoples, including horses, armor for his soldiers, and guns. In addition, Cortés' troops unknowingly transmitted smallpox to the Aztecs, which devastated their population as they had no immunity to this foreign illness. Vasco Núñez de Balboa was the first European explorer to view the Pacific Ocean when he crossed the Isthmus of Panama in 1513. Juan Ponce de León visited and claimed Florida in Spain's name in 1513. Álvar Núñez Cabeza de Vaca was one of only four men out of 400 to return from an expedition led by Pánfilo de Narváez in 1528 and was responsible for spreading the story of the Seven Cities of Cibola (the "cities of gold").

82. D: Keynes was an influential advocate of government intervention in a domestic economy for the purpose of stimulating economic growth. Keynes believed that appropriate government action could help end a recession more quickly; such measures might involve deficit spending. Because of this, and because Keynes is not associated with the view that deficit spending leads to inflation, option A can be eliminated. Additionally, Keynes is not closely associated with advocating government action to break up monopolies; this eliminates option B. Finally, option C can be eliminated because it describes Say's Law, which is in fact the opposite of Keynes's law: demand creates its own supply.

83. B: Although the nation faced recession, the US dollar made a comeback in world currency during the fall of 2008. Choice A cannot be concluded from the information because it is about the dollar and the euro, not the whole world. Choice C is incorrect as well; the euro fell in 2008 against the dollar. The wisdom of buying stocks cannot be known from the information given. So, choice D is incorrect.

84. C: A person who has taken out a fixed-rate loan can benefit from inflation by paying back the loan with dollars that are less valuable than they were when the loan was taken out. In the other examples, inflation harms the individual or entity.

85. C: With its emphasis on an individual's relationship with God and personal responsibility for salvation, the religious reformation sparked by Martin Luther in 1517 contributed to a rise in individualism. Rather than weakening the civil authorities in Europe, the Reformation served to strengthen many secular authorities by undermining the authority of the Catholic Church. This eliminates answer B. Although the Reformation deemphasized the Virgin Mary, it influenced improvements to education for women and girls, particularly in Germany. This eliminates answer A. Finally, option D can be rejected because the Catholic Church underwent its own internal reformation, in part due to Luther's Reformation.

86. D: According to Article III of the Constitution, Justices of the Supreme Court, judges of the courts of appeals and district courts, and judges of the Court of International Trade are appointed by the president with the confirmation of the Senate. The judicial branch of the government is the only one not elected by the people.

87. D: The Triple Alliance allowed the city-states to conquer city-states and land by combining forces against mutual enemies. The Triple Alliance and its conquered areas are commonly thought of as the Aztec Empire. While some conquered areas did rebel against the Aztec Empire at the time the Spanish conquistadores arrived, such rebellion did not specifically concern the city-states of the Triple Alliance. Texcoco and Tlacopan did not use the Alliance as a front against Tenochtitlan. The Triple Alliance had nothing to do with the number of annual human sacrifices. This eliminates options A, B, and C.

88. D: The Judiciary Act established the Supreme Court, district courts, circuit courts, and the office of attorney general in 1789. George Washington was inaugurated president in 1789.

89. C: One geographical concept is distance. For example, product prices are affected by the cost of transportation, which in turn is affected by how far away raw materials are from the factories that process them, and prices for land closer to highways are higher than for land farther away from them. Location is another geography concept. Absolute location is determined by a place's latitude and longitude, not land prices (A). Relative location is determined by a region's changing characteristics, which surrounding areas can influence; one example is that land costs more in urban than rural areas. Relative location is not determined by latitude and longitude (B). Achievability is related to the accessibility of a geographical area; for example, villages with surrounding forests or swamps are less accessible than those on beaches. The dependency of an area, and hence its achievability, *does* change (D) as its technology, transportation, and economy change.

90. D: Formulated during the Truman administration and enduring throughout the Cold War, the policy of containment was intended to prevent the spread of Communism after World War II. It served as a rationale for many military decisions during the Korean and Vietnamese conflicts.

91. C: Pennsylvania is most closely associated with William Penn, a Quaker of the Society of Friends. Penn hoped to establish a colony where Quakers would be free to practice their religion. This colony offered religious tolerance toward many other religions as well; Dutch Mennonites and German Baptists were among those who came to Pennsylvania. The desire for freedom of the press was not a salient concern in the motivation for colonizing Pennsylvania; this eliminates option A. Although some European colonists came to Pennsylvania for economic reasons, these are not best understood in terms of escaping high taxes or trade restrictions. This eliminates options B and D.

92. D: The West Bank contains a number of significant natural water reserves (aquifers). These aquifers are an important source of water not only to the Palestinians living in the West Bank but to Israel as well. Access to these aquifers is a significant motivation to Israel's continuing control of the West Bank. The West Bank does not border the Mediterranean Sea; this eliminates option A. There are no significant oil reserves in the West Bank; this eliminates option B. Though there are olive groves in the West Bank, olives and olive products are far less important resources to Israel than water.

93. D: The process of overriding a presidential veto is described in Article I, Section 7 of the Constitution. It requires a two-thirds vote from both the House and the Senate.

94. B: The Homestead Act, passed in 1862, gave settlers 160 acres of land at no monetary cost in exchange for a commitment to cultivating the land for five years. Other acts aided settlers in different ways, such as the Timber Culture Act, which provided farmers with 160 acres in exchange for planting trees on one quarter of the acreage. The Desert Land Act gave buyers a cheap price on acreage (25 cents per acre for 640 acres) if they would be willing to irrigate the land, therefore improving the quality of the land in the region. The Homestead Act was instrumental in promoting westward migration, in that it helped settlers establish themselves with a residence (homestead) and encouraged the production of tradeable goods through cultivating that land.

95. A: The earliest written language in Mesopotamia was Sumerian. Ancient Sumerians began writing this language around 3500 BC. Elamite, from Iran, was the language spoken by the ancient Elamites and was the official language of the Persian Empire from the 6th to 4th centuries BC. Written Linear Elamite was used for a very short time in the late 3rd century BC. The written Elamite cuneiform, used from about 2500 to 331 BC, was an adaptation of the Akkadian cuneiform. Akkadian is the earliest found Semitic language. Written Akkadian cuneiform first appeared in texts by circa 2800 BC, and full Akkadian texts appeared by circa 2500 BC. The Akkadian cuneiform writing system is ultimately a derivative of the ancient Sumerian cuneiform writing system, although these two spoken languages were not related linguistically. Aramaic is another Semitic language, but unlike Akkadian, Aramaic is not now extinct. Old Aramaic, the written language of the Old Testament and the spoken language used by Jesus Christ, was current from 1100 BC to 200 AD. Middle Aramaic, used from 200 to 1200 AD, included literary Syriac (Christian groups developed the writing system of Syriac in order to be able to write spoken Aramaic) and was the written language of the Jewish books of Biblical commentary (Namely, the Talmud, the Targum, and the Midrash). Modern Aramaic has been used from 1200 AD to the present.

96. B: The witch hunts reflect a time when belief in magic and superstition was widespread. Many historians view them as a reaction to the social and economic changes of the Early Modern period.

97. A: Samuel Morse invented a code of dots and dashes that became known as Morse Code, and in 1844 the first message was transmitted over a telegraph line. Morse code played an important role in communications during the Civil War.

98. D: America is a common law country because English common law was adopted in all states except Louisiana. Common law is based on precedent and changes over time. Each state develops its own common laws.

99. D: Local governments are usually divided into counties and municipalities. Municipalities oversee parks and recreation services, police and fire departments, housing services, emergency medical services, municipal courts, transportation services, and public works.

100. D: While rising prices may hurt many members of an economy, those same rising prices may benefit other members of the same economy. For example, rising prices may help those who sell goods and services and are able to keep their costs of production low, increasing their profit margin. Meanwhile, rising prices can hurt consumers because their income is now able to purchase fewer goods and services than before.

101. D: All of these statements are correct regarding consequences of the French Revolution. French historian and political analyst Alexis de Tocqueville (famous for his book Democracy in America) saw the French Revolution as signifying the increasing social self-awareness of the middle class as it gained wealth (A). Conservative, anti-French Revolution philosopher and political theorist Edmund Burke believed that the Revolution was started by a small faction of conspirators who had no valid claims (B) for revolting and who brainwashed the public into subversive action against the status quo. Those persons who subscribe to Marxist philosophy focus on the rising up of the lower and middle working classes (C) against elite royalty who enjoyed unfair privileges.

102. B: The Presidential Succession Act lists the Speaker of the House, president pro tempore of the Senate, and secretary of state next in succession after the vice president. However, anyone who succeeds as president must meet all of the legal qualifications.

103. D: Ziggurats were towers dedicated to gods; their prevalence indicates the importance of religion in Mesopotamian culture. The other options can be rejected because they pair accurate facts about Mesopotamia with inaccurate summaries of the purposes of the ziggurats. For example, while rulers of Mesopotamian cities fought among themselves, ziggurats were not used as lookouts. This eliminates option A. Although astrology was practiced in Mesopotamia, ziggurats did not function as places for stargazing or observing the sky. Finally, Mesopotamian cities were ruled by kings, but the ziggurats were not dedicated to them. This eliminates options B and C.

104. D: In 1954 the Warren Court unanimously reversed the separate but equal ruling of *Plessy* v. *Ferguson* in 1896.

105. B: The cost of the French and Indian War was high, and after the war, Great Britain sought to have the American colonies help pay for the war through measures such as higher taxes. This led to colonial resentment, in part because the colonists lacked representation in the British government. Option A can be rejected because, rather than limiting oversight on the American colonies, Great Britain reasserted its authority there. The Proclamation of 1763, although it did limit the location of new American colonies, was modified in response to colonial demands prior to the American Revolution. This eliminates choice C. Option D can be rejected because the French and Indian War (in which American colonists participated) actually decreased colonial dependence on the British military.

106. B: After World War I, the United States passed the Immigration Act of 1924, which regulated the number of immigrants in part according to their national origin. The United States sought to avoid the problems of Europe and other nations by limiting the number of foreigners who entered the United States. Option A can be rejected because quite soon after World War I, both inflation and unemployment were significant problems in the United States. Option C can be rejected because in the years immediately following World War I, the United States did not build its navy even to the extent allowed by treaty. Finally, option D can be rejected because after World War I, the United States made arrangements for the US to have access to oil in Colombia and in Middle Eastern countries.

107. D: Political Action Committees (PACs) raise money for political candidates and are formed by business, labor, or other special interest groups. They may donate $5,000 per candidate per election, but can contribute larger amounts for party-building activities.

108. A: In the 1780s, the French national debt was very high. The French nobility adamantly resisted attempts by King Louis XVI to reform tax laws, which led to a high tax burden on the French peasantry. The French government spent almost 50% of its national expenditures on debt-related payments during the 1780s; thus, it could not and did not spend almost 70% to finance luxuries for the French nobility. This eliminates choice B. King Louis XVI temporarily banned the guild system to bolster, rather than stifle, free trade. Because this system gave skilled craftsmen economic advantages, journeymen opposed ending the system. This eliminates choice D. Regardless of the status of guilds before the French Revolution, French society did not offer many opportunities for upward social mobility. Few peasants were able to advance. This eliminates choice C.

109. D: The popularity of hockey in Canada and the northern United States is an example of direct diffusion. Direct diffusion is the transfer of cultural practices and ideas between two groups living in close proximity to each other. Expansion diffusion, also known as forced diffusion, is the transfer of cultural practices from a subjugating culture to a subjugated culture. One example of expansion diffusion was the Western imposition of trading practices on China during the nineteenth and early twentieth centuries. Indirect diffusion is the spread of cultural traits over a long distance without there necessarily being any direct contact between the cultures. The popularity in the United States of henna tattoos, which originated in India, is an example of indirect diffusion.

110. B: The Virginia Company of London was based in London, not Massachusetts. It had a charter to colonize American land between the Hudson and Cape Fear rivers. The other Virginia Company was the Virginia Company of Plymouth, which was based in the American colony of Plymouth, Massachusetts. It had a charter to colonize North America between the Potomac River and the northern boundary of Maine. Both Virginia Companies were joint-stock companies, which had often been used by England for trading with other countries.

111. B: Most presidents have only served two terms, a precedent established by George Washington. Ulysses S. Grant and Theodore Roosevelt sought third terms; however, only Franklin D. Roosevelt served more than two terms. He served a third term and won a fourth, but died in its first year. The 22nd Amendment was passed by Congress in 1947 and ratified in 1951. It officially limited the president to two terms, and a vice president who serves two years as president only can be elected for one term.

112. B: Johann Gutenberg's printing press led to increased scientific knowledge and advancement as scientific texts were printed and dispersed throughout Europe. Because the distribution of such texts extended outside of Germany, options C and D may be eliminated. Gutenberg Bibles were printed using Gutenberg's press, and thus Gutenberg's invention was likely a factor in the Reformation of the Catholic Church. In fact, Martin Luther's Ninety-Five Theses (against the Catholic Church) were printed using a printing press. However, this reformation occurred alongside, rather than in place of, the advancement of scientific knowledge. This eliminates option A.

113. A: If there is a tie in the Electoral College, each state's delegation in the House of Representatives gets a vote, and the majority wins. The Senate votes on the Vice President who becomes acting President if the House does not come to a conclusion by Inauguration Day. It is possible for the Senate to tie because the former Vice President is not allowed to vote.

114. A: The federal government has three branches: executive, including the president, the vice president, and the president's cabinet; legislative, including the House of Representatives and the Senate; and judicial, including the Supreme Court and the court system.

115. B: A topographic map uses contour lines to show the shape and elevation of the land. Political maps identify state and national boundaries as well as capitals and major cities. Resource maps show the natural resources and economic activities in a region. Road maps are used mainly for driving directions and trip planning.

116. D: A relative location for Milwaukee is 100 miles north of Chicago. Relative location is a description of placement in terms of some other location. The latitude and longitude of Milwaukee are its absolute location because they describe its placement relative to an arbitrary but inalterable system of positioning. To say that Milwaukee is in Wisconsin or on Lake Michigan does not provide as much detail as answer choice D because Wisconsin is a big state and because Lake Michigan is a large body of water.

117. C: The Druids were neither ignored nor tolerated by the Romans. Conversely, the Druids were viewed as "non-Roman" and therefore were suppressed. Augustus (63 BC–14 AD) forbade Romans to practice Druid rites. According to Pliny, the Senate under Tiberius (42 BC–37 AD) issued a decree suppressing Druids, and in 54 AD, Claudius outlawed Druid rites entirely. It is correct that the Romans generally protected the Jews up until the rebellion in Judea in 66 AD. In fact, Julius Caesar circumvented the Roman laws against "secret societies" by designating Jewish synagogues as "colleges," which in essence permitted Jews to have freedom of worship. After the rebellion in Judea, according to Suetonius, the Emperor Claudius appeared to have expelled all Jews, probably including early Christians, from Rome. The Roman Empire viewed Christianity as a Jewish sect, which was how Christianity began, for 200 years following its emergence. It is also correct that according to Tacitus, when much of the public saw the Emperor Nero as responsible for the Great Fire of Rome in 64 AD, Nero blamed the Christians for the fire in order to deflect guilt from himself. Following their persecution of Jews, the Roman Empire would continue to persecute Christians for the next two centuries.

118. D: Political corruption was not an immediate effect of the rapid urban growth during this time. The accelerated growth of cities in America did soon result in services being unable to keep up with that growth. The results of this included deficiencies in clean water delivery and garbage collection, causing poor sanitation. That poor sanitation led to outbreaks of cholera and typhus, as well as typhoid fever epidemics. Police and fire fighting services could not keep up with the population increases, and were often inadequate. With people moving to the cities at such a fast rate, there were also deficits in housing and public transportation.

119. B: The Aztec was a Mesoamerican civilization of the pre-Columbian period. The Aztecs were ethnic groups of central Mexico dominant in large areas of Mesoamerica in the 14th-16th centuries. The Inca (A) was an Andean civilization from Peru. The Incas had the largest pre-Columbian empire, including Peru and major parts of Argentina, Bolivia, Chile, Colombia, and Ecuador in the 15th and 16th centuries. The Moche (C) was an Andean civilization in northern Peru between 100 and 800; this civilization is known for their artworks, architecture, and irrigation systems. They built the Huaca del Sol, an adobe pyramid that was the largest pre-Columbian construction in Peru before the Conquistadores destroyed part of it. The Cañaris (D) was an Andean tribe living in the south central part of Ecuador. The Incas eventually conquered the Cañaris, but the Cañaris resisted this conquest for many years. They were also known for their architecture, which had many Incan influences. They existed until their main city, Tumebamba, was destroyed by Atahualpa during the Inca Civil War in the 16th century.

120. D: Niccolò Machiavelli, perhaps best known for his book The Prince, was an Italian Renaissance political philosopher noted for writing more realistic representations and rational interpretations of politics. In The Prince, he popularized the political concept of "the ends justify the means." Dante Alighieri was a great poet famous for his Commedia (additionally labeled Divina by contemporary poet and author Boccaccio, who wrote the Decameron and other works) or Divine Comedy, a trilogy consisting of Inferno, Purgatorio, and Paradiso (Hell, Purgatory, and Heaven). Dante's work helped propel the transition from the Medieval period to the Renaissance. Francesco Petrarca, known in English as Petrarch, was famous for his lyrical poetry, particularly sonnets.

121. A: The attitudes of American colonists after the 1763 Treaty of Paris ended the French and Indian War was not a direct contributor to the American Revolution. American colonists had a supportive attitude toward Great Britain then, and were proud of the part they played in winning the war. Their good will was not returned by British leaders, who looked down on American colonials and sought to increase their imperial power over them. Even in 1761, a sign of Americans' objections to having their liberty curtailed by the British was seen when Boston attorney James Otis argued in court against the Writs of Assistance, search warrants to enforce England's mercantilist trade restrictions, as violating the kinds of natural laws espoused during the Enlightenment. Lord George Grenville's aggressive program to defend the North American frontier in the wake of Chief Pontiac's attacks included stricter enforcement of the Navigation Acts, the Proclamation of 1763, the Sugar Act (or Revenue Act), the Currency Act, and most of all the Stamp Act. Colonists objected to these as taxation without representation. Other events followed in this taxation dispute, which further eroded Americans' relationship with British government, including the Townshend Acts, the Massachusetts Circular Letter, the Boston Massacre, the Tea Act, and the resulting Boston Tea Party. Finally, with Britain's passage of the Intolerable Acts and the Americans' First Continental Congress, which was followed by Britain's military aggression against American resistance, actual warfare began in 1775. While not all of the colonies wanted war or independence by then, things changed by 1776, and Jefferson's Declaration of Independence was formalized. James Otis, Samuel Adams, Patrick Henry, the Sons of Liberty, and the Stamp Act Congress also contributed to the beginning of the American Revolution.

122. A: The postwar conference that brought US-Soviet differences to light was the Potsdam conference in July of 1945. The conference at Yalta, in February of 1945, resulted in the division of Germany into Allied-controlled zones. The Dumbarton Oaks conference (1944) established a Security Council, on which with the US, England, Soviet Union, France, and China served as the five permanent members. Each of the permanent members had veto power, and a General Assembly, with limited power, was also established. The Tehran conference included FDR's proposal for a new international organization to take the place of the League of Nations. This idea would later be realized in the form of the United Nations.

123. A: In geography, location—specifically, relative location—determines things like land prices based on the characteristics of an area, which are affected by nearby regions. An example of distance (B) is that land that is close to major highways is more expensive, while land far from main thoroughfares costs less. One example of pattern (C) in geography is that where rock folds form mountains (fold regions), the rivers accordingly form trellis patterns. Another example of pattern, in geographically oriented human behavior, is that settlements in mountainous areas form mainly spreading patterns. An example of interaction (D) in geography is when an industrial city needs raw materials from a rural village for production, and the village needs the city both as a market to buy its resources and for its industrial products: their mutual interdependence creates interaction between them.

124. C: Pope Urban II's plan for an army made up of previously trained military personnel was thwarted by the popular excitement concerning the First Crusade. This led to the creation of large armies primarily made up of untrained, unskilled, undisciplined, and ill- or unequipped soldiers, most of whom were recruited from the poorest levels of society. These armies were the first to set forth on the Crusade, which became known as the People's Crusade. Even though some of these armies contained knights, they were ultimately ineffective as fighting forces. These armies were prone to rioting and raiding surrounding areas for food and supplies and were viewed as a destabilizing influence by local leaders. They were defeated in battle and many converted to Islam to avoid being killed.

125. D: In the Dred Scott decision of 1857, the Court ruled that no slave or descendant of slaves could ever be a United States citizen. It also declared the Missouri Compromise of 1820 to be unconstitutional, clearing the way for the expansion of slavery in new American territories. This ruling pleased Southerners and outraged the North, further dividing the nation and setting the stage for war.

126. A: The distance between Buenos Aires and Tokyo is approximately 18,060 km. The process of converting a scaled distance to a real distance is fairly simple. In this case, multiply the number of centimeters by the number of kilometers represented by each of these centimeters. The calculation can be expressed as (35 cm) (516 km/1 cm). Because centimeters are in the numerator of the first term and the denominator of the second term, they cancel out, leaving kilometers as the unit.

127. A: Central to the Manifest Destiny (the belief that it was the right and duty of the United States to expand its borders) was the belief that the United States had a duty to spread democracy, offering a democratic example to the rest of the world. Option B was much less significant; proponents of the Manifest Destiny were more interested in spreading what they regarded as civilization than in spreading material prosperity in particular. Option C can be rejected because the issue of slavery was controversial; some proponents of the Manifest Destiny were decided supporters of slavery and others were not. Option D can be rejected because religious freedom was not a central issue for proponents of Manifest Destiny.

128. C: About 30 percent of the surface of the Earth is covered by land.

129. D: The Louisiana Purchase actually increased the US's territory by 100% overnight, not 50%. The Louisiana territory doubled the size of the nation. It is true that Jefferson initially sent a delegation to Paris to see if Napoleon would agree to sell only New Orleans to the United States. It is also true that Napoleon, who expected America to encroach on Louisiana, decided to avoid this by offering to sell the entire territory to the US It is likewise true that America only had authority to buy New Orleans. Nevertheless, the delegation accepted Napoleon's offer of all of Louisiana. Due to his belief in strict interpretation of the Constitution, Jefferson did require approval from Congress to make the purchase. When his advisors characterized the purchase as being within his purview based on the presidential power to make treaties, Congress agreed.

130. B: The Trail of Tears was the forcible removal of Native American tribes from their homes in the Southeastern US to Oklahoma. The name came due to the high number of Native Americans who died on the journey.

131. B: To determine the shortest route between Lima and Lisbon, Tracy should use an azimuthal projection with Lisbon at the center. An azimuthal projection depicts one hemisphere of the globe as a circle. A straight line drawn from the center of the map to any point represents the shortest possible distance between those two points. Tracy could obtain her objective, then, with an azimuthal projection in which either Lisbon or Lima were at the center. If the North Pole were at the center, the map would not include Lima because this city is in the Southern Hemisphere. A Robinson projection approximates the sizes and shapes of landmasses but does distort in some ways, particularly near the poles.

132. B: The Seven Years' War was a global military conflict. In the Americas, the conflict was largely between Western European countries, particularly Great Britain and France.

133. C: The New Kingdom was the period during which no more pyramids were built in Egypt. The Pyramids were built between the years of 2630 and 1814 BC, and the New Kingdom spanned from circa 1550–1070 BC. As a result, the last pyramid was built approximately 264 years before the New Kingdom began. 2630 BC marked the beginning of the reign of the first Pharaoh, Djoser, who had the first pyramid built at Saqqara. 1814 BC marked the end of the reign of the last Pharaoh, Amenemhat III, who had the last pyramid built at Hawara. In between these years, a succession of pharaohs built many pyramids. The Old Kingdom encompasses both the Third and Fourth Dynasties; therefore, all three of these choices encompass pyramid-building periods. Djoser's had his first pyramid built during the Third Dynasty. The Pharaohs Kufu, Khafre, and Menkaure, respectively, built the famous Pyramids of Giza during their reigns between circa 2575 and 2467 BC, the period of the Fourth Dynasty. The Middle Kingdom encompassed the 11th through 14th Dynasties, from circa 2080 to 1640 BC—also within the time period (2630–1814 BC) when pyramids were built by the Pharaohs.

134. D: Federalists who helped frame the Constitution believed the central government needed to be stronger than what was established under the Articles of Confederation. Anti-federalists were against this and feared a strong federal government. A system of checks and balances was established to prevent the central government from taking too much power.

135. C: The passage describes the 200-year period known as *Pax Romana.* Choice A is incorrect because the Julio-Claudian line held power in Rome for less than a century. Choice B refers to a succession of emperors that lasted less than one hundred years. The emperors in choice D only ruled from 69 AD to 96 AD.

136. D: The Battle of Chapultepec, a citadel outside Mexico City, was last major US assault prior to the US capture of Mexico City. When the United States won the battle, the Mexican defensive line collapsed, leaving the way open for US troops to march on the Mexican capital. The assault on Chapultepec was organized by US General Winfield Scott; although General Zachary Taylor was considered an American hero due in part to his performance during the US-Mexican War, this was not because of any involvement with the Battle of Chapultepec. This eliminates option A. Because the US won the battle, option B can be rejected. General Santa Ana was not personally involved in the battle, eliminating option C.

137. A: Nobles did not gain more power during the Age of Absolutism. Though the monarchs of that period often did require nobility to live in their royal palaces, this practice brought the nobility less power rather than more power, since it forced the nobles into dependence upon the monarchs for their income while officials of the state governed the noblemen's lands. In addition to the nobility, the Church also experienced a loss of influence (B) during this period as the monarch and the state gained more power, and state laws were developed. Partitioning common under the feudal system no longer took place (C) as most or all of the power was consolidated to the monarch. Since choice A was not a characteristic of the Age of Absolutism, choice D, all of these, is incorrect.

138. B: Economists understand the true cost of an action as not only its monetary cost but the cost of other opportunities missed as a result of pursuing that action. For example, if a person chooses to go to school rather than working, the cost of the action involves not only tuition and other associated fees and expenses, but the money one would have earned working, as well as the time one could have spent pursuing other activities. The concept of opportunity cost is not described by options (A), (C), or (D), each of which is concerned only with monetary costs. Each of these answers can be rejected on that basis.

139. B: James Madison was a close friend of Thomas Jefferson and supported a stronger central government. George Mason and Robert Yates were both against expanding federal authority over the states. Benjamin Franklin was a proponent of a strong federal government, but he was from Massachusetts.

140. A: In 1880, ill sentiment was high against Chinese laborers. This sentiment led to the reversal of the Burlingame Treaty of 1868, and thus legal immigration was stopped for a period of 10 years.

How to Overcome Test Anxiety

Just the thought of taking a test is enough to make most people a little nervous. A test is an important event that can have a long-term impact on your future, so it's important to take it seriously and it's natural to feel anxious about performing well. But just because anxiety is normal, that doesn't mean that it's helpful in test taking, or that you should simply accept it as part of your life. Anxiety can have a variety of effects. These effects can be mild, like making you feel slightly nervous, or severe, like blocking your ability to focus or remember even a simple detail.

If you experience test anxiety—whether severe or mild—it's important to know how to beat it. To discover this, first you need to understand what causes test anxiety.

Causes of Test Anxiety

While we often think of anxiety as an uncontrollable emotional state, it can actually be caused by simple, practical things. One of the most common causes of test anxiety is that a person does not feel adequately prepared for their test. This feeling can be the result of many different issues such as poor study habits or lack of organization, but the most common culprit is time management. Starting to study too late, failing to organize your study time to cover all of the material, or being distracted while you study will mean that you're not well prepared for the test. This may lead to cramming the night before, which will cause you to be physically and mentally exhausted for the test. Poor time management also contributes to feelings of stress, fear, and hopelessness as you realize you are not well prepared but don't know what to do about it.

Other times, test anxiety is not related to your preparation for the test but comes from unresolved fear. This may be a past failure on a test, or poor performance on tests in general. It may come from comparing yourself to others who seem to be performing better or from the stress of living up to expectations. Anxiety may be driven by fears of the future—how failure on this test would affect your educational and career goals. These fears are often completely irrational, but they can still negatively impact your test performance.

Elements of Test Anxiety

As mentioned earlier, test anxiety is considered to be an emotional state, but it has physical and mental components as well. Sometimes you may not even realize that you are suffering from test anxiety until you notice the physical symptoms. These can include trembling hands, rapid heartbeat, sweating, nausea, and tense muscles. Extreme anxiety may lead to fainting or vomiting. Obviously, any of these symptoms can have a negative impact on testing. It is important to recognize them as soon as they begin to occur so that you can address the problem before it damages your performance.

The mental components of test anxiety include trouble focusing and inability to remember learned information. During a test, your mind is on high alert, which can help you recall information and stay focused for an extended period of time. However, anxiety interferes with your mind's natural processes, causing you to blank out, even on the questions you know well. The strain of testing during anxiety makes it difficult to stay focused, especially on a test that may take several hours. Extreme anxiety can take a huge mental toll, making it difficult not only to recall test information but even to understand the test questions or pull your thoughts together.

Effects of Test Anxiety

Test anxiety is like a disease—if left untreated, it will get progressively worse. Anxiety leads to poor performance, and this reinforces the feelings of fear and failure, which in turn lead to poor performances on subsequent tests. It can grow from a mild nervousness to a crippling condition. If allowed to progress, test anxiety can have a big impact on your schooling, and consequently on your future.

Test anxiety can spread to other parts of your life. Anxiety on tests can become anxiety in any stressful situation, and blanking on a test can turn into panicking in a job situation. But fortunately, you don't have to let anxiety rule your testing and determine your grades. There are a number of relatively simple steps you can take to move past anxiety and function normally on a test and in the rest of life.

Physical Steps for Beating Test Anxiety

While test anxiety is a serious problem, the good news is that it can be overcome. It doesn't have to control your ability to think and remember information. While it may take time, you can begin taking steps today to beat anxiety.

Just as your first hint that you may be struggling with anxiety comes from the physical symptoms, the first step to treating it is also physical. Rest is crucial for having a clear, strong mind. If you are tired, it is much easier to give in to anxiety. But if you establish good sleep habits, your body and mind will be ready to perform optimally, without the strain of exhaustion. Additionally, sleeping well helps you to retain information better, so you're more likely to recall the answers when you see the test questions.

Getting good sleep means more than going to bed on time. It's important to allow your brain time to relax. Take study breaks from time to time so it doesn't get overworked, and don't study right before bed. Take time to rest your mind before trying to rest your body, or you may find it difficult to fall asleep.

Along with sleep, other aspects of physical health are important in preparing for a test. Good nutrition is vital for good brain function. Sugary foods and drinks may give a burst of energy but this burst is followed by a crash, both physically and emotionally. Instead, fuel your body with protein and vitamin-rich foods.

Also, drink plenty of water. Dehydration can lead to headaches and exhaustion, especially if your brain is already under stress from the rigors of the test. Particularly if your test is a long one, drink water during the breaks. And if possible, take an energy-boosting snack to eat between sections.

Along with sleep and diet, a third important part of physical health is exercise. Maintaining a steady workout schedule is helpful, but even taking 5-minute study breaks to walk can help get your blood pumping faster and clear your head. Exercise also releases endorphins, which contribute to a positive feeling and can help combat test anxiety.

When you nurture your physical health, you are also contributing to your mental health. If your body is healthy, your mind is much more likely to be healthy as well. So take time to rest, nourish your body with healthy food and water, and get moving as much as possible. Taking these physical steps will make you stronger and more able to take the mental steps necessary to overcome test anxiety.

Mental Steps for Beating Test Anxiety

Working on the mental side of test anxiety can be more challenging, but as with the physical side, there are clear steps you can take to overcome it. As mentioned earlier, test anxiety often stems from lack of preparation, so the obvious solution is to prepare for the test. Effective studying may be the most important weapon you have for beating test anxiety, but you can and should employ several other mental tools to combat fear.

First, boost your confidence by reminding yourself of past success—tests or projects that you aced. If you're putting as much effort into preparing for this test as you did for those, there's no reason you should expect to fail here. Work hard to prepare; then trust your preparation.

Second, surround yourself with encouraging people. It can be helpful to find a study group, but be sure that the people you're around will encourage a positive attitude. If you spend time with others who are anxious or cynical, this will only contribute to your own anxiety. Look for others who are motivated to study hard from a desire to succeed, not from a fear of failure.

Third, reward yourself. A test is physically and mentally tiring, even without anxiety, and it can be helpful to have something to look forward to. Plan an activity following the test, regardless of the outcome, such as going to a movie or getting ice cream.

When you are taking the test, if you find yourself beginning to feel anxious, remind yourself that you know the material. Visualize successfully completing the test. Then take a few deep, relaxing breaths and return to it. Work through the questions carefully but with confidence, knowing that you are capable of succeeding.

Developing a healthy mental approach to test taking will also aid in other areas of life. Test anxiety affects more than just the actual test—it can be damaging to your mental health and even contribute to depression. It's important to beat test anxiety before it becomes a problem for more than testing.

Study Strategy

Being prepared for the test is necessary to combat anxiety, but what does being prepared look like? You may study for hours on end and still not feel prepared. What you need is a strategy for test prep. The next few pages outline our recommended steps to help you plan out and conquer the challenge of preparation.

Step 1: Scope Out the Test

Learn everything you can about the format (multiple choice, essay, etc.) and what will be on the test. Gather any study materials, course outlines, or sample exams that may be available. Not only will this help you to prepare, but knowing what to expect can help to alleviate test anxiety.

Step 2: Map Out the Material

Look through the textbook or study guide and make note of how many chapters or sections it has. Then divide these over the time you have. For example, if a book has 15 chapters and you have five days to study, you need to cover three chapters each day. Even better, if you have the time, leave an extra day at the end for overall review after you have gone through the material in depth.

If time is limited, you may need to prioritize the material. Look through it and make note of which sections you think you already have a good grasp on, and which need review. While you are studying, skim quickly through the familiar sections and take more time on the challenging parts.

Write out your plan so you don't get lost as you go. Having a written plan also helps you feel more in control of the study, so anxiety is less likely to arise from feeling overwhelmed at the amount to cover.

Step 3: Gather Your Tools

Decide what study method works best for you. Do you prefer to highlight in the book as you study and then go back over the highlighted portions? Or do you type out notes of the important information? Or is it helpful to make flashcards that you can carry with you? Assemble the pens, index cards, highlighters, post-it notes, and any other materials you may need so you won't be distracted by getting up to find things while you study.

If you're having a hard time retaining the information or organizing your notes, experiment with different methods. For example, try color-coding by subject with colored pens, highlighters, or post-it notes. If you learn better by hearing, try recording yourself reading your notes so you can listen while in the car, working out, or simply sitting at your desk. Ask a friend to quiz you from your flashcards, or try teaching someone the material to solidify it in your mind.

Step 4: Create Your Environment

It's important to avoid distractions while you study. This includes both the obvious distractions like visitors and the subtle distractions like an uncomfortable chair (or a too-comfortable couch that makes you want to fall asleep). Set up the best study environment possible: good lighting and a comfortable work area. If background music helps you focus, you may want to turn it on, but otherwise keep the room quiet. If you are using a computer to take notes, be sure you don't have any other windows open, especially applications like social media, games, or anything else that could distract you. Silence your phone and turn off notifications. Be sure to keep water close by so you stay hydrated while you study (but avoid unhealthy drinks and snacks).

Also, take into account the best time of day to study. Are you freshest first thing in the morning? Try to set aside some time then to work through the material. Is your mind clearer in the afternoon or evening? Schedule your study session then. Another method is to study at the same time of day that you will take the test, so that your brain gets used to working on the material at that time and will be ready to focus at test time.

Step 5: Study!

Once you have done all the study preparation, it's time to settle into the actual studying. Sit down, take a few moments to settle your mind so you can focus, and begin to follow your study plan. Don't give in to distractions or let yourself procrastinate. This is your time to prepare so you'll be ready to fearlessly approach the test. Make the most of the time and stay focused.

Of course, you don't want to burn out. If you study too long you may find that you're not retaining the information very well. Take regular study breaks. For example, taking five minutes out of every hour to walk briskly, breathing deeply and swinging your arms, can help your mind stay fresh.

As you get to the end of each chapter or section, it's a good idea to do a quick review. Remind yourself of what you learned and work on any difficult parts. When you feel that you've mastered the material, move on to the next part. At the end of your study session, briefly skim through your notes again.

But while review is helpful, cramming last minute is NOT. If at all possible, work ahead so that you won't need to fit all your study into the last day. Cramming overloads your brain with more information than it can process and retain, and your tired mind may struggle to recall even previously learned information when it is overwhelmed with last-minute study. Also, the urgent nature of cramming and the stress placed on your brain contribute to anxiety. You'll be more likely to go to the test feeling unprepared and having trouble thinking clearly.

So don't cram, and don't stay up late before the test, even just to review your notes at a leisurely pace. Your brain needs rest more than it needs to go over the information again. In fact, plan to finish your studies by noon or early afternoon the day before the test. Give your brain the rest of the day to relax or focus on other things, and get a good night's sleep. Then you will be fresh for the test and better able to recall what you've studied.

Step 6: Take a Practice Test

Many courses offer sample tests, either online or in the study materials. This is an excellent resource to check whether you have mastered the material, as well as to prepare for the test format and environment.

Check the test format ahead of time: the number of questions, the type (multiple choice, free response, etc.), and the time limit. Then create a plan for working through them. For example, if you have 30 minutes to take a 60-question test, your limit is 30 seconds per question. Spend less time on the questions you know well so that you can take more time on the difficult ones.

If you have time to take several practice tests, take the first one open book, with no time limit. Work through the questions at your own pace and make sure you fully understand them. Gradually work up to taking a test under test conditions: sit at a desk with all study materials put away and set a timer. Pace yourself to make sure you finish the test with time to spare and go back to check your answers if you have time.

After each test, check your answers. On the questions you missed, be sure you understand why you missed them. Did you misread the question (tests can use tricky wording)? Did you forget the information? Or was it something you hadn't learned? Go back and study any shaky areas that the practice tests reveal.

Taking these tests not only helps with your grade, but also aids in combating test anxiety. If you're already used to the test conditions, you're less likely to worry about it, and working through tests until you're scoring well gives you a confidence boost. Go through the practice tests until you feel comfortable, and then you can go into the test knowing that you're ready for it.

Test Tips

On test day, you should be confident, knowing that you've prepared well and are ready to answer the questions. But aside from preparation, there are several test day strategies you can employ to maximize your performance.

First, as stated before, get a good night's sleep the night before the test (and for several nights before that, if possible). Go into the test with a fresh, alert mind rather than staying up late to study.

Try not to change too much about your normal routine on the day of the test. It's important to eat a nutritious breakfast, but if you normally don't eat breakfast at all, consider eating just a protein bar. If you're a coffee drinker, go ahead and have your normal coffee. Just make sure you time it so that the caffeine doesn't wear off right in the middle of your test. Avoid sugary beverages, and drink enough water to stay hydrated but not so much that you need a restroom break 10 minutes into the test. If your test isn't first thing in the morning, consider going for a walk or doing a light workout before the test to get your blood flowing.

Allow yourself enough time to get ready, and leave for the test with plenty of time to spare so you won't have the anxiety of scrambling to arrive in time. Another reason to be early is to select a good seat. It's helpful to sit away from doors and windows, which can be distracting. Find a good seat, get out your supplies, and settle your mind before the test begins.

When the test begins, start by going over the instructions carefully, even if you already know what to expect. Make sure you avoid any careless mistakes by following the directions.

Then begin working through the questions, pacing yourself as you've practiced. If you're not sure on an answer, don't spend too much time on it, and don't let it shake your confidence. Either skip it and come back later, or eliminate as many wrong answers as possible and guess among the remaining ones. Don't dwell on these questions as you continue—put them out of your mind and focus on what lies ahead.

Be sure to read all of the answer choices, even if you're sure the first one is the right answer. Sometimes you'll find a better one if you keep reading. But don't second-guess yourself if you do immediately know the answer. Your gut instinct is usually right. Don't let test anxiety rob you of the information you know.

If you have time at the end of the test (and if the test format allows), go back and review your answers. Be cautious about changing any, since your first instinct tends to be correct, but make sure you didn't misread any of the questions or accidentally mark the wrong answer choice. Look over any you skipped and make an educated guess.

At the end, leave the test feeling confident. You've done your best, so don't waste time worrying about your performance or wishing you could change anything. Instead, celebrate the successful completion of this test. And finally, use this test to learn how to deal with anxiety even better next time.

Review Video: Test Anxiety
Visit mometrix.com/academy and enter code: 100340

Important Qualification

Not all anxiety is created equal. If your test anxiety is causing major issues in your life beyond the classroom or testing center, or if you are experiencing troubling physical symptoms related to your anxiety, it may be a sign of a serious physiological or psychological condition. If this sounds like your situation, we strongly encourage you to seek professional help.

Online Resources

Due to our efforts to try to keep this book to a manageable length, we've created a link that will give you access to all of your online resources:

mometrix.com/resources719/praxsocst

It's Your Moment, Let's Celebrate It!

Share your story @mometrixtestpreparation